HISTORY OF ALABAMA.

VOL. I.

INDIANS EMPLOYED IN PLANTING CORN. Drawn from life by Jacob le Moyne, in 1564.

HISTORY

OF

ALABAMA,

AND INCIDENTALLY OF

GEORGIA AND MISSISSIPPI,

FROM THE EARLIEST PERIOD.

BY

ALBERT JAMES PICKETT,

Of Montgomery.

IN TWO VOLUMES,

VOL. I.

SECOND EDITION.

CHARLESTON:

WALKER AND JAMES,

1851.

CHARLESTON:
STEAM POWER-PRESS OF WALKER AND JAMES,
No. 101 East-Bay.

DEDICATION.

As a token of my sincere esteem, and of the high respect I feel for their talents and character, as well as in consideration of the deep interest which they have taken in my literary enterprises,

I DEDICATE THESE VOLUMES TO

BENJAMIN FITZPATRICK, JOHN ARCHIBALD CAMPBELL,

ARTHUR FRANCES HOPKINS, THOMAS JAMES JUDGE,

WILLIAM LOWNDES YANCEY, EDMUND STROTHER DARGAN,

FRANCIS BUGBEE, THADDEUS SANFORD,

WILLIAM PARISH CHILTON, BURWELL BOYKIN,

JOSHUA LANIER MARTIN, ALEXANDER BOWIE, BASIL MANLY,

SILAS PARSONS, NICHOLAS DAVIS AND CLEMENT C. CLAY, JR.,
Of Alabama;

GEORGE M. TROUP AND JOHN M. BERRIEN,
Of Georgia;

JOHN H. F. CLAIBORNE AND JOHN W. MONETTE,
Of Mississippi;

LESLIE A. THOMPSON AND WALKER ANDERSON,
Of Florida;

CHARLES GAYARRE AND SAMUEL F. WILSON,
Of Louisiana;

DANIEL GRAHAM,
Of Tennessee;

ARTHUR P. HAYNE, FRANCIS W. PICKENS,

JAMES H. HAMMOND, W. GILMORE SIMMS, RICHARD YEADON,

MITCHELL KING AND HENRY W. CONNER,
Of South-Carolina.

A. J. PICKETT.

PREFACE.

In submitting my first book to the public, I refrain from making apologies in its behalf, and shall only briefly allude to my labors, in order to show how strenuously I have endeavored to ensure its authenticity. I have sought materials for a correct history of my country, wherever they were to be procured, whether in Europe or America, and without regard to cost or trouble. All the Atlantic States have Historical Societies, and books and manuscripts relating to those States have been collected. In addition to this, agents have been sent to Europe, by different Legislatures, who have transcribed the colonial records which relate to their history. I have had none of these aids. I have been compelled to hunt up and buy books and manuscripts connected with the history of Alabama, and to collect oral information, in all directions. I rejoice, however, to know that a Historical Society has recently been formed at Tuscaloosa, by some literary gentlemen; and it gives me pleasure to reflect that the authors who may appear after my day, will not be subjected to the labor which it has been my lot to undergo. Believing that the historian ought to be the most conscientious of men, writing, as he does, not only for the present age, but for posterity, I have endeavored to divest myself of all prejudices, and to speak the truth in all cases. If it should be found, by the most scrutinizing reader, that any of my statements are incorrect, let me say in advance, that when I penned those statements I believed them to be true. So anxious have I been to record each incident as it really occurred, that upon several occasions I have travelled over four hundred miles, to learn merely a few facts.

About four years since, feeling impressed with the fact that it is the duty of every man to make himself, in some way, useful to his race, I looked around in search of some object, in the pursuit of which I could benefit my fellow-citizens; for, although much interested in agriculture, that did not occupy one-fourth of my time. Having no taste for politics, and never having studied a profession, I determined to write a History. I thought it would serve to amuse my leisure hours; but it has been the hardest work of my life. While exhausted by the labor of reconciling the statements of old authors, toiling over old French and Spanish manuscripts, travelling through Florida, Alabama and Mississippi, for information, and corresponding with persons in Europe and elsewhere, for facts, I have sometimes almost resolved to abandon the attempt to prepare a History of my State.

In reference to that portion of the work which relates to the Indians, I will state, that my father removed from Anson county, North-Carolina, and carried me to the wilds of the "Alabama Territory," in 1818, when I was a boy but eight years of age. He established a trading house, in connection with his plantation, in the present county of Autauga. During my youthful days, I was accustomed to be much with the Creek Indians—hundreds of whom came almost daily to the trading house. For twenty years I frequently visited the Creek nation. Their green corn dances, ball plays, war ceremonies, and manners and customs, are all fresh in my recollection. In my intercourse with them, I was thrown into the company of many old white men, called "Indian countrymen," who had for years conducted a commerce with them. Some of these men had come to the Creek nation before the revolutionary war, and others, being tories, had fled to it during the war, and after it, to escape from whig persecution. They were unquestionably the shrewdest and most interesting men with whom I ever conversed. Generally of Scotch decent, many of them were men of some education. All of them were married to Indian wives, and some of them had intelligent and handsome children. From these Indian countrymen I learned much concerning the manners and customs of the Creeks, with whom they had been so long associated, and more particularly with regard to the commerce which they carried on with them. In addition to this, I often conversed with the Chiefs while they were seated in the shades of the spreading mulberry and walnut, upon the banks of the beautiful Tallapoosa. As they leisurely smoked their pipes, some of them related to me the traditions of their country. I occasionally saw Choctaw and Cherokee traders, and learned much from them. I had no particular object in view, at that time, except the gratification of a curiosity, which led me, for my own satisfaction alone, to learn something of the early history of Alabama.

In relation to the invasion of Alabama by De Soto, which is related in the first chapter of this work, I have derived much information in regard to the route of that earliest discoverer, from statements of General McGillivray, a Creek of mixed blood, who ruled this country, with eminent ability, from

1776 to 1793. I have perused the manuscript history of the Creeks, by Stiggins, a half-breed, who also received some particulars of the route of De Soto, during his boyhood, from the lips of the oldest Indians. My library contains many old Spanish and French maps, with the towns through which De Soto passed, correctly laid down. The sites of many of these are familiar to the present population. Besides all these, I have procured, from England and France, three journals of De Soto's expedition.

One of these journals was written by a cavalier of the expedition, who was a native of Elvas, in Portugal. He finished his narrative on the 10th February, 1557, in the city of Evora, and it was printed in the house of Andrew de Burgos, printer and gentleman of the Lord Cardinal, and the Infanta. It was translated into English, by Richard Hakluyt, in 1609, and is to be found in the supplementary volume of his voyages and discoveries; London: 1812. It is also published at length in the Historical Collections of Peter Force, of Washington city.

Another journal of the expedition was written by the Inca Garcellasso de la Vega, a Peruvian by birth, and a native of the city of Cuzco. His father was a Spaniard of noble blood, and his mother the sister of Capac, one of the Indian sovereigns of Peru. Garcellasso was a distinguished writer of that age. He had heard of the remarkable invasion of Florida by De Soto, and he applied himself diligently to obtain the facts. He found out an intelligent cavalier of that expedition, with whom he had minute conversations of all the particulars of it. In addition to this, journals were placed in his hands, written in the camp of De Soto—one by Alonzo de Carmona, a native of the town of Priego, and the other, by Juan Coles, a native of Zafra. Garcellasso published his work, at an early period, in Spanish. It has been translated into French, but never into English. The copy in our hands is entitled "Histoire de la Conquete de la Floride ou relation, de ce qui s'est passé dans la découverte de ce pais, par Ferdinand De Soto, Composée en Espagnol, par L' Inca Garcellasso de la Vega, et traduite en François, par Sr. Pierre Richelet, en deux tomes; A Leide: 1731."

I have still another journal, and the last one, of the expedition of De Soto. It was written by Biedma, who accompanied De Soto, as his commissary. The journal is entitled "Relation de ce qui arriva pendant le voyage du Captaine Soto, et details sur la nature du pas qu'il parcourut; par Luis Hernandez de Biedma," contained in a volume entitled "Recuil de Pieces sur la Floride," one of a series of "Voyages et memoires originaux pour servir a la

L'Histoire de la decouverte de L'Amerique publies pour la premier fois en Francois; par H. Ternaux-Compans. Paris: 1841."

In Biedma there is an interesting letter written by De Soto, while he was at Tampa Bay, in Florida, which was addressed to some town authorities in Cuba. The journal of Biedma is much less in detail than those of the Portuguese Gentleman and Garcellasso, but agrees with them in the relation of the most important occurrences.

Our own accomplished writer, and earliest pioneer in Alabama history—Alexander B. Meek, of Mobile—has furnished a condensed, but well written and graphic account of De Soto's expedition, contained in a monthly magazine, entitled "The Southron," Tuscaloosa, 1839. He is correct as to the direction assumed by the Spaniards, over our soil, as well as to the character of that extraordinary conquest.

Theodore Irving, M.A., of New-York, has recently issued a revised edition of his Conquest of Florida. Its style is easy and flowing, when the author journalizes in regard to marches through the country, and is exceedingly graphic, when he gives us a description of De Soto's battles. As I have closely examined the sources from which Mr. Irving has collated his work, I am prepared to state that he has related all things as they are said to have occurred. For the complimentary terms which Mr. Irving has employed in the preface, and also in many of the notes of his late edition, in relation to my humble efforts in endeavoring to throw new light upon the expedition of De Soto, I beg him to accept my profound acknowledgments.

There are many gentlemen of talents and distinction, who have unselfishly, nobly and generously interested themselves in my behalf, while engaged in the arduous labors which are now brought to a close. I will name John A. Campbell and George N. Stewart, of Mobile; Alfred Hennen and J. D. B. DeBow, of New-Orleans; the Rev. Francis Hawks, of New-York; William H. Prescott and Jared Sparks, of Massachusetts; the Rev. William Bacon Stevens, of Philadelphia; W. Gilmore Simms, of South-Carolina; and particularly, John H. F. Claiborne, of Mississippi, who placed in my hands the manuscript papers of his father, Gen. F. L. Claiborne, who commanded the southern wing of the army, during the Creek war of 1813 and 1814. The son has requested me to present the manuscript papers of his father, as a contribution from him, to the Historical Society of Alabama. I shall comply with his request upon the first suitable occasion. There are many other persons who have manifested an interest in my behalf, to enumerate all of whom, would be extending this preface to an unreasonable length. While I omit the mention of their names, I shall ever cherish the memory of their attentions with the most grateful recollections.

THE AUTHOR.

May, 1851.

CONTENTS OF VOLUME I.

CHAPTER I.

CHAPTER II.

CHAPTER III.

CHAPTER IV.

CHAPTER V.

CHAPTER VI.

CHAPTER VII.

CHAPTER VIII.

CHAPTER IX.

CHAPTER X.

CHAPTER XI.

CHAPTER XII.

CHAPTER XIII.

HISTORY OF ALABAMA.

CHAPTER I.

DE SOTO IN ALABAMA, GEORGIA AND MISSISSIPPI.

THE first discovery of Alabama was by Hernando De Soto, a native of Spain, and the son of a squire of Xerez of Badajos. When a youth he went to Peru, enlisted under Pizarro, and, with no property but his sword, won distinguished military reputation. Returning to his native country, and making an imposing appearance at Court, he was made Governor of Cuba, and Adelantado of Florida. In the unknown regions of the latter, he resolved to embark his vast wealth in a splendid expedition, designed to conquer a people whom he believed to possess more gold than he had yet beheld in South America. Young men of the best blood in Spain and Portugal, sold their houses and their vineyards and flocked to his standard. Soon he was surrounded by an army of six hundred chosen men, with whom he put to sea, over the bar

CHAPTER I.

1533 April

CHAPTER I. of San Lucar de Barremeda. Arriving at Cuba, he consumed a year in arranging the affairs of his government, and in preparation for the great enterprise before him.* At the end of that period, he left his wife, Doña Isabel de Bobadilla, and
1539 May 12 the Lieutenant Governor in charge of the Island, and sailed for the coast of Florida, with a fleet of nine vessels—five large ships, together with caravals and brigantines.

A prosperous voyage soon enabled De Soto to pitch his
May 30 camp upon the shores of Tampa Bay, in Florida, with an army now increased to one thousand men. Sending out detachments to capture Indians, from whom he expected to learn something of the country, he found them skilful with the bow and too wily to be easily taken. In one of these sallies, the soldiers under Baltasar de Gallegos charged upon a small number of Indians. At that moment a voice cried out, "I am a christian! I am a christian!—slay me not." Instantly Alvaro Nieto, a stout trooper, drew back his lance, and lifting the unknown man up behind him, pranced off to join his comrades.

1528 Panfilo de Narvaez had attempted to overrun this country with a large expedition; but after disastrous wanderings, he reached Apalache without finding any gold,—and from thence went to the site of the present St. Marks, where his famished troops embarked for Cuba, in rude and hastily constructed boats, which were soon swallowed by

* Portuguese Narrative, pp. 695–700. Garcellasso de la Vega, pp. 59–60.

CHAPTER I.

the waves.* Jean Ortiz, the person taken prisoner, and who now, in all respects, resembled a savage, was a native of the town of Seville, in Spain. When a youth, he came to this coast with some others in search of Narvaez, and was captured by the Indians, who were about to burn him to death, when he was fortunately saved through the entreaties of the beautiful daughter of Uceta, the Chief. In the earlier periods of his slavery he was treated with barbarity, and compelled to guard, night and day, a lonely temple, in which the dead were deposited. After having been twelve years a prisoner among these savages, he was joyfully hastening to the camp of De Soto, when the Castilian words, which he so imploringly uttered, arrested the terrible lance of Alvaro Nieto.†

Gratified at the appearance of Jean Ortiz, who became his interpreter, De Soto gave him clothes and arms, and placed 1539 June
him upon a good charger. The Adelantado was now ready to penetrate the interior. His troops were provided with helmets, breastplates, shields, and coats of steel to repel the arrows of the Indians ; and with swords, Biscayan lances, rude guns called arquebuses, cross-bows, and one piece of artillery. His

* A history of the expedition of Narvaez will be found in Barcia, vol. 1, folio edition, Madrid, 1749, entitled " Navfragios de Alvar Nuñez Cabzea de Vaca y Relacion de la jornada que hizo a la Florida, con el Adelantado Panfilo de Narvaez." See, also, Herrera's History of America, vol. 4, pp. 27–38, vol. 5, pp. 91–105. London: 1740.

† Portuguese Narrative, pp. 702–704. Garcellasso, pp. 45–64.

CHAPTER cavaliers, mounted upon two hundred and thirteen horses,
I. were the most gallant and graceful men of all Spain. Grey-
hounds, of almost the fleetness of the winds, were ready to be
turned loose upon the retreating savages; and bloodhounds,
of prodigious size and noted ferocity, were at hand, to devour
them, if the bloody Spaniards deemed it necessary. To secure the unhappy Indian, handcuffs, chains and neck collars
abounded in the camp. Workmen of every trade, with their
various tools, and men of science, with their philosophical
instruments and crucibles for refining gold, were in attendance.
Tons of iron and steel, and much other metal, various merchandize, and provisions to last two years, were provided by
the munificence of the commander and his followers. A large
drove of hogs, which strangely multiplied upon the route,
together with cattle and mules, was also attached to the
expedition. The establishment of the Catholic religion ap-
1539 pears to have been one of the objects; for, associated with
June the army, were twelve priests, eight clergymen of inferior
rank, and four monks, with their robes, holy relics, and sacra-
mental bread and wine. Most of them were relatives of the
superior officers. Never was an expedition more complete,
owing to the experience of De Soto, who, upon the plains of
Peru, had ridden down hundreds in his powerful charges, and
had poured out streams of savage blood with his broad and
sweeping sword! It is not within our scope to detail the
bloody engagements which attended the wanderings of this
daring son of Spain, upon the territory of the now State of

Florida. Every where, but especially in narrow defiles, the natives showered clouds of arrows upon the invaders. Strong in numbers, and made revengeful by the cruelties inflicted by Narvaez, they had determined to fight De Soto until his army was destroyed or driven from their soil. No where in Florida did he find peace. His gallant troops, however, were successful. The Indians, often put to flight, and as often captured, were laden with chains, while the ponderous baggage of the expedition was unfeelingly thrown upon their backs for transportation. When in camp, they were made to pound corn, and to perform the most laborious and servile drudgery. CHAPTER I.

Cutting his way from Tampa, De Soto arrived at Anaica Apalache, in the neighborhood of the modern Tallahassee. Then, as it is yet, a fertile region, he drew from this town, and from others which surrounded it, breadstuffs to last him during the winter. The sea, only thirty miles distant, was explored by a detachment, and at the present St. Marks the bones of horses, hewn timbers, and other evidences of Narvaez, were discovered. During the winter all the detachments, in their various expeditions, were attacked by the Indians, and the main camp at Apalache was harrassed, day and night, in the fiercest manner, and with the most sanguinary results. At length Captain Maldinado, who had been ordered to sail to the west in some brigantines, which arrived from Tampa Bay, in search of a good harbor, returned in February, and reported the discovery of the bay of Ochus, since called Pensacola, which had a spacious channel, and was protected from the winds on

1539 October 27

1540 February

CHAPTER I. all sides.* Delighted at this good news, which enabled the Governor to make a wide circuit in the interior, he now ordered Maldinado to put to sea in the brigantines which then lay in the Apalache Bay, and to sail for Cuba. He was commanded to sail from thence to Ochus with a fleet of provisions, clothes, and military supplies, with which to recruit the expedition, when it should have met him at that point in October.†

1540 March 3 Learning from an Indian slave that a country to the north-east abounded in gold, De Soto broke up his winter encampment, and set out in that direction. He entered the territory of the present Georgia at its south-western border, and successively crossing the Ockmulgee, Oconee and Ogechee,‡ finally rested upon the banks of the Savannah, immediately opposite the modern Silver Bluff. On the eastern side was the town of Cutifachiqui,§ where lived an Indian Queen, young, beau-

* The Portuguese Narrative asserts that Maldinado was sent to the west, at the head of a detachment, by land; but I adopt the more reasonable statement of Garcellasso, especially as he is sustained by Biedma, De Soto's commissary. See "Relation de ce qui arriva pendant le voyage du Captaine Soto par Luis Hernandez de Biedma," p. 59.

† Portuguese Narrative, p. 709. Garcellasso, pp. 211–214.

‡ Biedma states that De Soto crossed a river (while in this part of the country) called the Altapaha. The substitution of only one letter would make it the Altamaha. p. 62.

§ All Indian tradition locates this town at the modern Silver Bluff, which is situated on the east bank of the Savannah, in Barnwell

tiful and unmarried, and who ruled the country around to a vast extent. She glided across the river in a magnificent canoe, with many attendants, and, after an interesting interview with De Soto, in which they exchanged presents, and passed many agreeable compliments, she invited him and his numerous followers over to her town. The next day the expedition crossed the Savannah upon log rafts and in canoes, and quartered in the wigwams and under the spreading shades of the mulberry. Many interesting things occurred at this place, which are mentioned at length by both of the journalists of De Soto, particularly by Garcellasso, but which are here reluctantly omitted in our anxiety to reach the borders of Alabama.

CHAPTER I.

1540 April

District, South-Carolina, and which is now the property of Governor Hammond.

In 1736, George Golphin, then a young Irishman, established himself as an Indian trader at this point, and gave the old site of Cutifachiqui the name of Silver Bluff. The most ancient Indians informed him that this was the place where De Soto found the Indian Princess; and this tradition agrees with that preserved by *other* old traders, and handed down to me. Golphin became a very wealthy man, and was for many years one of the most influential persons in Georgia and South-Carolina, as we will see hereafter. He left many descendants; among others, the wife of the late Governor Millege, was his daughter; Dr. Thomas G. Holmes, an intelligent man, of Baldwin county, Alabama, is his grandson.

Bartram, in his "Travels," page 313, speaking of Silver Bluff, says: "The Spaniards formerly fixed themselves at this place in the hopes of finding silver."

CHAPTER I. After a halt of several weeks at Cutifachiqui, De Soto broke up his camp, and, in company with the beautiful young Queen, whom he retained about his person as a hostage, to
1540 May 3 ensure obedience among her subjects, and who did not escape from him until the army had nearly accomplished its route through northern Georgia,—marched up the Savannah to its head waters, and rested, for a short time, at a town in the present Habersham county, Georgia. From this place the expedition assumed a direct western course, across northern Georgia, until they struck the head waters of the Coosa river, where they advanced upon the town of Guaxule, containing three hundred houses, and situated between several streams which had their sources in the surrounding mountains. The Chief met De Soto with five hundred warriors clothed in light costume, after the fashion of the country, and conducted him to his own house,—surrendered at the instance of his wife,—which stood upon a mound, and was surrounded by a terrace wide enough for six men to promenade abreast.* Having but little corn for the famished troops, the natives collected and gave them three hundred dogs, which the Spaniards had been accustomed to eat in the pine barrens of lower Georgia, "esteeming them as though they had been fat wethers."† Gaining much information about the country, in conversations with the Chief, conducted by the interpreter,
1540 May Jean Ortiz, the Governor, after the fourth day's sojourn at Guaxule, marched to the town of Conasauga, in the modern

* Garcellasso, p. 294. † Portuguese Narrative, p. 712.

county of Murray, Georgia. Crossing the Conasauga creek, and journeying down its western banks, the Spaniards found it to increase in size, and being joined by other streams, it presently grew larger than the Guadalquiver which passes by Seville.* This was the Oostanaula; and following its western side, De Soto, after a very slow march, advanced within seven miles of Chiaha, where he was met by fifteen Indians, laden with corn, bearing a message from the Chief, inviting him to hasten to his capital, where abundant supplies awaited him. Soon the eager Spaniards stood before the town of Chiaha, which is the site of the modern Rome.

CHAPTER I.

1540 May

The most ancient Cherokee Indians, whose tradition has been handed down to us through old Indian traders, disagree as to the precise place where De Soto crossed the Oostanaula to get over into the town of Chiaha—some asserting that he passed over that river seven miles above its junction with the Etowa, and that he marched from thence down to Chiaha, which, all contend, lay immediately at the confluence of the two rivers; while other ancient Indians asserted that he crossed, with his army, immediately opposite the town. But this is not very important. Coupling the Indian traditions with the account by Garcellasso, and that by the Portuguese eye-witness, we are inclined to believe the latter tradition that the expedition continued to advance down the western side of the Oostanaula, until they halted in view of the mouth of the Etowa.

* Garcellasso, 295.

CHAPTER I. 1540 June 5

De Soto having arrived immediately opposite the great town of Chiaha, now the site of Rome, crossed the Oostanaula in canoes and upon rafts made of logs prepared by the Indians, and took up his quarters in the town.*

The noble young Chief received De Soto with unaffected joy, and made him the following address:

Mighty Chief: Nothing could have made me so happy as to be the means of serving you and your warriors. You sent me word from Guaxule to have corn collected to last your army two months. Here I have twenty barns full of the best which the country can afford. If I have not met your wishes, respect my tender age, and receive my good will to do for you whatever I am able.†

The Governor responded in a kind manner, and was then conducted to the Chief's own house, prepared for his accommodation.

Chiaha contained a great quantity of bear's oil in gourds, and walnut oil as clear as butter and equally palatable; and for the only time upon the entire route were seen pots of honey.‡ The Spaniards, irregularly quartered in the fields,

* Garcellasso, p. 295. † Portuguese Narrative, p. 717.

‡ I have often been informed by old bee hunters and Indian countrymen, that after the territory of Alabama became partially settled by an American population, wild bees were much more abundant than they were in their earliest recollection. They were introduced into the country from Georgia and the Carolinas, and often escaping from their hives to the woods, became wild,—hence De Soto found no honey in the country at the early period in which he invaded it, except at Chiaha.

and scattered about at their will, reposed under trees and loitered upon the banks of the rivers. The horses, reduced in flesh and unfit for battle, grazed upon the meadows. Unaccustomed to allow such loose discipline, De Soto now winked at it, for the natives were friendly, and every soul in the camp needed repose. One day the Chief presented the Governor with a string of pearls, two yards in length, and as large as filberts, for which he received in return pieces of velvet and other cloth much esteemed by the Indians. He said that the temple of this town, where the remains of his ancestors were deposited, contained a vast quantity of these valuables. He invited his distinguished guest to take from it as many as he desired. But the latter declined, remarking that he wished to appropriate nothing to himself from so sacred a place. The Chief, to gratify him in regard to the manner of obtaining these pearls, immediately despatched some of his subjects in four canoes, with instructions to fish all night for the oysters which contained them. In the morning he caused a fire to be made upon the bank. The canoes returned laden, and the natives throwing the oysters upon the glowing coals, succeeded in finding many pearls the size of peas, which De Soto pronounced beautiful, but for the fire which had robbed them of some of their brilliancy. A soldier, in eating some of the oysters, or, rather, muscles, found one of great size uninjured, and offered it to the commander for Doña Isabel. He declined the kindness intended his wife, and urged the generous fellow to keep it to buy horses with at Havana. Con-

1540 June

CHAPTER I. noisseurs in camp valued it at four hundred ducats.* While here, a cavalier, named Luis Bravo de Xeres, walking one day upon the bank of the river, threw his lance at a dog, which suddenly disappeared under the bluff. Coming up to recover his weapon, he found, to his horror, that it had pierced the temple of Jean Mateos and had killed him. The poor man was quietly fishing on the margin of the stream, and little sus-
1540 June pecting that death was at hand. The accident caused deep regret in the camp, the deceased being much esteemed, and, having the only gray head in the army, was called, by way of pleasantry, Father Mateos.†

About this time a principal Indian from Costa, a town below, informed De Soto that in the mountains to the north,

* Garcellasso, p. 297. The oyster mentioned was the muscle to be found in all the rivers of Alabama. Heaps of muscle shells are now to be seen on our river banks wherever Indians used to live. They were much used by the ancient Indians for some purpose, and old warriors have informed me that their ancestors once used the shells to temper the clay with which they made their vessels. But as thousands of the shells lie banked up, some deep in the ground, we may also suppose that the Indians, in De Soto's time, everywhere in Alabama, obtained pearls from them. There can be no doubt about the quantity of pearls found in this State and Georgia in 1540, but they were of a coarser and more vauleless kind than the Spaniards supposed. The Indians used to perforate them with a heated copper spindle, and string them around their necks and arms like beads—others made toy babies and birds of them.

† Garcellasso, p. 298.

at a place called Chisca, were mines of copper, and of a yellow metal, still finer and softer. Having seen, upon the Savannah, copper hatchets, supposed to be mixed with gold, his attention was deeply aroused upon the subject. Villabos and Silvera, two fearless soldiers, volunteered to explore that region. Furnished with guides by the Chief of Chiaha, they departed upon their perilous journey.

CHAPTER I. 1540 June

The Spaniards had basked upon the delightful spot where now stands the town of Rome, for the space of thirty days. The horses had recruited, and the troops had grown vigorous and ready for desperate deeds. De Soto demanded of the hospitable Chief, through the persuasion of some of his unprincipled officers, a number of females to accompany them in their wanderings. That night the inhabitants quietly left the town and hid themselves in the bordering forests. The Chief entreated the Governor not to hold him responsible for their conduct, for, during his minority, an arbitrary uncle ruled them with a despotic will. With sixty troopers De Soto ravaged the surrounding country, and, provoked at not finding the fugitives, laid waste their flourishing fields of corn. When afterwards informed that men only would be required to bear the baggage, the Indians returned to Chiaha, apologized for their flight, and yielded to the last proposition.* De Soto then broke up his camp, re-crossed the Oostanaula, and marched down the west side of the Coosa, leaving the generous people of Chiaha well satisfied with presents. On the

1540 June

* Portuguese Narrative, pp. 718–719.

CHAPTER I.

1540 July

2d July, and after seven days slow march, he entered the town of Costa.* The Spaniards were now in Alabama, in the territory embraced in the county of Cherokee, and by the side of the Coosa, one of our noblest streams. Never before had our soil been trodden by European feet! Never before had our natives beheld white faces, long beards, strange apparel, glittering armor, and, stranger than all, the singular animals bestrode by the dashing cavaliers! De Soto had discovered Alabama, not by sea, but after dangerous and difficult marches had penetrated her north-eastern border with a splendid and well-equipped land expedition! The Atlantic States were quietly discovered by voyagers entering their harbors. Alabama was marched upon by an army, whose soldiers sickened with famine upon the barrens of Georgia, and left tracks of blood upon the soil of Florida!

Commanding his camp to be pitched two cross-bow shots from the town, De Soto, with eight men of his guard, approached the Chief of Costa, who received him with apparent friendship. While they were conversing together, some unscrupulous footmen entered the town and plundered several of the houses. The justly incensed Indians fell upon them with their clubs. Seeing himself surrounded by the natives, and in great personal danger, the Governor seized a cudgel, and, with his usual presence of mind, commenced beating his own men. The savages observing that he took their part, became pacified for a moment. In the meantime, taking the Chief

* Portuguese Narrative, pp. 718–719.

by the hand, he led him, with flattering words, towards the camp, where he was presently surrounded by a guard and held as a hostage.* The Spaniards remained under arms all night. Fifteen hundred Indians, armed complete, often made dispositions to charge upon them, vociferating angry and insulting language. Averse to war since he had been so repeatedly attacked by the Floridians, De Soto restrained his anxious troops. His coolness, together with the influence of a prominent Indian who followed him from Chiaha, put an end to the serious affair.† Three days after this, Villabos and Silvera returned from Chisca. They passed into the mountains, found no gold, but a country abounding with lofty hills and stupendous rocks. Dispirited, they returned to a poor town, where the inhabitants gave them a buffalo robe, which they supposed once covered a tremendous animal, partaking of the qualities of the ox and the sheep.‡ According to Garcellasso, the mines which they reached were of a highly colored copper, and were doubtless situated in the territory of the county of De Kalb. The sick, who were placed in canoes at Chiaha, had by this time arrived down the river. Furnished with the burden carriers by the Chief, who was to the last hour held a prisoner, the Governor left Costa on the 9th of July, 1540, and crossed over to the east side of the Coosa upon rafts and canoes. Proceeding down its eastern bank, he encamped the first night at the town of Talle. The Chief

CHAPTER I.

1540 July 9

* Portuguese Narrative, pp. 718–719. † Garcellasso, p. 300.

‡ Portuguese Narrative, p. 719.

CHAPTER I. came forth to receive him, and, in a formal speech, begged him to command his services. Here the Spaniards remained two days, sharing the hospitality of the natives. Upon their departure they were supplied with two women and four men. Indeed, De Soto brought from the forests of Florida over five hundred unhappy men and women, secured with chains, driven by keepers, and made to transport the effects of the expedition. When any of them became sick, died, or escaped, it was his policy to supply their places at the first town upon which he marched. He always, however, distributed among the principal Indians presents, which were gratifying to them, and left at many of the towns pairs of swine to stock the country.

The expedition now began to enter the far-famed province of Coosa, the beauty and fertility of which were known to all
1540 July the Indians, even upon the sea-side. Garcellasso asserts that it extended three hundred miles, and other authors agree that it reached over the territory now embraced in the counties of Cherokee, Benton, Talladega and Coosa. Continuing through the rich lands of Benton, the expedition passed many towns subject to the Chief of Coosa. Every day they met ambassadors, "one going and another coming," by which De Soto was assured of a hearty welcome at the capital.* With joyful faces the Indians rushed to his lines every mile upon the route, furnishing supplies and assisting the troops from one town to another. The same generous reception attended him upon entering the soil of the county of Talladega. The

* Portuguese Narrative, p. 719.

hospitality of the Coosas surpassed that of any people whom he had yet discovered. The trail was lined with towns, villages and hamlets, and "many sown fields which reached from one to the other."* With a delightful climate, and abounding in fine meadows and beautiful little rivers, this region was charming to De Soto and his followers. The numerous barns were full of corn, while acres of that which was growing bent to the warm rays of the sun and rustled in the breeze. In the plains were plum-trees peculiar to the country, and others resembling those of Spain. Wild fruit clambered to the tops of the loftiest trees, and lower branches were laden with delicious Isabella grapes.

On the 26th of July, 1540, the army came in sight of the town of Coosa. Far in the outskirts, De Soto was met by the Chief, seated upon a cushion, and riding in a chair supported upon the shoulders of four of his chief men. One thousand warriors, tall, active, sprightly and admirably proportioned, with large plumes of various colors on their heads, followed him, marching in regular order. His dress consisted of a splendid mantle of martin skins, thrown gracefully over his shoulder, while his head was adorned with a diadem of brilliant feathers. Around him many Indians raised their voices in song, and others made music upon flutes.† The steel-clad warriors of Spain, with their glittering armor, scarcely equalled the magnificent display made by these natives of Alabama.

1540 July 26

* Portuguese Narrative, p. 719. † Garcellasso, p. 300.

CHAPTER I. The Chief, receiving De Soto with the warmth of a generous heart, made him the following speech :

Mighty Chief! above all others of the earth! Although I come now to receive you, yet I received you many days ago deep in my heart. If I had the whole world, it would not give me as much pleasure as I now enjoy at the presence of yourself and your incomparable warriors. My person, lands and subjects, are at your service. I will now march you to your quarters with playing and singing.*

De Soto responded in his best style, after which he advanced to the town, conversing with the Chief, who rode in his sedan chair, while the lofty Spaniard sat upon his fiery steed. The royal house was set apart for the accommodation of the Adelantado, and one half of the other houses

1540 July were surrendered to the troops. The town of Coosa was situated upon the east bank of the river of that name, between the mouths of the two creeks, now known as Talladega and Tallasehatchee, one of which is sometimes called Kiamulgee.† It contained five hundred houses, and was the capital of this rich and extensive province.

* Portuguese Narrative, pp. 719-720.

† In 1798, Col. Benjamin Hawkins, then Creek Agent, visited the Coosa town, now embraced in the county of Talladega. He accurately describes the inhabitants and the location of the town, which he says was situated on the bank of the Coosa, between the mouths of two creeks, the Indian names of which were Natche and Ufaula. When he French expelled the Natchez from the Mississippi in 1730, some of

The Chief of Coosa was twenty-six years of age, well formed, intelligent, with a face beautifully expressive, and a heart honest and generous. He always dined with De Soto. One day he rose from the table, and, in an earnest manner, besought the Governor to select a region any where in his dominions, and immediately establish upon it a large Spanish colony. De Soto had contemplated peopling some beautiful country, and was better pleased with this section than any other, but his imagination still pointed him to some gold region, like Peru. He returned the Chief his profound thanks, adduced many reasons for declining the liberal offer, among others, that Maldinado's ships would await him at the bay of Pensacola. Yet, in the face of all this kindness, the politic and suspicious De Soto kept the Chief about his person, as a hostage, to preserve peace among the Indians, and to extort slaves and provisions. Enraged at the imprisonment of their Chief, the Indians fled to the woods to

CHAPTER I.

1540 August

that tribe sought refuge among the Talladegas—hence the name of one of these creeks in Hawkins' day. When the Americans, in 1832, began to settle this country, they changed the name of these creeks to Talladega, or Kiamulgee, and Tallasehatchee. In addition to the testimony of Col. Hawkins, many old Indian countrymen have informed me that here was the site of the Coosa town, which was known by that name in their early days. Several ancient French and Spanish maps, in my possession, lay down the town of Coosa at the place described.

See Hawkins' sketch of the Creek Country in 1798–1799, published by the Historical Society of Georgia, Savannah, 1848.

CHAPTER I. prepare for war. Four captains, with their companies, were despatched in different directions in pursuit, and returned with many women and men in chains. Some of the principal of these were released at the entreaty of the Chief, while others were carried off with the expedition, laden with irons and baggage, and those who were not destroyed at the battle of Maubila, were conducted far beyond the Mississippi river.*

The Indians returned from the forest, and remained at peace with the Spaniards, but were still dissatisfied at the restrictions imposed upon the liberties of their Chief. After

1540 August twenty-five days had been passed at the capital of Coosa, De Soto marched in the direction of the Tallapoosa, leaving behind a christian negro, too sick to travel, whom the Indians desired to retain among them on account of his singular hair and sable complexion. He recovered, and was doubtless the distant ancestor of the dark-colored savages seen in that region in more modern times.† The first day the army

* Portuguese Narrative, p. 720.

†The negro left at Coosa was not the only memorial of De Soto that remained with these people. George Stiggins, whose mother was a Natchez Indian, and whose father was a Scotchman, was born in the Talladega country. He was a fair English scholar, and a pretty good writer. He had been for years engaged in writing a history of the Creeks, and died some years ago, leaving it in an unfinished state. His son permitted me to peruse it one day. Stiggins asserts that the Talladegas had, at a late day, a brass kettle-drum and several shields which

CHAPTER I.

passed through the large town of Tallemuchasa, within a few hours after it had been abandoned by its inhabitants. The next day the town of Utaua was reached, where De Soto encamped six days, awaiting the abatement of the stream which ran by it, now violently swollen by incessant rains. As the expedition had not crossed any stream since leaving Coosa, it is probable the one alluded to was the modern Tallasehatchee. The march was continued to Ullebahale, situated upon Hatchet creek, which was called a "small river." The town was surrounded by a wall composed of two rows of posts driven deep in the ground, with poles laid horizontally between them, the inner and outside of the frame work neatly stuccoed with clay and straw. Port-holes were left at proper distances, forming a defence "as high as a lance." Such was the character of the Indian fortifications from this place onward. In consequence of the duresse of the Chief of Coosa, whom De Soto carried along with him, but treated with respect and kindness, the Indians of Ullebahale were in arms. Before the Spaniards entered the suburbs, twelve principal men, armed with bows, and with lofty plumes upon their heads, 1540 September 14
advanced and volunteered to rescue their beloved Chief by arraying a formidable force; but he dissuaded them from it. On the opposite side of the creek lived a sub-Chief, who fur-

once belonged to the army of De Soto, and that he had often seen them. The Coosas used them as trophies in their annual festivals. Besides these, De Soto left hogs and sometimes cattle, among the Alabama towns, and such is the origin of these animals among the Indians. Horses and mules were too valuable to be given away.

CHAPTER I. nished De Soto with thirty women for slaves, and to carry burdens. Then the Adelantado pursued his wanderings, leaving behind Mansano, a native of Salamanca, of noble parentage, who was lost while rambling in the hills for grapes, which were found in great abundance. The route lay along the modern Socapatoy region, in the county of Coosa. The expedition passed the town of Toase and several others, subject to the Chief of Tallase, and arrived at the great town of that
1540 name on the 18th September, 1540.

September 18 Tallase was an extensive town, the principal part of which was encompassed by a wall, similar to that just described, with the addition of terraces. It reposed upon a point of land "almost surrounded by a main river," which was the Tallapoosa.* Extensive fields of corn reached up and down the banks. On the opposite side were other towns, skirted with rich fields laden with heavy ears of maize. The beautiful river, rolling its silvery waters through these fertile lands, and the delightful climate, contributed to render the whole

* Some years after De Soto passed through this country, the Muscogees or Creeks came from the Mexican empire, of which they were subjects, and overrun all East Alabama and the greater portion of Georgia, killing and making slaves of many of the Alabamas, Ockmulgees, Oconees and Uchees, the latter of whom then lived near the modern city of Savannah. Upon the ruins of the Tallase discovered by De Soto, the Muscogees built the town of Tookabatcha, but immediately opposite, across the river, the name of Tallase was preserved until they moved to Arkansas, in 1836. This ancient and extensive Indian settlement is now in large cotton plantations.

prospect most pleasing. But the reception of De Soto among these people was cool and scarcely civil. Some had abandoned their houses at his approach, and gone into the woods. However, the Chief gave him forty Indians. After a few days, a noble-looking young savage, of gigantic proportions, and with a face extremely handsome and interesting, visited the marquee. He was the son of Tuscaloosa, a potent Chief, whose domains commenced thirty miles below, and extended to the distant Tombigby. He bore an invitation from his father to De Soto to hasten to his capital, where he was making preparations to receive him upon a magnificent scale, and then awaited him upon the eastern confines of his territory. The son was despatched with a suitable reply, and presents for the father.

Having remained at Tallase twenty days, De Soto dismissed the Chief of Coosa, with whom he parted upon good terms, crossed the Tallapoosa in canoes and upon rafts, marched down the eastern side, and encamped the first night at Casista, probably the site of the modern Autose. Delayed in passing the river, he could not have advanced further that day. In the morning the march was resumed. During this day a large town was discovered, and at night the camp was pitched upon the borders of another. The next day, advancing within six miles of the temporary residence of Tuscaloosa, a halt was made in the woods. Louis de Moscoso, the camp-master, with fifteen horsemen, was despatched to inform the Chief of the proximity of the Governor. Moscoso found the proud Mobilian seated upon two cushions, placed on a large

1540 October

CHAPTER I. and elegant matting, upon an eminence which commanded a delightful prospect. His numerous attendants posted themselves around him, leaving space for the nearer position of his chief men. One of these held over his head a round deerskin shield, with a staff in the middle, resembling an umbrella. Painted with stripes of different colors, it was used as a banner in his wars, but was employed at present in protecting his head from the rays of the sun. Tuscaloosa was forty years of age, of great stature, with immense limbs. He was spare around the waist, and his whole form was admirably proportioned. His countenance was handsome, but grave and severe. "He was lord of many territories and much people, and was feared by his neighbors and subjects." In vain did Moscoso endeavor to excite his curiosity, by prancing his horses before him. Sometimes he scarcely deigned to raise his eyes, and then, again, he bestowed upon the troopers the most contemptuous smiles. Even when De Soto arrived, he preserved the same haughty demeanor; but, in consideration of his position as commander-in-chief, he reluctantly advanced, and made the following address:

Mighty Chief: I bid you welcome. I greet you as I would my brother. It is needless to talk long. What I have to say can be said in a few words. You shall know how willing I am to serve you. I am thankful for the things which you 1540 October have sent me, chiefly because they were yours. I am now ready to comply with your desires.

The Governor replied in true Spanish style, failing not to assure the Chief that, even in distant Indian countries through

which he passed, he had heard of his greatness and power. CHAPTER I.
This interesting scene occurred below Line Creek, in the present county of Montgomery. Both journalists agree that De Soto had advanced thirty-six miles below Tallase. Reposing at this town the space of two days, preparations were made to advance. An officer was sent among the horses, to find one large enough to sustain the giant Indian. A large pack-horse, the property of the Governor, was selected. Appareled in a rich suit of scarlet, and a cap of the same, given to him by De Soto, the Chieftain, who was a head taller than any of his attendants, mounted upon his horse, with his feet nearly trailing on the ground. Onward the lofty and graceful Mobilian rode, side by side with the Governor. Marching 1540 October
through the territory embraced in the present counties of Montgomery, Lowndes, and the south-eastern part of Dallas, the expedition arrived at a town called Piache, seated on a peninsula formed by the windings of a large river, "the same which runs by Tallase, but here grown much wider and deeper." * This was the Alabama. On the march hither, a distressing disease broke out among the Spaniards, from the want of salt. The death of several, together with the loathsome condition of the sufferers, spread alarm in the camp. Those who afterwards used ashes with their food, from a weed recommended by the Indians, escaped the dreadful malady.†

* Garcellasso, p. 310. Portuguese Narrative, p. 722.

† Garcellasso, pp. 369–370.

CHAPTER I. The town of Piache was strongly fortified. Its name is probably preserved in a large creek which flows into the Alabama, on the northern side, called Chilache. The Indians having no canoes, soon constructed rafts of dry logs and cane, upon which the troops were wafted to the northern or western side of the Alabama—according to the conviction of the writer, in the upper part of the county of Wilcox.*

1540 October The expedition assumed a southern direction, and marched down the western side of the Alabama, over the soil of the present county of Wilcox. De Soto began to read the Mobilian Chief. He was still proud and distant, and evidently felt that he was a prisoner. Upon the whole route he had been studiously engaged in consulting with his principal men, and in constantly sending runners to the capital with messages. De Soto suspected that he meditated schemes, which aimed at the destruction of the Spaniards. His suspicions were further awakened, when Villabos and another cavalier were believed to have been killed by his subjects. When asked about them, Tuscaloosa indignantly replied, "I am not their keeper." High words ensued between him and De Soto; but the latter restrained himself until an opportunity offered of taking deep revenge on the Chief for his insolence and the death

* Biedma says that De Soto occupied two days in passing the river; and he learned from the Indians that Narvaez's barques touched at the mouth of the river (the Alabama) in search of water, and that a christian, named Teodoro, was still among the Indians below,—and they exhibited to De Soto a dagger which they had obtained from him. p. 72.

of the two Spaniards. On the third day of the march from Piache, they passed through many populous towns, well stored with corn, beans, pumpkins, and other provisions. In the meantime, Charamilla and Vasques, two able and discreet cavaliers, were despatched in advance to discover if any conspiracy was going on at the capital. Before daylight, on the fourth morning, De Soto placed himself at the head of one hundred horse, and an equal number of foot, and marched rapidly in that direction with the Chief, leaving Moscoso, the camp-master, to bring up the larger portion of the troops. At eight o'clock the same morning, the 18th October, 1540, De Soto and Tuscaloosa arrived at the capital, called Maubila. It stood by the side of a large river, upon a beautiful plain, and consisted of eighty handsome houses, each capacious enough to contain a thousand men. They all fronted a large public square. They were encompassed by a high wall, made of immense trunks of trees, set deep in the ground and close together, strengthened with cross-timbers, and interwoven with large vines. A thick mud plaster, resembling handsome masonry, concealed the wood work, while port-holes were abundant, together with towers, capable of containing eight men each, at the distance of fifty paces apart. An eastern and a western gate opened into the town. The writer is satisfied that Maubila was upon the north bank of the Alabama, and at a place now called Choctaw Bluff, in the county of Clarke, about twenty-five miles above the confluence of the Alabama and Tombigby. The march from Piache, the time occupied, the distance from Maubila to the bay of Pensacola—

1540 October 18

CHAPTER I. computed by Garcellasso and the Portuguese Gentleman at eighty-five miles—and the representations of aged Indians and Indian countrymen, that here was fought the great battle between De Soto and the brave Mobilians, have forcibly contributed to make that impression upon his mind.

De Soto and Tuscaloosa were ushered into the great public square of Maubila with songs, music upon Indian flutes, and the graceful dancing of beautiful brown girls. They alighted from their chargers, and seated themselves under a "canopy of state." Remaining here a short time, the Chief requested that he should no longer be held as a hostage, nor required to follow the army any further. The Adelantado hesitated in reply, which brought Tuscaloosa immediately to his feet, who walked off with a lofty and independent bearing,
1540 October 18 and entered one of the houses. De Soto had scarcely recovered from his surprise, when Jean Ortiz followed the Chief and announced that breakfast awaited him at the Governor's table. Tuscaloosa refused to return, and added, "If your Chief knows what is best for him, he will immediately take his troops out of my territory." In the meantime, Charamilla, one of the spies, informed the Governor that he had discovered over ten thousand men in the houses, the subjects of Tuscaloosa and other neighboring Chiefs; that other houses were filled with bows, arrows, stones and clubs; that the old women and children had been sent out of the town, and the Indians were at that moment debating the most suitable hour to capture the Spaniards. The General received this startling intelligence with the deepest solicitude. He secretly sent word to his men

to be ready for an attack. Then, anxious to avert a rupture, by regaining possession of the person of the Chief, he approached him with smiles and kind words, but Tuscaloosa scornfully turned his back upon him, and was soon lost among the host of excited warriors. At that moment a principal Indian rushed out of the same house, and loudly denounced the Spaniards as ROBBERS, THIEVES and ASSASSINS, who should no longer impose on their great Chief, by depriving him of a liberty with which he was born, and his fathers before him. His insolence, and the motions which he made to shoot at a squad of Spaniards with a drawn bow, so incensed Baltasar de Gallegos, that, with a powerful sweep of his sword, he split down his body and let out his bowels! Like bees in a swarm the savages now poured out upon the Spaniards. De Soto placed himself at the head of his men, and fought face to face with the enemy, retreating slowly and passing the gate into the plain. His cavalry had rushed to rescue their horses, tied outside the walls, some of which the Indians came upon in time to kill. Still receding, to get out of the reach of the enemy, De Soto at length paused at a considerable distance upon the plain. The Mobilians seized the Indian slaves, packed upon their backs the effects of the expedition, which had now arrived and lay scattered about, drove the poor devils within the walls, knocked off their irons, placed bows in their hands, and arrayed them in battle against their former masters. In the first sally, De Soto had five men killed and many wounded, himself among the latter number. Having captured the baggage, the victors covered the ground in advance

1540 October 18

CHAPTER I. of the gate, and rent the air with exulting shouts. At that moment the Governor headed his cavalry, and followed by his footmen, charged upon the savage masses; and, with a terrible slaughter, drove them back into the town. The Indians rushed to the port-holes and towers, and shot upon the invaders clouds of arrows, compelling them again to retire from the walls. A small party of Spaniards were left in a perilous situation. Three cross-bow men, an armed friendly Indian, five of De Soto's guard, some servants and two priests, not having time to join the others when first attacked in the square, took refuge in the house set apart for their commander. The savages sought an entrance at the door, but the unhappy inmates bravely defended it, killing many of the assailants. Others clambered upon the roof to open the covering, but were as successfully repulsed. Separated from their friends by a thick wall, and in the midst of thousands of enemies panting to lap their blood, their destruction appeared
1540 October 18 inevitable. During the long struggle for existence, the holy fathers engaged in earnest prayer for their deliverance, while the others fought with a desperation which rose with the occasion.

Seeing the Spaniards again retreat, the Indians rushed through the gates, and dropping down from the walls, engaged fiercely with the soldiers, seizing their sweeping swords and piercing lances! Three long hours were consumed in the terrible conflict, first one side giving way and then the other. Occasionally, De Soto was strengthened by small squads of horsemen who arrived, and without orders, charged into the midst of the bloody melée. The Governor was every where present in the fight, and his vigorous arm hewed down the lustiest warriors. That sword, which had often been dyed in the blood of Peruvians, was now crimsoned with the gore of a still braver race. The invincible Baltasar de Gallegos, who struck the first blow, followed it up, and was only equalled by the commander in the profuse outpouring of savage blood. Far on the borders of the exciting scene rode his brother, Fray Juan, a Dominican friar, who constantly beckoned him to quit the engagement on foot, and take the horse which he bestrode, in order to fight the better. But Baltasar, gloating on blood, heeded him not; when presently an Indian arrow, which made a slight wound upon the back of the worthy father, caused him to retire to a less dangerous distance. Indeed, during the whole battle the priests kept the plain, watched the awful carnage with intense anxiety, and often fell upon their knees, imploring Almighty God to give victory to the Spaniards.

1540 October 18

At length the matchless daring of De Soto and his troops forced the Indians to take a permanent position within Maubila, closing after them its ponderous gates. The sun began to lower towards the tops of the loftiest trees, when Moscoso and the last of the army arrived. He had strangely loitered by the way, allowing the soldiers to scatter in the woods and hunt at their leisure. His advanced guard heard at a distance the alarum of drums and the clangor of trumpets. With beating hearts they passed back the word along the scattered lines, from one to the other, and soon the hindmost rushed to

CHAPTER I. the support of their exhausted and crimson-stained comrades. Joined by all his force, De Soto formed the best armed into four divisions of foot. Provided with bucklers for defence, and battle-axes to demolish the walls, they made a simultaneous charge, at the firing of an arquebuse. Upon the first onset, they were assailed with showers of arrows and dreadful missiles. Repeated blows against the gates forced them open. The avenues were filled with eager soldiers, rushing into the square. Others, impatient to get in, battered the stucco from the walls, and aided each other to climb over the skeleton works. A horrible and unparalleled carnage ensued. The horsemen remained on the outside to overtake those who 1540 October 18 might attempt to escape. The Indians fought in the streets, in the square, from the tops of the houses and walls. The ground was covered with their dead, but not one of the living entreated for quarters. The Spaniards were protected with bucklers and coats of mail, while the poor Indians were only covered with the thin shield which the Great Spirit gave them at the dawn of their existence. The troops entered the town in time to save the two priests and their companions, who had so long held out against such fearful odds. The battle, which now waxed hotter and more sanguinary than ever, cannot be as graphically described as the heroic deeds on either side so justly deserve. Often the Indians drove the troops out of the town, and as often they returned with increased desperation. Near the wall lay a large pool of delicious water, fed by many springs. It was now discolored with blood. Here soldiers fell down to slake the intense thirst created by heat and wounds, and those who were able rose again, and once more pitched into a combat characterized by the most revolting destruction of human life. For some time the young females had joined in the fight, and they now contended side by side with the foremost warriors, sharing in the indiscriminate slaughter. Heated with excitement, smarting with his wounds, and provoked at the unsubdued fierceness of the natives, De Soto rushed out alone by the gate, threw himself into his saddle, and charged into the town. Calling, with a loud voice, upon "Our Lady and Santiago," he forced his charger over hundreds of fighting men and women, followed by the brave Nuno Tobar. While opening lanes through the savage ranks and sprinkling his tracks with blood, he rose on one occasion to cast his lance into a gigantic warrior. At that instant, a powerful winged arrow went deep into the bottom of his thigh. Unable to extract it, or to sit in his saddle, he continued to fight to the end of the battle, standing in his stirrups. Everywhere, that mighty son of Spain now gorged upon Alabama blood! His fearless bounds filled the boldest soldiers with renewed courage. At length the houses were set on fire, and the wind blew the smoke and flames in all directions, adding horror to the scene. The flames ascended in mighty volumes! The sun went down, hiding himself from the awful sight! Maubila was in ruins, and her inhabitants destroyed!

CHAPTER I.

1540 October 18

The battle of Maubila had lasted nine hours. It was disastrous to De Soto. Eighty-two Spaniards were slain, or died

CHAPTER I.

in a few days after the engagement. Among these were Diego de Soto, the nephew of the Governor, Don Carlos Enriquez, who had married his niece, and Men-Rodriquez, a cavalier of Portugal, who had served with distinction in Africa and upon the Portuguese frontiers. Other men of rank and blood lost their lives in the terrible conflict, some of whom died in great agony, being shot in the eyes and in the joints of their limbs. Forty-five horses were slain—an irreparable loss, mourned by the whole expedition. All the camp equipage and baggage were consumed in the house where the Indians had stored it, except that of Captain Andres de Vasconcellos, which arrived late in the evening. All the clothes, medicines, instruments, books, much of the armor, all the pearls, the relics and robes of the priests, their flour and wine, used in the holy sacrament, with a thousand other things which a wilderness could not supply, perished in the flames. The Mobilians were nearly all destroyed. Garcellasso asserts that above eleven thousand were slain. The Portuguese Gentleman sets down the number at two thousand five hundred killed within the walls alone. Assuming a point between the two estimates, it is safe to say that at least six thousand were killed in the town and upon the plains, or were afterwards

1540 October 18

found dead in the woods. These authors also disagree as to the fate of Tuscaloosa—the one contending that he was consumed in the flames, and the other that he decamped upon the arrival of Moscoso, at the solicitation of his people, attended by a small guard, and laden with rich Spanish spoils.

It is more probable that the Black Warrior remained in his capital, desiring not to survive the downfall of his people.*

Upon the ruins of Maubila the Spaniards passed the first night, in confusion and pain, sending forth groans and cries that fell upon the distant air like the ravings of the damned! In every direction a sickening and revolting sight was presented. In the slowly receding fire, piles of brave Mobilians cracked and fried upon the glowing coals! Upon the great square, pyramids of bodies, smeared with blood and brains, lay still unburnt. Outside the walls, hundreds lay in the sleep of death, still hot from their last desperate exertions, and copiously bleeding from the large orifices made by lances and swords, and discoloring the beautiful grounds upon which they had so often sported in their native games. All the Spaniards were wounded except the holy fathers, and were, besides, exhausted, famished, and intoxicated with the most fiendish desperation. Seventeen hundred dangerous wounds demanded immediate attention. It was often that a soldier had a dozen severe ones, with barbed arrows rankling in his flesh. But one surgeon of the expedition survived, and he was slow and unskilful. Everything, in his department, was devoured by the terrible element. Those who were slightly wounded, administered to those whom the Indians had pierced

1540 October 18

* In describing the battle of Maubila, I have carefully consulted the Portuguese Narrative and Garcellasso. I find that they are, in the main, sustained by Biedma. See Garcellasso, pp. 312–331—Portuguese Narrative, pp. 722–725—Biedma, pp. 74–78.

CHAPTER I. deepest. As the soldiers of Cortez did in Mexico, they opened the bodies of some of the savages, and with the fat obtained, bound up the wounds with bandages torn from the garments of the soldiers who were killed. Others rushed to the woods, obtained straw and boughs, and formed against the walls beds and imperfect covering for the wounded and dying. Although severely pierced himself with arrows, and bruised with missiles, yet the generous De Soto unselfishly gave his whole attention to his men. 1540 October 18 During that miserable night, many of the unhappy Spaniards joined the priests in fervent appeals to their Heavenly Father, for the alleviation of their wretched condition.

They remained within the walls eight days, and then removed to the Indian huts upon the plain. De Soto sent out foraging detachments, who found the villages abounding in provisions. In the woods and ravines, Indians were found dead, and others lay wounded. The latter were treated with kindness by the Spaniards, who fed them and dressed their wounds. Females of incomparable beauty were captured upon these excursions, and added to those who were taken at the close of the battle. From them, the Governor was astounded to learn the deep schemes which Tuscaloosa had planned to capture his army, weeks before his arrival at Maubila. To the Tallases, who complained to him that their Chief had given their people to De Soto as slaves, he replied: "Fear nothing; I shall shortly send the Spaniards back from my country to Tallase in chains, led by your people, whom they have enslaved."

The priests, monks, and best informed laymen, went into convention to determine the propriety of substituting corn meal for flour in the celebration of Mass. They decided that bread made of pure wheat, and wine of the juice of the grape, were required for consecration. After this, the fathers, in lieu of the chalices, altar dresses, chasubles, and other sacred ornaments, which had been consumed by fire, made some robes of dressed deer skins, erected rude altars and read the *introitus* and other prayers of the Mass on Sundays and feasts, omitting the consecration. This unusual ceremony was denominated the DRY MASS. CHAPTER I.

While referring to the religious exercises of the Spaniards, it is proper to allude to some of their vices. Upon the whole journey from Tampa Bay to this place, they had passed much of their leisure time in gambling. This vice was common to all classes; those of rank often bet high, staking their money, jewels, horses, effects, and even their female slaves! The fire of Maubila destroyed their cards. They now made others of parchment, painted them with admirable skill, and loaned these packs from one company to another, continuing to gamble under trees, upon the river banks, and in their rude huts. 1540 October

The report which De Soto had received upon his first arrival at Maubila, that Maldinado and his vessels awaited him at the bay of Pensacola, was now fully confirmed by the females whom he had captured. Refreshed by this good news, which determined him to plant a colony in the wilderness, he dismissed a Chief of that country whom Maldinado had brought into his camp, while at Apalache Anaica. He had

CHAPTER I.

always treated him with kindness, and they parted upon the most friendly terms. The Chief set out for Ochus. When it became known in camp that the ships had arrived, joy succeeded the sadness which had universally prevailed. Some of the most distinguished cavaliers secretly talked of sailing from Ochus to Spain, and others to Peru, each resolved upon quitting De Soto and his fortunes. He heard of the conspiracy with painful solicitude, and determined to ascertain if it was founded in seriousness. One dark night he disguised himself and cautiously moved about the camp. Approaching the hut of Juan Caitan, the treasurer, he overheard an earnest conversation, which satisfied him of the truth of what

1540 November

had been intimated. De Soto was startled at the faithless schemers. It altered his plans. He now dreaded to march to Ochus, for he well knew that some of these cavaliers had once deserted Pizarro, leaving him on the island of Gorgonne. He reflected, that his means were exhausted, his hopes of finding a gold country, thus far, blasted, and that he had nothing to tempt the cupidity of recruits; even the pearls, all he had to exhibit of his discoveries, having shared the fate of the other effects. These things, connected with a desire to thwart the plans of the conspirators, influenced him to turn his back upon his ships, laden with provisions, clothes, arms, and every thing which the whole army needed.

De Soto became gloomy and morose. Sometimes, in the midst of his desponding fits, a hope of yet finding a gold region shot across his mind, but, like a flashing meteor, it exploded in darkness, leaving him in deeper despair! He resolved, however, to strike into the wilderness. The wounded had recovered enough to march, and he gave orders to break up the camp. On Sunday, the 18th of November, 1540, a direction was assumed to the north. The order fell like a clap of thunder upon the unwilling cavaliers. But they obeyed, for he threatened to put to death the first man who should even think of Maldinado and his ships.* The expedition traversed an extremely fertile, but uninhabited country, called Pafallaya, now embraced in the counties of Clarke, Marengo, and Greene, and, at the expiration of five days, passed the town of Talepataua, and reached another called Cabusto. This was "near a river, wide, deep and with high bluffs." † The Spaniards had now arrived upon the Black Warrior, and near the modern town of Erie. Fifteen hundred Indians advanced in battle array, shouting that a war of "fire and blood" was what they desired. They remembered the destruction of their friends at Maubila, and they were determined to be revenged. Severe skirmishing ensued. The Spaniards drove the savages into the river; some crossed over in canoes and others swam; and on the opposite side they were joined by a force estimated

1540 November 18

* De Soto had no doubt determined to settle a colony in the province of Coosa. The desperate resolution, now formed, of again plunging into unknown regions, was unfortunate for him and his followers, and for the historians of Alabama. A colony in Alabama, at that early period, would have afforded many rich historic incidents.

† "Etoit sur un fleuve, grand, profond et haut de bord." Garcellasso, p. 348. The American rivers, of ordinary size, appeared large to the Spaniards, and do even now to all Europeans.

CHAPTER I. at eight thousand. For six miles they stretched along the western bank, to oppose the crossing of the army. De Soto occupied Cabusto, and was attacked every night by detachments of the enemy, who came over secretly in canoes from different directions, and sprang upon him. He at length caused ditches to be cut near the landings, in which he posted cross-bow men and those armed with arquebuses. After the Indians were repulsed three times from these intrenchments, they ceased to annoy the Spaniards at night. In the meantime, one hundred men completed in the woods two large boats. They were placed upon sledges, and by the force of horses and mules, and with the assistance of the soldiers, were conveyed to a convenient landing one and a half miles up the river, and launched before day. Ten cavalry and forty infantry entered each of these boats, the former keeping the saddle while the latter rowed rapidly across. Five hundred Indians rushed down the banks and overwhelmed the voyagers with

1540 November arrows. However, the boats reached the shore, one of them coming to with great difficulty. The soldiers, all of whom were wounded, sprang out, and, headed by the impetuous Silvestre and Garcia, charged the Indians with great resolution. A severe conflict continued until the boats returned and brought over De Soto with eighty men, who, joining in the fight, forced the Indians to retreat to a distant forest. The advanced wing keeping off the enemy, the whole army soon crossed the river. When all were over, the Indians were driven to their first position, which they had strengthened with pallisades, and from which they continually sallied, skirmishing with the invaders until the sun was lost behind the hills.* Upon the Warrior, De Soto found a delightful country, with towns and villages well supplied with corn, beans and other provisions. The next day he caused the boats to be broken up, for the iron which they contained, and the expedition marched in a northern direction, passing through a portion of Greene and Pickens. After five days they reached the Little Tombigby, somewhere in the county of Lowndes, Mississippi. Here the Indians had collected to dispute the passage. Having recently suffered so severely in contentions with the natives of Alabama, De Soto felt unwilling to expose his army to further loss. Halting two days for the construction of a small boat, he despatched in it an Indian, who bore a message to the Chief, with offers of peace and friendship. Immediately upon reaching the opposite bank, the poor fellow was seized and barbarously killed, in the sight of the Governor. His murderers then rent the air with terrific yells, and dispersed. De Soto conducted his troops unmolested across the river, and marched until he arrived at the town of Chickasa, in the province of that name. It consisted of two hundred houses, and reposed upon a hill extending towards the north, shaded by oak and walnut trees, and watered by several rivulets. The Spaniards had now reached the territory embraced in the county of Yalobusha. The region was fertile, well-peopled and dotted with villages. The cold weather set in with much severity. In the midst of snow and ice, the army encamped 1540 November

* Portuguese Narrative, p. 725. Garcellasso, pp. 348–352.

CHAPTER I. upon the fields opposite the town, until houses could be erected; for here De Soto had determined to pass the winter. Foraging parties scoured the country, collected provisions and captured Indians. The latter were invariably dismissed, with presents for their Chief.

The Chief at length came to see De Soto, and offered him his lands, person and subjects. He returned, shortly after, with two neighboring Chiefs—Alibamo and Nicalaso. The august trio gave the Adelantado one hundred and fifty rabbits, besides mantles and skins. The Chief of Chickasa became a frequent visitor, and De Soto often sent him home on one of the horses. Having besought the General to aid him in over-

1541 January coming a prominent and rebellious subject, for the purpose of dividing and destroying the army, as was afterwards ascertained, De Soto marched, with thirty horsemen and two hundred Indians, upon Saquechuma, and destroyed that place by fire. Upon their return to the camp, the principal Indians were feasted upon the flesh of swine. They were pleased with the first dish of an animal never before seen, and from that time the place where the hogs were kept was often broken in upon dark nights, and many stolen. Three of the rogues were caught on one occasion, and two of them put to death. The hands of the other were chopped off, and in that painful and helpless situation, he was sent to his Chief. On the other side, the Spaniards robbed the Indians. One day, four horsemen, Francisco Osario, a servant of the Marquis of Astorga, called Raynoso, Ribera, the page of the Governor, and Fuentes, his chamberlain, entered a neighboring village

and forcibly carried off some valuable skins and mantles. CHAPTER I.
The enraged Indians forsook their town and went into the woods to prepare for war. The robbers were arrested, and Fuentes and Osario were condemned to die. The priests and some of the most distinguished cavaliers pleaded, in vain, for the pardon of the latter. De Soto had them brought out to have their heads chopped off, when Indians arrived with a message from the Chief, informing him of the outrage upon his people. At the suggestion of Baltasar de Gallegos, the interpreter cunningly turned it to the advantage of the prisoners. He said to De Soto, that the Chief desired him not to execute the robbers, for they had not molested his subjects. He said to the Indian ambassadors, that they might return home 1541 March
well assured that the plunderers would be immediately put to death, according to the wishes of the Chief. The prisoners, in consequence, were all set at liberty, much to the joy of the army.*

Upon the appearance of March, 1541, the thoughts of the unhappy De Soto occasionally turned upon pursuing the journey. He demanded of the Chief two hundred men for

* Poor Ortiz never reached his native country, but died in Arkansas. He was of great service as an interpreter. Understanding only the Floridian language, he conducted conversations through the Indians of different tribes who understood each other, and who attended the expedition. In conversing with the Chickasaws, for instance, he commenced with a Floridian, who carried the word to a Georgian, the Georgian to the Coosa, the Coosa to the Mobilian, and the latter to the Chickasaw. In the same tedious manner the answer was conveyed to him and reported to De Soto.

CHAPTER I. burden bearers. An evasive answer was given, and for several days the Governor was apprehensive of an attack. He posted sentinels, under the supervision of Moscoso. One dark night, when the cold wind was howling awfully, the Chickasaws rushed upon the camp, in four squadrons, sending up yells the most terrific, and adding horror to the scene by the sound of wooden drums and the discordant blasts of conch shells. The houses of the town, in which the larger portion of the troops now lodged, were set on fire by arrows containing burning matches, made of a vegetable substance, which shot through the air like flashing meteors and fell upon the roofs! Constructed of straw and cane, the wigwams were soon wrapped in flames. The Spaniards, blinded by the smoke, ran out of the houses half dressed, and, in their dismay, knew not the best way to oppose the assailants. Some of the horses were burned in the stables and others broke their halters, and running in all directions among the soldiers, increased the unparalleled confusion. De Soto and a soldier named Tapier, the first to mount, charged upon the enemy, the former being enveloped in an overcoat, quilted with cotton three inches thick, to shield him from the arrows. His saddle, which, in the haste, had not been girted, turned with him in one of his sweeping bounds, and he fell heavily to the ground, at the moment his lance had pierced a savage. The soldiers drove off the Indians, who had surrounded him
1541 March with clubs, and adjusted his saddle. Vaulting into it, he charged in the thickest of the enemy, and revelled in blood! The Spaniards were now seen in all directions, engaged in

a dreadful fight. Many, however, had just awoke, and now crawled upon their hands and knees out of the devouring flames above them. In a house, at some distance, lay the sick, and those who had not recovered from the wounds which they had received at Maubila and Cabusto. Hordes of savages pressed upon the poor fellows, and, before they were rescued, several fell victims. In the meantime, the cavaliers, some without saddles and others without clothes, joined the intrepid De Soto; and now the awful wind, the flames, the yells and the clangour of arms, made the scene frightfully sublime, and the night one long to be remembered. Fifty infantry took flight, which was the first instance of cowardice upon the march. Nuno Tobar, sword in hand, 1541
rushed before them, and with the assistance of a detachment March
of thirty men under Juan de Guzman, arrayed them against the enemy. At that instant, Andres de Vasconcelos, at the head of twenty Portuguese hidalgos, most of whom had served as horsemen upon the African frontier, accompanied by Nuno Tobar on foot, forced the savages to retire on one side of the town. At length the Indians fled from the battle field, and were pursued by De Soto and his troops as long as they could distinguish objects by the light of the burning town. Returning from the chase, the Governer found that the engagement had resulted in considerable loss. Forty Spaniards were killed, and among them the only white woman in camp, the wife of a soldier, whom she had followed from Spain. Fifty horses were lost, either burned or pierced with arrows. Dreading these singular quadrupeds in war, the Indians aimed

CHAPTER I. at their entire destruction, and many were found shot entirely through in the most vital parts. The swine, the increase of which had often kept the Spaniards from starving, when hard pressed for food, were confined in a roofed enclosure, and a number of them were consumed by the fire. De Soto surveyed the scene with deep mortification. He blamed Moscoso for the unfortunate attack. His negligence here, reminded him of his tardy advance upon Maubila, and, in his anger, he deposed his old brother in arms from the rank of camp-master, and bestowed it upon the bold Baltasar de Gallegos. A
1541 March succession of losses had attended him since he crossed the Alabama at Piache. Indeed, from his first landing at Tampa Bay, over three hundred men had fallen by the assaults of the natives. The fire at Chickasa swept the few things saved at Maubila, together with half their wearing apparel. And now many of the unfortunate soldiers shivered in the cold, with scarcely a vestige of clothing.

In the fit of deep despondency into which he was thrown, De Soto did not forget the duties which a commanding officer owes to his suffering troops. The dead were buried and the wounded properly attended. The Indians, thick upon the plain, and upon the ruined town, remained, a prey for the hungry wolves and birds of carrion. The Spaniards abandoned the sickening spot, and encamped three miles distant, at Chickasilla, or little Chickasa, where they erected a forge and tempered their swords, now seriously injured by the fire. They busied themselves in making shields, lances and saddles. The remainder of the winter was passed in great wretchedness.

Intense cold and grievous wounds were not all they had to bear, but often the natives assailed them at night, with the agility and ferocity of tigers! At sunset they were compelled to evacuate the town, and take position in the field, for fear that fire might be applied to the houses. The ingenuity of one of the soldiers devised mattings, four inches in thickness, made of a long soft grass, in which those who were not upon guard wrapped themselves, and were somewhat protected from the piercing air. Often De Soto sent forth detachments, who cut down every Indian they overtook; yet, in a few succeeding nights, the savages would return and attack the camp. Before daylight on Wednesday, the 15th March, 1541, Capt. Juan de Guzman, a man of delicate form, but of indomitable courage, was seized by the collar by an athletic Indian, who carried a banner, and jerked from his horse. The soldiers, rushing up, cut the bold fellow to pieces. Others dashed after the main body of Indians, and deep revenge would have been taken, if a monk, fearful that they would be led into an ambush, had not arrested the charge by the cry of, "to the camp!—to the camp!" Forty Indians fell,—two horses were killed and two soldiers wounded.

On the 25th of April, 1541, De Soto marched north-west, through a champaign country, thickly populated, and journeying twelve miles, halted in a plain not far from the town of Alibamo. Juan de Anasco, with a foraging party, came in sight of this fortress, which was garrisoned by a large number of savages, whose bodies were painted in stripes of white, black and red, while their faces were frightfully blackened.

1541 April

CHAPTER I. Red circles surrounded their eyes. These, with head-dresses of feathers and horns, gave them a fantastic and ferocious appearance. The drums sounded alarums, and they rushed out of the fort with fearful whoops, forcing Anasco to retreat to the open fields. The enemy, scorning the inferiority of the detachment, pretended to knock one of the warriors in the head with a club, in front of the fort; and swinging him by the head and heels near a fire, in insulting mockery, indicated the fate of the Spaniards who should fall into their hands. The irritated Anasco sent three troopers to the camp, who returned with De Soto at the head of a considerable force. The latter assaulted the fortress of Alibamo, leading on his men in
1541 April 27 three squadrons, commanded by Guzman, Avaro Romo de Cardenoso, and the stout Gonzalo Silvestre. A hundred Alabamas poured out from each portal and met the Spaniards. Upon the first encounter, Diego de Castro, Louis Bravo and Francisco de Figarro, fell mortally wounded. An arrow struck the casque of the Governor with such force that it made his eyes flash fire. The victorious Spaniards forced the Alabamas into the fort, pressing them to death by the united shock of cavalry and infantry—the passes of the gates admitting but few of the Indians at once. The soldiers remembered that they had united with the Chickasaws, and they knew no bounds to the revenge which they now sought. In the rear many savages escaped, by climbing over the walls and through the back portals, pitching into the river which ran by the fort, but far below its foundation. In a short time, De Soto held possession of the interior. Alibamo stood upon the

Yazoo river, in the county of Tallahatchie.* It was built of pallisades, in the form of a quadrangle, four hundred paces long on either side. Inner walls divided it into separate parts, enabling the besieged to retreat from one to the other. The centre wall, on the back side, was immediately upon a perpendicular bluff, beneath which flowed a deep and narrow river, across which were thrown a few rude bridges. Portions of the fort appeared to have been recently constructed for defence against the horses. It was decidedly the best fortified place yet discovered, except Maubila, but the garrison was greatly inferior in numbers to that of the latter. The outside portals were too low and narrow for a cavalier to enter on his horse.

1541 April 27

* General Le Clerc Milfort, an intelligent Frenchman, lived in the Creek Nation from 1776 until 1796. He wrote a history of the Muscogees or Creeks, and published his work in Paris in 1802. He married the sister of General Alexander McGillivray of the Creek tribe. When he arrived in France, Bonaparte made him a General of Brigade; and in 1814 he was attacked in his house by a party of Russians, and rescued by some grenadiers. Shortly afterwards he died.

Milfort states that the Alabamas wandered from the northern part of Mexico, and settled upon the Yazoo, and afterwards removed to the river which bears their name. This fact, connected with that of the Alibamo fort, mentioned by the journals of De Soto, establishes, conclusively, that they were the same people. The Alabamas, after De Soto's time, settled on the site of the modern Montgomery, Coosawda and Washington, below the confluence of the Coosa and Tallapoosa. From these people the river and state took their names.

"Memoire ou coup d'œil rapide sur mes differens voyages et mon sejour dans la Nation Crëck, par Le Clerc Milfort."—pp. 229–288.

CHAPTER I. De Soto crossed the river at a ford below the plain, and pursued the savages until twilight, leaving many of them in the sleep of death. Four days were consumed at Alibamo in attending to the wounded. Fifteen Spaniards died—among them the cavaliers first wounded, who were young, valiant and of the best blood of Spain. So terminated the battle of Alibamo,—the last one of the many De Soto fought, which it is within our province to describe. We have followed that extraordinary adventurer through our State, into the heart of Mississippi. A few more words must close the account of his nomadic march, as far as it rests in our hands.

The Spaniards reached the Mississippi river in May, 1541, and were the first to discover it, unless Cabaca de Vaca crossed it twelve years before, in wandering to Mexico with his four companions,—which is not probable, from the evidence afforded by his journal. De Soto consumed a year in marching over Arkansas, and returned to the "Father of Waters," at the town of Guachaya, below the mouth of the Arkansas river, on the last of May, 1542. He here engaged in the construction of two brigantines to communicate with Cuba. That
1542 May great man, whose spirits had long since forsaken him—who had met with nothing but disappointments—and who had, in his most perilous wanderings, discovered no country like Peru and Mexico,—became sick with a slow and malignant fever. He appointed Moscoso to the command—bid his officers and soldiers farewell—exhorted them to keep together, in order to reach that country which he was destined never to see—and then CLOSED HIS EYES IN DEATH! Thus died Hernando De

Soto, one of the most distinguished captains of that or any age. To conceal his death and protect his body from Indian brutalities, he was placed in an oaken trough, and silently plunged into the middle of the Mississippi, on a dark and gloomy night. Long did the muddy waters wash the bones of one of the bravest sons of Spain! He was the first to behold that river—the first to close his eyes in death upon it—and the first to find a grave in its deep and turbid channel.

Moscoso and the remaining troops again plunged into the wilderness west of the Mississippi, with the hope of reaching Mexico. Departing on the 1st of June, 1542, he returned on the 1st December to the Mississippi river, at a point fifty miles above the place where De Soto died. The Spaniards began the construction of seven brigantines, the building of which required the chains of the slaves, saddle-stirrups, and every thing which contained a particle of iron, made into nails by the erection of forges, the Indian mantles stitched together for sails, and the inner bark of trees made into ropes. When these were completed, Gov. Moscoso departed down the vast stream, the 2d July, 1543. The once splendid army of one thousand men, was reduced to three hundred and twenty! Five hundred slaves were left at the place of embarkation, and Moscoso took with him one hundred, among others, the beautiful women of Maubila. Twenty-two of the best horses were embarked; the others were killed and dried for food, as were the hogs, a large number of which still remained.. The Spaniards were attacked, in descending the river, by fleets of Indian canoes. In one of these engagements, the brave Guzman and

1543 July 2

CHAPTER I. eleven others were drowned, and twenty-five wounded. In sixteen days they reached the Gulf, and put to sea on the 18th July, 1543. Having landed at Tampa Bay on the 30th of May, 1539, they had consumed a little over four years in wandering through Florida, Georgia, Alabama, Mississippi and the vast regions of the Arkansas Territory. Tossed by the waves, famished with hunger, parched with thirst, and several times wrecked by tornadoes, the poor Spaniards finally reached the mouth of the river Panuco, upon the Mexican coast, on the 10th September, 1543. From thence they went to the town of Panuco. Appareled in skins of deer, buffalo, bear and other animals—with faces haggard, blackened, shriveled, and but 1543 September 10 faintly resembling human beings—they repaired to the church and offered up thanks to God for the preservation of their lives. Repairing to the city of Mexico, the Viceroy extended to them every hospitality. So did the elegant Castilian ladies of his court, who were enraptured with the beauty of the Mobilian females—the high-spirited daughters of Alabama.*

Maldinado, whom we left at Pensacola bay, awaited, in vain, the arrival of De Soto. He and his distinguished associate, Gomez Arias, at length weighed anchor and sailed along the coast in different directions, hoping to meet the expedition at some point. They left signals upon the trees, and at-

* An interesting account of the expedition, from the battle of Alibamo to their entrance into the city of Mexico, which I have rapidly glanced at, may be found in the Portuguese Narrative, pp. 728–762, Garcellasso de la Vega, pp. 372–557.

tached letters to the bark. Returning to Cuba they again sailed in search of De Soto in the summer of 1541, and touched frequently upon the Floridian and Mexican coasts, but heard nothing of him. Again, in the summer of 1542, they made a similar voyage, with no better success. Determined not to give up the search for the lost Spaniards, Maldinado and Arias, in the spring of 1543, departed on a long voyage. On the 15th of October they touched at Vera Cruz, and learned that De Soto had died upon the Mississippi, and that three hundred of his army only had lived to reach Mexico. When this sad intelligence was conveyed to Havana, every one grieved, and Doña Isabel, long racked with anxiety, died of a broken heart!

CHAPTER I.

1543 October 15

CHAPTER II.

PART I.

THE ABORIGINES OF ALABAMA, AND THE SURROUNDING STATES.

THE Indians of Alabama, Florida, Georgia and Mississippi, were so similar in form, mode of living and general habits, in the time of De Soto and of others who succeeded him in penetrating these wilds, that they will all be treated, on the pages of this chapter, as one people. Their color was like that of the Indians of our day. The males were admirably propor-
1540 tioned, athletic, active and graceful in their movements, and possessed open and manly countenances. The females, not inferior in form, were smaller, and many of them beautiful. No ugly or ill-formed Indians were seen, except at the town of Tula, west of the Mississippi. Corpulency was rare; nevertheless, it was excessive in a few instances. In the neighborhood of Apalache, in Florida, the Chief was so fat that he was compelled to move about his house upon his hands and knees.

The dress of the men consisted of a mantle of the size of a common blanket, made of the inner bark of trees, and a species of flax, interwoven. It was thrown over the shoulders,

with the right arm exposed. One of these mantles encircled CHAPTER
the body of the female, commencing below the breast and II.
extending nearly to the knees, while another was grace- Part 1. 1540
fully thrown over the shoulders, also with the right arm exposed. Upon the St. Johns river, the females, although 156
equally advanced in civilization, appeared in a much greater state of nudity—often with no covering, in summer, except a moss drapery suspended round the waist, and which hung down in graceful negligence. Both sexes there, were, however, adorned with ornaments, consisting of pretty shells and shining pearls, while the better classes wore moccasins and buskins of dressed deer leather. In Georgia and Alabama the towns contained store-houses, filled with rich and comfortable clothing, such as mantles of hemp, and of feathers of
every color, exquisitely arranged, forming admirable cloaks 1540
for winter; with a variety of dressed deer skin garments, and skins of the martin, bear and panther, nicely packed away in baskets.* Fond of trinkets, the natives collected shells from the sea-side and pearls from the beds of the interior rivers. The latter they pierced with heated copper spindles, and strung them around their legs, necks and arms.† The Queen upon the Savannah took from her neck a magnificent cordon of pearls, and twined it round the neck of the warlike but courteous De Soto.‡ In the interior of the country,
pearls were worn in the ears; but upon the coast, fish blad- 1564

* Portuguese Narrative, p. 711. † Portuguese Narrative, p. 701.

‡ Portuguese Narrative, p. 714.

CHAPTER II. Part 1.

ders, inflated after they had been inserted, were greatly preferred.* The Chiefs and their wives, the Prophets and principal men, painted their breasts and the front part of their bodies with a variety of stripes and characters. Others, like sea-faring people, had their skins punctured with bone needles and indelible ink rubbed in, which gave them the appear-
1539 ance of being tattoed.† Jean Ortiz, so long a prisoner among the Floridians, when discovered by De Soto, was taken for an Indian, on account of his body being "razed" in this manner.‡ It will be remembered that the Alabamas, upon the Yazoo, painted in stripes of white, yellow, black and red, and

* Le Moyne's Florida plate, 38. Renaud de Laudouniere, an admiral of France, made a second voyage to Florida, and landed upon its shore in 1564. Attached to this expedition was a Frenchman, named Jacob Le Moyne, who was an admirable painter. Laudouniere left some soldiers at a Fort which he built upon the St. John's, and with them this accomplished artist. Le Moyne was frequently despatched with small detachments along the coast, and to some distance in the interior, to make surveys of the rivers and to cultivate the friendship of the natives. During these excursions he made admirable drawings of the Indians, their houses, farms, games, amusements, manners, customs and religious ceremonies. Returning to France, he related his adventures to Charles IX., and exhibited to him his pictures. These, with his explanatory notes, were published by Theodore de Bry, in 1591, in the Latin language, at Frankfort. The copy in my possession, a most interesting book upon the ancient Indians of Florida and the adjoining States, contains forty-two plates, a few specimens of which are introduced in this volume.

† La Moyne, plate 38. ‡ Portuguese Narrative, p. 702.

CHIEFS, WITH THEIR ORNAMENTS AND WAR IMPLEMENTS, UPON THEIR MARCH AGAINST THE ENEMY.
Drawn from life, by Jacob le Moyne, in 1564

"seemed as though they were dressed in hose and doublets."* Lofty plumes of the feathers of the eagle, and other noted birds, adorned the heads of the warriors. At the battle of Vitachuco, in Middle Florida, ten thousand warriors appeared in this magnificent native head-dress. They also punished and deformed themselves in the display of their more peculiar ornaments. Upon an island in West Florida, they wore reeds thrust through their nipples and under lips.† Indian grandees were 1528
often seen promenading, of an evening, enveloped in beautiful mantles of deer skins, and of the martin, trailing behind them, and often held up by attendants. Among the prettiest ornaments were flat shells, of varied colors, which they suspended from girdles around their waists, and which hung down around their hips.

The bow, the most formidable weapon of the ancient Indians, was long, elastic and exceedingly strong. The string was made of the sinews of the deer. The arrows, of strong 1540
young cane, hardened before the fire, were often tipped with buck-horn, and invariably pointed either with palm or other hard wood, flints, long and sharp like a dagger, fish-bones shaped like a chisel, or diamond flints.‡ The Spaniards soon ascertained that they pierced as deep as those which they themselves shot from the cross-bow, and were discharged

* Portuguese Narrative, p. 727.

† Expedition of Narvaez, contained in Herrera's History of America—vol. 4, p. 33.

‡ Garcellasso de la Vega, p. 266.

CHAPTER II. Part 1. 1564

more rapidly.* The quiver which held them was made of fawn or some other spotted skin, and was cased at the lower end with thick hide of the bear or the alligator. It was always suspended by a leather strap, passing round the neck, which permitted it to rest on the left hip, like a sword. It was capable of holding a great many arrows. Shields were universal appendages in war, and were made either of wood, split canes strongly interwoven, alligator hide, and sometimes that of buffalo. The latter was often the case west of the Mississippi. Of various sizes, but ordinarily large enough to cover the breast, these round shields were painted with rings and stripes, and suspended from the neck by a band. Sometimes a noted Chief protected his breast and a portion of his abdomen with three of them. These, with a piece of bark covering the left arm, to prevent the severe rebound of the bow-string, were all that shielded the natives in time of war. Wooden spears, of the usual length, pointed with excellent darts of fish-bone or flint, were, also, much used. And, strange to say, swords of palm wood, of the proper shape, were often seen. A Chief, in Georgia, seized one of this description, which was born by one of his servants, and began to cut and thrust with it to the admiration of De Soto and his officers. The war clubs were of two kinds—one, small at the handle, gradually enlarging at the top in oval form; and the other, with two sharp edges at the end, usually employed in executions. Decoration with plumes, appears to have been more common in general cos-

* Portuguese Narrative, p. 102.

A Chief addressing his Warriors, who are armed, painted and plumed, and ready to march against the enemy. Drawn from life, by Jacob le Moyne, in 1564.

tume and pleasure excursions, than in war. In enterprises of CHAPTER
the latter character, the natives sought to appear as ferocious II.
as possible. The skins of the eagle, of the wolf and of the Part 1.
panther, with the heads of these animals attached, and well
preserved, were worn by warriors, while the talons and claws 1564
were inserted as ear ornaments.*

When about to make war, a Chief despatched a party, who
approached near the town of the enemy, and by night stuck
arrows into the cross-paths and public places, with long locks
of human hair waving from them.† After this declaration of
war, he assembled his men, who, painted and decorated in the
most fantastic and frightful manner, surrounded him on all
sides. Excited with seeming anger, he rolled his eyes,
spoke in guttural accents, and often sent forth tremendous
war whoops. The warriors responded in chorus, and struck
their weapons against their sides. With a wooden spear he
turned himself reverentially towards the sun, and implored, of
that luminary, victory over his enemies. Turning to his men, 1564
he took water from a vessel on his right and sprinkled it
about, saying, "Thus may you do with the blood of your
enemies." Then raising another vessel of water, he poured its
entire contents on a fire which had been kindled on his left,
and repeated, "Thus may you destroy your enemies and bring
home their scalps."‡ Having marched his army within the
vicinity of the enemy, he bid his Prophet to inform him of

* Le Moyne, plates 11, 12, 13, 14. † Le Moyne, plate 33.

‡ Le Moyne, plate 11.

CHAPTER II. Part 1.

their number and position, and in what manner it was best to bring on the attack. The old man, usually a hundred years of age, advanced, and a large circle was immediately formed around him. He placed a shield upon the ground, drew a ring around it five feet in diameter, in which he inscribed various characters. Then kneeling on the shield, and sitting on his feet, so as to touch the earth with no part of his body, he made the most horrible grimaces, uttered the most un-
1564 natural howls, and distorted his limbs until his very bones appeared to be flexible. In twenty minutes he ceased his infernal juggling, assumed his natural look, with apparently no fatigue, and gave the Chief the information which he desired.* Some of our ancient natives marched in regular order, with the Chief in the centre, but it was their common habit to scatter in small parties, and take the enemy by surprise. But in the arrangement of their camp, which was always made at sunset, they were exceedingly particular. They then stationed detachments around the Chief, forming a compact and well-arranged defence.†

The women who had lost their husbands in battle, at a convenient time surrounded the Chief, stooped at his feet, covered their faces with their hands, wept, and implored him to be revenged for the death of their companions. They entreated him to grant them an allowance during their widowhood, and to permit them to marry again when the time appointed by law expired. They afterwards visited the graves of

* Le Moyne, plate 12. † Le Moyne, plate 14.

their husbands and deposited upon them the arms which they CHAPTER
used in hunts and wars, and the shells out of which they II.
Part 1.
were accustomed to drink. Having cut off their long hair, they 1564
sprinkled it also over their graves, and then returned home.
They did not marry until it had attained its ordinary length.*

The natives drank a tea, which, in modern times, was
called black drink. It was made by boiling the leaves of the
cacina plant, until a strong decoction was produced. The Chief
took his seat, made of nine small poles, in the centre of a
semi-circle of seats; but his was the most elevated of all. His
principal officers approached him by turns, one at a time, and
placing their hands upon the top of their heads, sung *ha*, 1564
he, *ya*, *ha*, *ha*. The whole assembly responded, *ha*, *ha*.
After which, they seated themselves upon his right and left.
The women, in the meantime, had prepared the black drink,
which was served up in conch shells and handed to certain
men, who distributed it around. The warriors drank large
potions of it, and presently vomited it with great ease. It 1564
seemed to have been used at the early period of 1564, as it
is at present, to purify the system, and also to fulfil a kind of
religious rite.†

The punishments of that day were summary and cruel.
For a crime deserving death, the criminal was conducted to
the square and made to kneel with his body inclined forward.
The executioner placed his left foot upon his back, and with
a murderous blow with the sharp-sided club, dashed out his 1564

* Le Moyne, plate 19. † Le Moyne's Florida, plate 29.

CHAPTER II. Part 1. 1539 brains.* Jean Ortiz and his companions were stripped naked, and forced to run from corner to corner through the town, while the exulting savages shot at them by turns with deadly arrows. Ortiz alone survived, and they next proceeded to roast him upon a wooden gridiron, when he was saved by the entreaties of a noble girl.† Whenever they made prisoners of each other, those who were captured were often put to menial services. To prevent them from running away, it was

1540 customary to cut the nerves of their legs just above the instep.‡

When a battle was fought, the victors seized upon the enemy and mutilated their bodies in the most brutal manner. With cane knives the arms and legs were cut around, and then severed from the body by blows upon the bones, from wooden cleavers. They thus amputated with great skill and rapidity. The head was also cut around, with these knives, just above the ears, and the whole scalp jerked off. These were then rapidly smoked over a fire, kindled in a small round hole, and borne off in triumph towards home, together with the arms and legs, suspended upon spears.§ The joyous and excited inhabitants now assembled upon the square and formed a large area, in which these trophies were hung

1564 upon high poles. An old Prophet took a position on one side of the circle, held in his hand a small image of a child, and danced and muttered over it a thousand imprecations

* Le Moyne's Florida, plate 32.

† Garcellasso de la Vega.

‡ Garcellasso de la Vega.

§ Le Moyne, plate 15.

Indians engaged in scalping and cutting up the slain enemy. Drawn from life, by Jacob le Moyne, in 1564.

upon the enemy. On the other side, and opposite to him, three warriors fell upon their knees. One of them, who was in the middle, constantly brought down a club, with great force, on a smooth stone, placed before him, while the others, on either side of him, rattled gourds filled with shells and pebbles, all keeping exact time with the Prophet.*

The houses of the Chiefs, with but few exceptions, stood upon large and elevated artificial mounds. When the Indians of 1540 resolved to build a town, the site of which was usually selected upon low, rich land, by the side of a beautiful stream, they were accustomed, first, to turn their attention to the erection of a mound from twenty to fifty feet high, round on the sides, but flat on top. The top was capable of sustaining the houses of the Chief, and those of his family and attendants; making a little village by itself of from ten to twenty cabins, elevated high in the air. The earth to make this mound was brought to the spot. At the foot of this eminence a square was marked out, around which the principal men placed their houses. The inferior classes joined these with 1540
their wigwams. Some of these mounds had several stairways to ascend them, made by cutting out incline-planes fifteen or twenty feet wide, flanking the sides with posts, and laying poles horizontally across the earthen steps—thus forming a kind of wooden stairway. But, generally, the lofty residence of the Chief was approached by only one flight of steps. These mounds were perpendicular, and inaccessible, except by the

* Le Moyne, plate 16.

CHAPTER II. Part 1. avenues already mentioned, which rendered the houses upon them secure from the attacks of an Indian enemy. Besides the motive for security, a disposition to place the Chief and his family in a commanding position, and to raise him above his subjects, caused the formation of these singular elevations.*

Upon the coasts of Florida, the houses were built of timber, covered with palm leaves, and thatched with straw. Those of Toalli, between Apalache and the Savannah, and for some distance beyond, were covered with reeds in the manner
1540 of tiles, while the walls were extremely neat. In the colder regions of the territories of Georgia, Alabama and Mississippi, every family possessed a house daubed inside and out with clay, for a winter house, and another, open all round, for summer; while a crib and kitchen, also, stood near by. The houses of the Chiefs, much larger than the others, had piazzas in front, in the rear of which were cane benches of comfortable dimensions. They contained, also, lofts, in which were stored skins, mantles and corn, the tribute of the subjects.† Upon the head waters of the Coosa, it will be recollected, that De Soto found the house of the Chief standing upon a mound,
1540 with a piazza in front, "large enough for six men to promenade abreast."‡ The town of Ochille, in Middle Florida, contained fifty very substantial houses. The Chief's house was built in the form of a large pavilion, upwards of one hundred and twenty feet in length by forty in width, with

* Garcellasso de la Vega, p. 136. † Portuguese Narrative, p. 701.

‡ Garcellasso de la Vega, p. 294.

a number of small buildings, connected like offices.* Narvaez found a house large enough to contain three hundred men, in which were fishing nets and a tabor with gold bells.† The Indian grandeur and spacious dimensions of the houses of Maubila, in Alabama, have already been described. In the province of Palisema, west of the Mississippi, the house of the Chief was covered with deer skins, which were painted with stripes of various colors, and with animals, while the walls were hung, and the floor carpeted, with the same materials.‡ In the first town which De Soto discovered, at Tampa Bay, was found a large temple, on the top of which was a wooden bird with gilded eyes.§ The Chief, Uceta, made Jean Ortiz keeper of the temple, situated in a lonely forest in the outskirts of the town. In this temple were deposited dead Indians, contained in wooden boxes, the lids of which, having no hinges, were kept down with weights. The bodies and bones were sometimes carried off by panthers and wolves. In this horrible place was poor Ortiz stationed to watch, day and night, and threatened with instant death if he allowed a single body to be taken away. At length, constant anxiety and fatigue overcame him, and one night he fell asleep. The heavy falling of a coffin-lid awoke him. In his terror he seized a bow, and running out, heard the cracking of bones amid a dark clump of bushes! He winged a powerful arrow in that direction. A scuffle ensued, and then

CHAPTER II. Part 1. 1528

1529

1529

* Garcellasso de la Vega, p. 101.

† Herrera, vol. 4.

‡ Portuguese Narrative.

§ Portuguese Narrative, p. 701.

CHAPTER II. Part 1.

all was still! He moved towards the spot, and found an enormous panther, dead, by the side of the body of the child of a principal Indian. He replaced the latter in its box, exultingly dragged the animal into the town, and was from that
1528 time respected by the Indians.* Narvaez, upon first landing in Florida, found a temple in which were chests, each containing a dead body, covered with painted deer skins. The Commissary, John Xuarez, considering it to be idolatrous, ordered them to be burned.† A remarkable temple was situated in the town of Talomeco, upon the Savannah river, three miles distant from Cutifachiqui, now Silver Bluff. It was more than one hundred feet in length, and forty in width. The walls were high in proportion, and the roof steep and covered with mats of split cane, interwoven so compactly that they resembled the rush carpeting of the Moors. (The inhabitants of this part of the country all covered their houses with this matting.) Shells of different sizes, arranged in an ingenious manner, were placed on the outside of the roof. On the inside, beautiful plumes, shells and pearls were suspended in
1540 the form of festoons, from one to the other, down to the floor. The temple was entered by three gates, at each of which were stationed gigantic wooden statues, presenting fierce and menacing attitudes. Some of them were armed with clubs, maces, canoe-paddles, and copper hatchets, and others with drawn bows and long pikes. All these implements were ornamented with

* Garcellasso de la Vega, pp. 274–282.

† Herrera, vol. 4, p. 30.

rings of pearls and bands of copper. Below the ceiling, on CHAPTER
four sides of the temple, arranged in niches, were two rows of II.
wooden statues of the natural size—one of men, with pearls Part 1.
suspended from their hands, and the other of women. On the 1540
side of the walls were large benches on which sat boxes containing the deceased Chiefs and their families. Two feet below these were statues of the persons entombed, the space between them being filled with shields of various sizes, made of strong woven reeds, adorned with pearls and colored tassels. Three rows of chests, full of valuable pearls, occupied the middle of the temple. Deer skins, of a variety of colors, were packed away in chests, together with a large amount of clothing made of the skins of wild cat, martin and other animals. The temple abounded in the most splendid mantles of feathers. Adjoining was a store-house, divided into eight apartments, which contained long pikes of copper, around which rings of pearl were coiled, while clubs, maces, wooden swords, paddles, arrows, quivers, bows, round wooden shields, and those of reed and buffalo hide, were decorated in like manner.* Everywhere upon the route through Alabama and the neighboring States, De Soto found
the temples full of human bones. They were held sacred, 1540
but sometimes were wantonly violated by tribes at war with each other. On the west bank of the Mississippi, De Soto, joined by the Indian forces of the Chief Casquin, sacked the town of Pacaha. The invading Indians entered the temple, threw down the wooden boxes containing the dead, trampled

* Garcellasso de la Vega, pp. 274–282.

CHAPTER II. Part 1.

upon the bodies and bones, and wreaked upon them every insult and indignity. A few days after, the Chief of Pacaha and his people come back to the ruined town, and gathering up the scattered bones in mournful silence, kissed and returned them reverentially to their coffins.*

1540 The productions of the country were abundant. Peas, beans, squashes, pumpkins and corn grew as if by magic. Persimons, formed into large cakes, were eaten in winter, together with walnut and bear's oil. A small pumpkin when roasted in the embers, was delightful, and resembled, in taste, boiled chesnuts. Corn was pounded in mortars, but Narvaez
1528 saw stones for grinding it, upon the Florida coast.† The Indians prepared their fields by digging up the ground with
1564 hoes made of fish-bone. When the earth was levelled in this manner, others followed with canes, with which they made holes, certain distances apart. The women next came with corn, in baskets, which they dropped in the holes. The virginity and richness of the soil produced the crop without further labor. [See Frontispiece.] The granaries were sometimes erected in the woods, near navigable streams, and were constructed with stone and dirt, and covered with cane mats. Here were deposited corn, fruits and all kinds of cured meat,
1564 for subsistence during the winter hunts in that part of the country. The universal honesty of the people was a guarantee that the contents of these granaries would remain undisturbed, until consumed by the owners.

* Portuguese Narrative, p. 701. † Herrera, vol. 4, p. 30.

Indians preparing Meats to be deposited in their Winter Hunt Houses. Drawn from life by Jacob le Moyne, in 1564.

Hunting and fishing occupied much of the time of the natives. The hunter threw over his body the skin of a deer, with the head, horns and legs admirably preserved. Round wooden hoops gave the body of the skin its proper shape, inside of which the Indian placed his body. Then, in a stooping position, so as to allow the feet to touch the ground, he moved along and peeped through the eye-holes of the deer's head, all the time having a drawn bow. When near enough to the deer, he let fly a fatal arrow. The deer, in that day, unaccustomed to the noise of fire-arms, were gentle and numerous, and easily killed by a stratagem like this.* 1564

At certain periods, the Indians were a social people, and indulged in large feasts. At other times, they resorted to bow-shooting, ball-plays and dancing.†

The population was much greater when De Soto was in the country, than it has been since. Large armies were frequently arrayed against him. In Patofa, Florida, he was even furnished with seven hundred burden bearers. In Ocute, Georgia, he was supplied with two hundred of these indispensable men. At Cafeque, in the same State, four thousand warriors escorted him, while four thousand more transported the effects of his army. It has been seen what a numerous population was found in the province of Coosa, and what forces opposed him at Maubila, Chickasa and Alibamo. 1540

* Le Moyne's Florida, plate 25. Bossu's Travels in Louisiana, vol. 1, p. 259.

† Le Moyne, plate 28.

CHAPTER II. Part 1.

The ingenuity of the natives, displayed in the construction of mounds, arms, houses and ornaments, was by no means inconsiderable. At Chaquate, west of the Mississippi, earthenware was manufactured equal to that of Estremos or Mon-
1541 tremor.* At Tulla, in Arkansas, salt was made from the deposite formed upon the shores of a lake; and again, at several saline springs. The salt was made into small cakes, and vended among other tribes for skins and mantles.† The walls which surrounded the towns, with their towers and terraces, have already been mentioned in the preceding chapter. Entrenchments and ditches were also found over the country. The most remarkable of the latter was at Pacha, west of the Mississippi. Here a large ditch, "wide enough for two canoes to pass abreast without the paddles touching," surrounded a walled town. It was cut nine miles
1541 long, communicated with the Mississippi, supplied the natives with fish and afforded them the privileges of navigation.

1541 The construction of canoes and barges, connected with the things which have already been enumerated, affords abundant proof that our aborigines were superior, in some respects, to the tribes who afterwards occupied Alabama, but who were also ingenious in the manufacture of articles. The Queen of Savannah, borne out of her house in a sedan chair, supported
1540 upon the shoulders of four of her principal men, entered a

* Portuguese Narrative and Garcellasso.

† Portuguese Narrative and Garcellasso

CHAPTER II. Part 1.

handsome barge which had a tilted top at the stern—under which she took a seat upon soft cushions. Many principal Indians likewise entered similar barges, and accompanied her to the western side, in the style of a splendid water procession. When De Soto first discovered the Mississippi, a Chief approached from the other side with two hundred handsome canoes of great size, filled with painted and plumed warriors, who stood erect, with bows in their hands, to protect those who paddled. The boats of the Chiefs and principal men had tops,—like that of the Georgia Queen,—decorated with waving flags and plumes, which floated on the breeze from poles to which they were attached. They are described by the journalists to have been equal to a beautiful army of gallies.* 1541

The natives worshipped the sun, and entertained great veneration for the moon, and certain stars. Whether they also believed in a Great Spirit is not stated. When the Indian ambassadors crossed the Savannah to meet De Soto, they made three profound bows towards the east, intended for the sun; three towards the west, for the moon; and three to the Governor.† Upon the east bank of the Mississippi, all the Indians approached him without uttering a word, and went through precisely the same ceremony; making, however, to him three bows, much less reverential than those made to the sun and moon. On the other side of that river, he was surrounded by the Chief and his subjects. Presently, his Indian majesty sneezed in a loud manner. The subjects bowed their

* Portuguese Narrative, p. 729. † Garcellasso de la Vega, p. 256.

heads, opened and closed their arms, and saluted the Chief
with these words, "may the sun guard you"—"may the sun
be with you"—"may the sun shine upon you," and "may
the sun prosper and defend you."* About the first of March,
1541 annually, the natives selected the skin of the largest deer,
with the head and legs attached. They filled it with a variety of fruit and grain, and sewed it up again. The horns were, also, hung with garlands of fruit. This skin, in all respects resembling a large buck, was carried by all the inhabitants to a plain. There it was placed upon a high post, and just at the rising of the sun, the Indians fell down on their knees around it, and implored that bright luminary to grant them, the ensuing season, an abundance of fruits and provisions, as good as those contained in the skin of the deer.† This was the practice upon the coast of East Florida, and,
1564 doubtless, it was observed all over the country. It was certainly a very practical mode of asking favors of the sun.

When a Chief or Prophet died upon the St. Johns, he was placed in the ground, and a small mound, of conical form, was erected over him. The base of this mound was surrounded with arrows, stuck in regular order. Some sat, and others kneeled around it, and continued to weep and howl for the space of three nights. Chosen women next visited the mound for a long time, every morning at the break of day, at noon, and at night.‡ Indeed, great respect appears to have been paid

* Garcellasso de la Vega, pp. 439–440.

† Le Moyne, plate 35. ‡ Le Moyne, plate 40.

Indians bearing in a chair, a young girl, who has been selected as one of the future wives of the king, Drawn from life, by Jacob le Moyne, in 1564.

to the Chief when alive, and to him a cruel sacrifice was ac- CHAPTER
customed to be made. The first born male child was always II.
brought out before the Chief, who sat upon a bench on one Part 1. 1564
side of a large circle. Before him was a block, two feet high,
and near it stooped the young mother, weeping in great
agony. The child was brought forward by a dancing woman,
placed upon the block, and a Prophet dashed out its brains
with a club; at the same time, many females danced, and
raised their voices in song.*

If a Chief desired to marry, he was accustomed to send his
principal men to select, from the girls of nobility, one of the
youngest and most beautiful. Painted with various colors,
and adorned with shells and pearls, the chosen one was then
placed in a sedan chair, the top of which formed an arch of 1564
green boughs. When placed by his side, on an elevated seat,
great pomp and ceremony, an array of ornaments of all kinds,
and music and dancing, characterized the affair, while she and
her lord were fanned with beautiful feathers.

The treatment of diseases in that day, were few and simple.
The doctor sometimes scarified the patient with shells and
fishes teeth, and sucked out the blood with his mouth. This
he spurted in a bowl, and it was drunk by nursing women
who stood by, if the patient was an athletic young man, in
order to give their children the same vigor. It was customary,
also, to smoke the patient with tobacco and other weeds, until 1564
perspiration ensued and re-action was produced.†

* Le Moyne, plate 34. † Le Moyne, plate 20.

PART II.

THE MODERN INDIANS OF ALABAMA, GEORGIA AND MISSISSIPPI.

CHAPTER II. Part 2. 1540 July September October November 1541 April

It has been seen that the Indians living in that part of Alabama through which De Soto passed, were the Coosas, inhabiting the territory embraced in the present counties of Benton, Talladega, Coosa, and a portion of Cherokee; the Tallases, living upon the Tallapoosa and its tributary streams; the Mobilians, extending from near the present city of Montgomery to the commercial emporium which now bears their name; the Pafallayas or Choctaws, inhabiting the territory of the modern counties of Greene, Marengo, Tuscaloosa, Sumpter and Pickens; and, in the present State of Mississippi, the Chickasaws, in the valley of the Yalobusha; and the Alabamas, upon the Yazoo. It will, also, be recollected, that this remarkable Spaniard overrun the rich province of Chiaha, in the territory of the present north-western Georgia, and that he there found the Chalaques, which all writers upon aboriginal history decide to be the original name of the Cherokees.

1540 March April May

The invasion of De Soto resulted in the destruction of an immense Indian population, in all the territory through which he passed, except that of Georgia, where he fought no battles.

The European diseases, which the natives inherited from the Spaniards, served, also, to thin their population. Again, the constant bloody wars in which they were engaged afterwards, among each other, still further reduced their numbers. And while the bloody Spaniards were wandering over this beautiful country, the Muscogees were living upon the Ohio.* They heard of the desolation of Alabama, and after a long time came to occupy and re-people it. The remarkable migration of this powerful tribe, and that of the Alabamas, will now, for the first time, be related, and that, too, upon the authority of a reliable person, who must here be introduced to the reader.

Le Clerc Milfort, a young, handsome, and well educated Frenchman, left his native country, sailed across the Atlantic, 1775
made the tour of the New England States, and came, at length, to Savannah. A love of adventure led him to the Creek na-

* Alexander McGillivray, whose blood was Scotch, French and Indian, who was made a Colonel in the British service, afterwards a Spanish Commissary with the rank and pay of Colonel, then a Brigadier General by Washington, with full pay,—a man of towering intellect and vast information, and who ruled the Creek country for a quarter of a century,—obtained the information that the Creeks were living upon the Ohio when De Soto was here in 1540. He was informed, upon the best traditional authority, that the Creek Indians then heard of De Soto, and the strange people with him; and, that, like those whom they had seen in Mexico, they had "hair over their bodies, and carried thunder and lightning in their hands."

CHAPTER II. Part 2. 1776 May

tion, and in May, 1776, he arrived at the great town of Coweta, situated on the Chattahoochee river, two miles below the present city of Columbus. There he became acquainted with Colonel McGillivray, the great Chieftain of the nation, and accompanied him to the Hickory Ground, upon the banks of the Coosa. Fascinated with the society of this great man, the hospitality of the Indians, and the wide field afforded for exciting enterprise, Milfort resolved to become a permanent inmate of McGillivray's house, then situated at Little Tallase,

1780 May 5

four miles above Wetumpka. He married his sister, was created Tustenuggee, or Grand Chief of War, and often led Indian expeditions against the Whig population of Georgia, during the American Revolution A fine writer, and much of an antiquarian, he employed some of his leisure hours in preparing a history of the Creeks. Remaining in the nation twenty years, he resolved to return to France. In 1796 he sailed from Philadelphia, and it was not long before he was among the gay people from whom he had so long been absent. Bonaparte, at length, heard of this adventurous man, and honored him with an audience. He desired to engage his services in forming alliances with the Alabama and Mississippi Indians, for the purpose of strengthening his Louisiana possessions. But, finally giving up those possessions, and turning his whole attention to the wars in which he was deeply engaged with the allied powers, he still retained Milfort, conferring upon him the pay and rank of General of Brigade, but without active employment. In the meantime, General

1814

Milfort had published his work upon the Creek Indians.* In 1814, his house was attacked by a party of Russians, who had heard of his daring exploits in assisting to repel the allied invaders. He barricaded it, and defended himself with desperation. His French wife assisted him to load his guns. At length he was rescued by a troop of grenadiers. Shortly after this, General Milfort closed, by death, a career which had been full of event in the savage as well as the civilized world. His wife, at an advanced age, was recently burned to death in her own house at Rheims.†

1776 July

When Milfort arrived among the Creeks, the old men often spoke of their ancestors, and they exhibited to him strands of pearl which contained their history and constituted their archives. Upon their arrangement depended their signification; and only principal events were thus preserved. One of their chaplets sometimes related the history of thirty years. Each year was rapidly distinguished by those who understood them. The old men, therefore, with the assistance of these singular records and strong memories, were enabled to impart to Milfort a correct tradition, the substance of which we give.‡

Hernando Cortez, with some Spanish troops, landed at Vera Cruz, in 1519. He fought his way thence to the City

* Memoire ou coup d'œil rapide sur mes differens voyages et mon sejour dans la nation Crëck, by Le Clerc Milfort, Tastanegry ou Grand Chef de Guerre de la nation Crëck et General de Brigade ou service de la Republique Francaise. A Paris. 1802.

† Extract from a Paris paper, published by Galignani. ‡ Milfort, p. 47.

CHAPTER II. Part 2. 1519 of Mexico. In the meantime, Montezuma had assembled his forces from all parts of his empire to exterminate the invaders. The Muscogees then formed a separate republic on the north-west of Mexico. Hitherto invincible in war, they now rallied to his aid, engaging in the defence of that greatest of aboriginal cities. At length Cortez was successful—Montezuma was killed, his government overthrown, and thousands of his subjects put to the sword. Having lost many of their own warriors, and unwilling to live in a country conquered by foreign assassins, the Muscogees determined to seek some other land. The whole tribe took up the line of march, and conti-
1520 nued eastward until they struck the sources of the Red river. The route lay over vast prairies, abounding with wild animals and fruits, which afforded them all the means of subsistence. In journeying down the banks of the Red river, they discovered salt lakes and ponds, which were covered with fowl of every description. Consuming months upon the journey, they finally reached a large forest, in which they encamped. The young men, sent in advance to explore the country, returned in a month, and announced the discovery of a forest on the banks of the Red river, in which were beautiful subterranean habitations. Marching thither, they found that these caves had been made by buffalo and other animals who came there to lick the earth, which was impregnated with salt. A town was here laid out, houses constructed, an extensive field enclosed, and corn, which they had brought with them, planted. Subsisting by the chase and the products of the earth, they passed here several years in health and tran-

quillity. But even in this remote retreat they eventually found those who would molest them. The Alabamas, who seem also to have been wandering from the west, attacked a party of Muscogees, who were hunting, and killed several of them. The Muscogees abandoned their town, which they believed did not afford them sufficient protection from the buffalo and human foes. They resumed their march in the direction of the camps of the Alabamas, upon whom they had resolved to be revenged. Traversing immense plains, they reached a grove on the Missouri river, having shaped their course in a northern direction from their last settlement. Here they came upon the footprints of the Alabamas. The most aristocratic among the Muscogees, called the Family of the Wind, passed the muddy river first. They were followed by the Family of the Bear; then by that of the Tiger; and thus, till the humblest of the tribe had crossed over. Resuming the march, the young warriors and the Chiefs formed the advanced guard; the old men were placed in the rear, and those of an age less advanced on the flanks, while the women and children occupied the centre. Coming within the neighborhood of the enemy, the main party halted, while the Tustenuggee or Grand Chief of War, at the head of the young warriors, advanced to the attack. The Alabamas, temporarily dwelling in subterranean habitations, were taken by surprise, and many of them slain. Forced to abandon this place, and retreat from the victors, they did not rally again until they had fled a great distance down on the eastern side of the Missouri. After a time they were overtaken, when several

Probably in 1527

Probably in 1528

CHAPTER II. Part 2. bloody engagements ensued. The Muscogees were triumphant, and the vanquished retreated in terror and dismay to the banks of the Mississippi. The enemy again coming upon them with invincible charges, precipitated many of them into the river. Thus, alternately fighting, constructing new towns, and again breaking up their last establishments, these two warlike tribes gradually reached the Ohio river, and proceeded along its banks almost to the Wabash.* Here, for a long time, the Muscogees resided, and lost sight of the Alabamas, who had established themselves upon the Yazoo, and were there living when De Soto, in 1541, attacked their fortress.† The Muscogees abandoned their home in the
1520 to 1535 north-western province of Mexico about the period of 1520, had consumed fifteen years in reaching the Ohio, and were there residing when the Spanish invasion occurred. How long they occupied that country Milfort does not inform us; but he states that they finally crossed the Ohio and Tennessee, and settled upon the Yazoo—thus continuing to pursue the unfortunate Alabamas. Delighted with the genial climate, the abundance of fruit and game with which it abounded, they established towns upon the Yazoo, constructed subterranean habitations, and for some years passed their time most agreeably. It is probable the Alabamas had fled before their arrival, for the Spaniards had so thinned the number of the latter that it was folly to resist the Muscogees, who had conquered them when they were much stronger.

* Milfort, pp. 234–259. † Other Indian traditions in my possession.

Milfort states that the Alabamas finally advanced to the river which now bears their name. Here, finding a region charming in climate, rich in soil, convenient in navigation, and remote from the country of their enemies, they made permanent establishments, from the confluence of the Coosa and Tallapoosa some distance down the Alabama.

Remembering how often they had been surprised by the Muscogees, and how insecure from their attacks was even a distant retreat, the Alabamas sent forth young warriors westward, to see if their foes were still wandering upon their heels. It happened that a party of the latter were reconnoitering eastward. They met, fought, and some of the Muscogees were killed. In the meantime, the latter tribe had learned what a delightful country was occupied by the Alabamas, and this new outrage, coupled with a desire to go further south-east, induced them to break up their establishments upon the Yazoo. Without opposition the Muscogees took possession of the lands upon the Alabama, and also those upon the Coosa and Tallapoosa. The Alabamas fled in all directions, seeking asylums among the Choctaws and other tribes.

Supposed to be in 1620

Gaining a firm footing in the new region, enjoying good health, and increasing in population, the Muscogees advanced to the Ockmulgee, Oconee, and Ogechee, and even established a town where now reposes the beautiful city of Augusta. With the Indians of the present State of Georgia, they had combats, but overcome them. Pushing on their conquests, they reduced a warlike tribe called the Uchees, lower down upon the Savannah, and brought the prisoners in slavery to

CHAPTER II. Part 2.

the Chattahoochie.* In 1822, the Big Warrior, who then ruled the Creek confederacy, confirmed this tradition, even going further back than Milfort,— taking the Muscogees from Asia, bringing them over the Pacific, landing them near the Isthmus of Darien, and conducting them from thence to this country. "My ancestors were a mighty people. After they reached the waters of the Alabama and took possession of all this country, they went further,—conquered the tribes upon the Chattahoochie, and upon all the rivers from thence to the Savannah,—yes, and even whipped the Indians then living in the territory of South-Carolina, and wrested much of their country from them." The Big Warrior concluded this sentence with great exultation, when Mr. Compere, to whom he was speaking, interposed an unfortunate question:—"If this is the way your ancestors acquired all the territory now lying
1822 in Georgia, how can you blame the American population in that State for endeavoring to take it from you?" Never after that could the worthy missionary extract a solitary item from the Chieftain, in relation to the history of his people.†

*Milfort, pp. 269–263. Bartram's Travels in Florida, pp. 53, 54, 464. Also traditional MS. notes in my possession.

†Rev. Lee Compere's MS. notes, in my possession. This gentleman was born in England, on Nov. 3d, 1790. He came to South Carolina in 1817. The Baptist Missionary Board and that of the General Convention, sent him as a missionary to the Creek nation in 1822. He and his wife, who was an English lady, resided at Tookabatcha (the capital) six years. Mr. Compere made but little progress towards the conversion of the Creeks, owing to the opposition of the Chiefs to the

Sometime after these conquests, the French established themselves at Mobile. The Alabamas, scattered as we have seen, and made to flee before superior numbers, became desirous to place themselves under their protection. Anxious to cultivate a good understanding with all the Indian tribes, and to heal old animosities existing among them, the French caused an interview between the Chiefs of the Alabamas and those of the Muscogees, at Mobile. In the presence of M. Bienville, the Commandant of that place, a peace was made, which has not since been violated. The Alabamas returned to their towns, upon the river of that name, which were called Coosawda, Econchate, Pauwocte, Towassau and Autauga, situated on both sides of the river, and embracing a country from the junction of the Coosa and Tallapoosa, for forty miles down. They consented to become members of the Muscogee confederacy, and to observe their national laws, but stipulated to retain their ancient manners and customs.

CHAPTER II. Part 2. 1701

1702

Not long afterwards, the Tookabatchas, who had nearly been destroyed by the Iroquois and Hurons, wandered from the Ohio country, and obtained permission from the Muscogees to form a part of their nation. They were willingly received

abolition of p imitive customs. He was a learned man and a respectable writer. He furnished the Indian Bureau, at Washington, with a complete vocabulary of the Muscogee language, and also the Lord's Prayer, all of which is published in the 11th vol. of "Transactions of the American Antiquarian Society," Cambridge, 1836, pp. 381–422. In 1833, I often heard Mr. Compere and his wife sing beautiful hymns in the Creek tongue. He lives in the State of Mississippi.

CHAPTER II. Part 2. by the cunning Muscogees, who were anxious to gain all the strength they could, to prevent the encroachments of the English from South-Carolina. Upon the ruins of the western Tallase, where De Soto encamped twenty days, the Tookabatchas built a town and gave it their name.*

The Tookabatchas brought with them to the Tallapoosa some curious brass plates, the origin and objects of which have much puzzled the Americans of our day, who have seen them. Such information respecting them as has fallen into
1759 July 27 our possession, will be given. On the 27th July, 1759, at the Tookabatcha square, William Balsover, a British trader, made inquiries concerning their ancient relics, of an old Indian Chief named Bracket, near an hundred years of age. There were two plates of brass and five of copper. The Indians esteemed them so much, that they were preserved in a private place, known only to a few Chiefs, to whom they were annually entrusted. They were never brought to light but once in a year, and that was upon the occasion of the Green Corn Celebration, when, on the fourth day, they were introduced in what was termed the "brass plate dance." Then one of the high Prophets carried one before him, under his arm, ahead of the dancers—next to him the head warrior carried another, and then others followed with the remainder, bearing aloft, at the same time, white canes, with the feathers of the swan at the tops.

* Milfort, pp. 263–266.

CHAPTER II. Part 2.

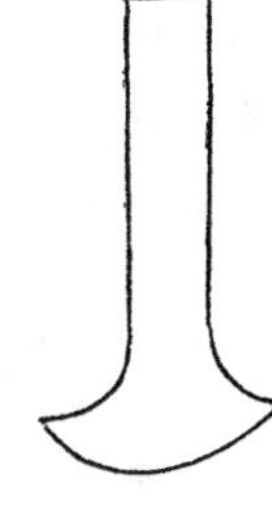

Shape of the five copper plates: one a foot and a half long, and seven inches wide; the other four a little shorter and narrower.

Shape of the two brass plates: eighteen inches in diameter, about the thickness of a dollar, and stamped as exhibited upon the face.

Formerly, the Tookabatcha tribe had many more of these relics, of different sizes and shapes, with letters and inscriptions upon them, which were given to their ancestors by the Great Spirit, who instructed them that they were only to be handled by particular men, who must at the moment be engaged in fasting, and that no unclean woman must be suffered to come near them or the place where they were deposited. Bracket further related, that several of these plates were then buried under the Micco's cabin in Tookabatcha, and had lain there ever since the first settlement of the town; that formerly it was the custom to place one or more of them in the grave by the side of a deceased Chief of the pure Tookabatcha blood, and that no other Indians in the whole

1759 July 27

CHAPTER II. Part 2. 1759 July 27 Creek nation had such sacred relics.* Similar accounts of these plates were obtained from four other British traders, "at the most eminent trading house of all English America."† The town of Tookabatcha became, in later times, the capitol of the Creek nation; and many reliable citizens of Alabama have seen these mysterious pieces at the Green Corn Dances, upon which occasions they were used precisely as in the more ancient days.‡ When the inhabitants of this town, in the autumn of 1836, took up the line of march for their present home in the Arkansas Territory, these plates were transported thence by six Indians, remarkable for their sobriety and moral character, at the head of whom was the Chief, Spoke-oak, Micco. Medicine, made expressly for their safe transportation, was carried along by these warriors. Each one had a plate strapped behind his back, enveloped nicely in buckskin. They
1836 carried nothing else, but marched on, one before the other, the whole distance to Arkansas, neither communicating nor conversing with a soul but themselves, although several thousands were emigrating in company; and walking, with a solemn

* Adair's "American Indians," pp. 178–179.

† Adair's "American Indians," p. 179.

‡ Conversations with Barent Dubois, Abraham Mordecai, James Moore, Capt. William Walker, Lacklan Durant, Mrs. Sophia McComb, and other persons, who stated that these plates had Roman characters upon them, as well as they could determine from the rapid glances which they could occasionally bestow upon them, while they were being used in the "brass plate dance."

CHAPTER II. Part 2.

religious air, one mile in advance of the others.* How much their march resembled that of the ancient Trojans, bearing off their household gods! Another tradition is, that the Shawnees gave these plates to the Tookabatchas, as tokens of their friendship, with an injunction that they would annually introduce them in their religious observance of the new corn season. But the opinion of Opothleoholo, one of the most gifted Chiefs of the modern Creeks, went to corroborate the general tradition that they were gifts from the Great Spirit.† It will be recollected that our aborigines, in the time of De Soto, understood the use of copper, and that hatchets and ornaments were made of that metal. The ancient Indians may have made them, and engraved upon their face hieroglyphics, which were supposed, from the glance only permitted to be given them, to be Roman characters. An intelligent New-Englander, named Barent Dubois, who had long lived among the Tookabatchas, believed that these plates originally formed some portion of the armor or musical instruments of De Soto, and that the Indians stole them, as they did the shields, in the Talladega country, and hence he accounts for the Roman letters on them. We give no opinion, but leave the reader to determine for himself—having discharged our duty by placing all the available evidence before him.

1833 December

The reputation which the Muscogees had acquired for strength and a warlike spirit, induced other tribes who had be-

* Conversations with Barent Dubois.

† Conversations with Opothleoholo in 1833

CHAPTER II. Part 2. [illegible]

come weak to seek an asylum among them. The Tuskegees wandered down into East Alabama, were received with open arms, and permitted to occupy the territory immediately in the fork of the Coosa and Tallapoosa. Upon the east bank of the former, a town was erected and called after the name of the tribe. Sometime after this, the French fort, Toulouse, was built here; and, one hundred years afterwards, Fort Jackson was placed upon the same foundation by the Americans.

A tribe of Ozeailles came at the same time, and were located eighteen miles above, on a beautiful plain, through
1700 which meandered a fine creek.* A large tribe of Uchees, made prisoners and brought to Cusseta, upon the Chattahoochie, not long afterwards, were liberated and assigned residences upon the creeks which bear their name, flowing through the eastern portion of the county of Russell. Or, upon the authority of Col. Hawkins, the Uchees, formerly living upon the Savannah in small villages at Ponpon, Saltketchers and Silver Bluff, and also upon the Ogechee, were continually at war with the Creeks, Cherokees and Cataubas; but in 1729, an old Chief of Cusseta, called Captain Ellick, married three Uchee women and brought them to Cusseta, which greatly displeased his friends. Their opposition determined him to move from Cusseta. With three of his brothers, two of whom also had Uchee wives, he settled upon the Uchee creek. Afterwards he collected all that tribe, and with them formed there a distinct community, which, however,

* Milfort, p. 267.

became amenable, nationally, to the government of the Musco- gees.* CHAPTER II. Part 2.

1729 In 1729, the Natchez massacred the French at Fort Rosalie, now the site of the city of Natchez, and were in turn overpowered, and many of them made slaves, while others escaped to the Coosa. In the Talladega country, they built two towns, one called Natche and the other Abecouche. Thus a branch of the Natchez also became members of the Muscogee confederacy. At the close of the Revolutionary War, a party of Savannahs came from that river in company with some Shaw- 1783
nees, from Florida, and formed a town on the east side of the Tallapoosa, called Souvanogee; upon the ruins of which the Americans, in 1819, established the village of Augusta—no remains of which now exist. Souvanogee was laid out in conformity with their usages and habits, which they retained; but they willingly came under the national government of the confederacy.†

Thus did the Muscogee confederacy gain strength, from time to time, by the migration of broken tribes. When the English began to explore their country, and to transport goods into all parts of it, they gave all the inhabitants, collectively,

* "Sketch of the Creek Country in 1798–1799," by Benjamin Hawkins, pp. 61, 62, 63.

Also, manuscript traditional notes in my possession, taken from the lips of aged Indian countrymen.

† Milfort, pp. 282-283. "Sketch of the Creek Country," by Hawkins, p. 34. Also, conversations with Indian countrymen.

CHAPTER II. Part 2.

the name of the "CREEKS," on account of the many beautiful rivers and streams which flowed through their extensive domain.* By that name they will, in the future pages of this history, be called.

The Creek woman was short in stature, but well formed.
Her cheeks were rather high, but her features were generally
regular and pretty. Her brow was high and arched, her
eye large, black and languishing, expressive of modesty and
diffidence. Her feet and hands were small, and the latter
exquisitely shaped. The warrior was larger than the ordinary
race of Europeans, often above six feet in height, but was in-
1777 variably well formed, erect in his carriage, and graceful in
every movement. They were proud, haughty and arrogant;
brave and valiant in war; ambitious of conquest; restless, and
perpetually exercising their arms, yet magnanimous and merciful to a vanquished *Indian* enemy who afterwards sought their
friendship and protection.† Encountering fatigue with ease,
they were great travellers, and sometimes went three or four
hundred leagues on a hunting expedition. "Formerly they
1780 were cruel, but at the present day they are brave, yet peaceable, when not forced to abandon their character."‡

Like all other Indians they were fond of ornaments, which consisted of stones, beads, wampum, porcupine quills, eagles' feathers, beautiful plumes, and ear-rings of various descriptions. The higher classes were often fantastic in their

* Hawkins, p. 19.

† Bartram's Travels, pp. 482, 500, 506.

‡ Milfort, p. 216–217.

wearing apparel. Sometimes a warrior put on a ruffled shirt of fine linen, and went out with no other garment except a flap of blue broadcloth, with buskins made of the same. The stillapica or moccasin, embroidered with beads, adorned the feet of the better classes. Mantles of good broadcloth, of a blue or scarlet color, decorated with fringe and lace, and hung with round silver or brass buttons, were worn by those who could afford them. When they desired to be particularly gay, vermilion was freely applied to the face, neck and arms. Again, the skin was often inscribed with hieroglyphics, and representations of the sun, moon, stars and various animals.* This was performed by puncturing the parts with gar's-teeth, and rubbing in a dye made of the drippings of rich pine roots. These characters were inscribed during youth, and frequently in manhood, every time that a warrior distinguished himself in slaying the enemy. Hence, when he was unfortunately taken prisoner, he was severely punished in proportion to the marks upon his skin, by which he was known to have shed the blood of many of the kindred of those into whose hands he had fallen.† The Creeks wore many ornaments of silver. Crescents or gorgets, very massive, suspended around the neck by ribbons, reposed upon the breast, while the arms, fingers, hats, and even sometimes the necks, had silver bands around them.

The female wore a petticoat which reached to the middle

* Bartram's Travels, pp. 482–506.

† Adair's American Indians, p. 389.

of her leg. A waistcoat or wrapper, made of calico, printed linen, or fine cloth, ornamented with lace and beads, enveloped the upper part of the body. They never wore boots or stockings, but their buskins reached to the middle of the leg. Their hair, black, long and rather coarse, was plaited in wreaths, and ordinarily turned up and fastened to the crown with a silver band. This description of dress and ornaments were
1777 worn only by the better classes. The others were more upon the primitive Indian order. They were fond of music, both vocal and instrumental; but the instruments they used were of an inferior kind, such as the tambour, rattle-gourd, and a kind of flute, made of the joint of a cane or the tibia of the deer's leg. Dancing was practised to a great extent, and they employed an endless variety of steps.*

Their most manly and important game was the "ball play." It was the most exciting and interesting game imaginable, and was the admiration of all the curious and learned travellers who witnessed it. The warriors of one town challenged those of another, and they agreed to meet at one town, or the other, as may have been decided. For several days previous to the time, those who intended to engage in the amusement, took medicine, as though they were going to war. The night immediately preceding was spent in dancing and other ceremonious preparations. On the morning of the play, they painted and decorated themselves. In the meantime, the news had spread abroad in the neighboring towns, which

* Bartram's Travels, pp. 482–506.

collected, at the place designated, an immense concourse of men, women and children—the young and the gay—the old and the grave,—together with hundreds of ponies, Indian merchandize, extra wearing apparel, and various articles brought there to stake upon the result. CHAPTER II. Part 2.

The players were all nearly naked, wearing only a piece of cloth called "flap." They advanced towards the immense plain upon which they were presently to exhibit astonishing feats of strength and agility. From eighty to a hundred men were usually on a side. They now approached each other, and were first seen at the distance of a quarter of a mile apart, but their war songs and yells had previously been heard. Intense excitement and anxiety was depicted upon the countenances of the immense throng of spectators. Presently the parties appeared in full trot, as if about to encounter fiercely in fight. They 1790 met and soon became intermingled together, dancing and stamping while a dreadful artillery of noise and shouts went up and rent the air. An awful silence then succeeded. The players retired from each other, and fell back one hundred and fifty yards from the centre. Thus they were three hundred yards apart. In the centre were erected two poles, between which the ball must pass to count one. Every warrior was provided with two rackets or hurls, of singular construction, resembling a ladle or hoop-net with handles nearly three feet long. The handle was of wood, and the netting of the thongs of raw hide or the tendons of an animal. The play was commenced by a ball, covered with buckskin, being thrown in the air. The players rushed together with a

CHAPTER II. Part 2. 1790 mighty shock, and he who caught the ball between his two rackets, ran off with it and hurled it again in the air, endeavoring to throw it between the poles in the direction of the town to which he belonged. They seized hold of each others' limbs and hair, tumbled each other over, first trampled upon those that were down, and did every thing to obtain the ball, and afterwards to make him who had it, drop it, before he could make a successful throw. The game was usually from twelve to twenty. It was kept up for hours, and during the time the players used the greatest exertions, exhibited the most infatuated devotion to their side, were often severely hurt, and sometimes killed in the rough and unfeeling scramble which prevailed. It sometimes happened that the inhabitants of a town gamed away all their ponies, jewels, and wearing apparel, even stripping themselves, upon the issue of the ball play. In the meantime, the women were constantly on the alert with vessels and gourds filled with water, watching every opportunity to supply the players.*

If a Creek warrior wished to marry, he sent his sister, mother, or some female relation, to the female relations of the girl whom he loved. Her female relations then consulted the
1798 uncles, and if none, the brothers on the maternal side, who decided upon the case. If it was an agreeable alliance, the bridegroom was informed of it, and he sent, soon after, a blanket and articles of clothing to the female part of the family of

* The "Narrative of a Mission to the Creek Nation, by Col. Marinus Willett," pp. 108–110. Bartram's Travels, pp. 482–506.

the bride. If they received these presents, the match was made, and the man was at liberty to go to the house of his wife as soon as he deemed it proper. When he had built a residence, produced a crop, gathered it in, made a hunt and brought home the game, and tendered a general delivery of all to the girl, then they were considered man and wife. 1798

Divorce was at the choice of either party. The man, however, had the advantage, for he could again marry another woman if he wished; but the woman was obliged to lead a life of celibacy until the Boosketuh or Green Corn Dance was over. Marriage gave no right to the husband over the property of the wife, or the control or management of the children which he might have by her.

Adultery was punished by the family of the husband, who collected together, consulted and agreed upon the course to pursue. One half of them then went to the house of the woman, and the other half to the residence of the guilty warrior. They apprehended, stripped, and beat them with long poles until they were insensible. Then they cropped off their ears, and sometimes their noses, with knives, the edges of which were made rough and saw-like. The hair of the woman was carried in triumph to the square. Strange to say, they generally recovered from this inhuman treatment. If one of the offenders escaped, satisfaction was taken by similar 1798
punishment inflicted upon the nearest relative. If both of the parties fled unpunished, and the party aggrieved returned home and laid down the poles, the offence was considered satisfied. But one family in the Creek nation had authority to

CHAPTER II. Part 2.

take up the poles the second time, and that was the Ho-tul-gee, or family of the *Wind*. The parties might absent themselves until the Boosketuh was over, and then they were free from punishment for this and all other offences, except murder, which had to be atoned for by death inflicted upon the guilty one or his nearest relative.*

The Creeks buried their dead in the earth, in a square pit, under the bed where the deceased lay in his house. The grave was lined on the sides with cypress bark, like the curbing of a well. The corpse, before it became cold, was drawn up with cords, and made to assume a squatting position; and in this manner it was placed in the grave, and covered with earth. The gun, tomahawk, pipe, and other articles of the deceased, were buried with him.†

In 1777, Bartram found, in the Creek nation, fifty towns, with a population of eleven thousand, which lay upon the rivers Coosa, Tallapoosa, Alabama, Chattahoochie and Flint, and the prominent creeks which flowed into them. The Muscogee was the national language, although, in some of these towns, the Uchee or Savannah, Alabama, Natchez and Shawnee tongues prevailed. But the Muscogee was called, by the traders, the "mother tongue," while the others, mentioned, were termed the "stinkard lingo."‡

The general council of the nation was always held in the principal town, in the centre of which was a large public

* Hawkins' "Sketch of the Creek Country," pp. 73–74.

† Bartram, pp. 513–514. ‡ Bartram's Travels, pp. 461–462.

square, with three cabins of different sizes in each angle,
making twelve in all. Four avenues led into the square.
The cabins, capable of containing sixty persons each, were so
situated that from one of them a person might see into the 1776
others. One belonging to the Grand Chief fronted the rising
sun, to remind him that he should watch the interests of his
people. Near it was the grand cabin, where the councils were
held. In the opposite angle, three others belonged to the old
men, and faced the setting sun, to remind them that they were
growing feeble, and should not go to war. In the two remaining corners were the cabins of the different Chiefs of the
nation, the dimensions of which were in proportion to the rank
and services of those Chiefs. The whole number in the square 1776
was painted red, except those facing the west, which were
white, symbolical of virtue and old age. The former, during
war, were decorated with wooden pieces sustaining a chain of
rings of wood. This was a sign of grief, and told the warriors that they should hold themselves in readiness, for their
country needed their services. These chains were replaced by
garlands of ivy leaves, during peace.

In the month of May, annually, the Chiefs and principal
Indians assembled in the large square formed by these houses,
to deliberate upon all subjects of general interest. When they
were organized, they remained in the square until the council
broke up. Here they legislated, eat and slept. During the
session, no person, except the principal Chiefs, could approach
within less than twenty feet of the grand cabin. The women
prepared the food, and deposited it at a prescribed distance, 1776

when it was borne to the grand cabin by the subordinate Chiefs. In the centre of the square was a fire constantly burning. At sunset the council adjourned for the day, and then the young people of both sexes danced around this fire until a certain hour. As soon as the sun appeared above the horizon, a drum-beat called the Chiefs to the duties of the day.*

Besides this National Legislature, each principal town in the nation had its separate public buildings, as do the States of this American Union; and, like them, regulated their own local affairs. The public square at Auttose, upon the Tallapoosa, in 1777, consisted of four square buildings, of the same dimensions and uniform in shape, so situated as to form a tetragon, enclosing an area of an half acre. Four passages, of equal width at the corners, admitted persons into it. The
1777 frames of these buildings were of wood, but a mud plaster, inside and out, was employed to form neat walls; except two feet all around under the eaves, left open to admit light and air. One of them was the council house, where the Micco (King), Chiefs and Warriors, with the white citizens, who had business, daily assembled to hear and decide upon all grievances—adopt measures for the better government of the people, and the improvement of the town—and to receive ambassadors from other towns. This building was enclosed on three sides, while a partition, from end to end, divided it into two apartments,—the back one of which was totally dark, having only three arched holes large enough for a per-

* Milfort, pp. 206–208.

son to crawl into. It was a sanctuary of priestcraft, in which were deposited physic-pots, rattles, chaplets of deer's hoofs, the great pipe of peace, the imperial eagle-tail standard, displayed like an open fan, attached to which was a staff as white and clean as it could be scoured. The front part of 1777
this building was open like a piazza, divided into three apartments, breast high—each containing three rows of seats, rising one above the other, for the legislators. The other three buildings fronting the square, were similar to the one just described, except that they had no sanctuary, and served to accommodate the spectators; they were also used for banqueting houses.

The pillars and walls of the houses of the square abounded with sculptures and caricature paintings, representing men in different ludicrous attitudes; some with the human shape, having the heads of the duck, turkey, bear, fox, wolf, and deer. Again, these animals were represented with the human head. These designs were not ill-executed, and the outlines were bold and well proportioned. The pillars of 1777
the council house were ingeniously formed, in the likeness of vast speckled snakes ascending—the Auttoses being of the Snake family.*

Rude paintings were quite common among the Creeks, and they often conveyed ideas by drawings. No people could present a more comprehensive view of the topography of a country with which they were acquainted, than the Creeks

* Bartram's Travels, pp. 448–454.

CHAPTER II. Part 2. 1771 September 30 could, in a few moments, by drawing upon the ground. Barnard Roman, a Captain in the British Army, saw at Hoopa Ulla, a Choctaw town, not far from Mobile, the following drawing, executed by the Creeks, which had fallen into the possession of the Choctaws.

This represents that ten Creek warriors, of the family of the Deer, went into the Choctaw country in three canoes; that six of them landed, and in marching along a path, met two Choc-
1771 taw men, two women, and a dog; that the Creeks killed and scalped them. The scalp, in the deer's foot, implies the horror of the action to the whole Deer family.*

The great council house in Auttose, was appropriated to much the same purpose as the square, but was more private. It was a vast conical building, capable of accommodating many hundred people. Those appointed to take care of it, daily

* Barnard Roman's Florida, p. 102.

swept it clean, and provided canes for fuel and to give lights. CHAPTER II. Part 2.
Besides using this rotundo for political purposes, of a private
nature, the inhabitants of Auttose were accustomed to take
their "black drink" in it. The officer who had charge of this
ceremony, ordered the cacina tea to be prepared under an 1777
open shed opposite the door of the council house; he directed
bundles of dry cane to be brought in, which were previously
split in pieces two feet long. "They were now placed
obliquely across upon one another on the floor, forming a
spiral line round about the great centre pillar, eighteen inches in
thickness. This spiral line, spreading as it proceeded round and
round, often repeated from right to left, every revolution increased its diameter, and at length extended to the distance
of ten or twelve feet from the centre, according to the time
the assembly was to continue." By the time these preparations were completed, it was night, and the assembly had
taken their seats. The outer end of the spiral line was
fired. It gradually crept round the centre pillar, with the
course of the sun, feeding on the cane, and affording a bright
and cheerful light. The aged Chiefs and warriors sat upon
their cane sofas, which were elevated one above the other, and 1777
fixed against the back side of the house, opposite the door.
The white people and Indians of confederate towns sat, in like
order, on the left—a transverse range of pillars, supporting a
thin clay wall, breast high, separating them. The King's seat
was in front; back of it were the seats of the head warriors, and
those of a subordinate condition. Two middle-aged men now
entered at the door, bearing large conch shells full of black

CHAPTER II. Part 2.

drink. They advanced with slow, uniform and steady steps, with eyes elevated, and singing in a very low tone. Coming within a few feet of the King, they stopped, and rested their shells on little tables. Presently they took them up again, crossed each other, and advanced obsequiously. One presented his shell to the King, and the other to the principal man among the white audience. As soon as they raised them to their mouths,
1777 the attendants uttered two notes—*hoo-ojah!* and *a-lu-yah!*—which they spun out as long as they could hold their breath. As long as the notes continued, so long did the person drink or hold the shell to his mouth. In this manner all the assembly were served with the "black drink." But when the drinking begun, tobacco, contained in pouches made of the skins of the wild cat, otter, bear and rattlesnake, was distributed among the assembly, together with pipes, and a general smoking commenced. The King began first, with a few whiffs from the great pipe, blowing it, ceremoniously, first towards the sun, next towards the four cardinal points, and then towards the white audience. Then the attendants passed this pipe to others of distinction. In this manner, these dignified and singular people occupied some hours in the night, until the spiral line of canes was consumed, which was a signal for retiring.*

* Bartram's Travels, pp. 448–454. The site of Auttose is now embraced in Macon county, and is in a cotton plantation, the property of the Hon. George Goldthwaite, Judge of the Eighth Judicial Circuit. On the morning of the 29th of Nov., 1813, a battle was fought here between the Creeks and the Georgians—the latter commanded by Gen. John Floyd.

Twenty-one years after the visit of Bartram to the Creek
nation, Col. Benjamin Hawkins, to whom Washington had
confided important trusts in relation to the tribes south of the 1798
Ohio, penetrated these wilds. He found the public buildings, at that period, similar to those already described, with, however, some exceptions, which may have been the result of a slight change of ancient customs.

Every town had a separate government, and public buildings for business and pleasure, with a presiding officer, who was called a King, by the traders, and a Micco, by the Indians. This functionary received all public characters, heard their talks, laid them before his people, and, in return, delivered the
talk of his own town. He was always chosen from some noted 1798
family. The Micco of Tookabatcha was of the Eagle tribe (Lum-ul-gee). When they were put into office, they held their stations for life, and when dead, were succeeded by their nephews. The Micco could select an assistant when he became infirm, or for other causes, subject to the approval of the principal men of the town. They generally bore the name of the town which they governed, as Cusseta Micco, Tookabatcha Micco, &c.

"Choo-co-thluc-co, (big house,) the town house or public 1798
square, consists of four square buildings of one story, facing each other, forty by sixteen feet, eight feet pitch; the entrance at each corner. Each building is a wooden frame supported on posts set in the ground, covered with slabs, open in front like a piazza, divided into three rooms, the back and ends clayed up to the plates. Each division is divided lengthwise into

two seats. The front, two feet high, extending back half way, covered with reed mats or slabs; then a rise of one foot and it extends back, covered in like manner, to the side of the building. On these seats they lie or sit at pleasure.

"THE RANK OF THE BUILDINGS WHICH FORM THE SQUARE.

1798 "1st. Mic-ul-gee in-too-pau, the *Micco's cabin.* This fronts the east, and is occupied by those of the highest rank. The centre of the building is always occupied by the Micco of the town, by the Agent for Indian Affairs, when he pays a visit to a town, by the Miccos of other towns, and by respectable white people.

"The division to the right is occupied by the Mic-ug-gee (Miccos, there being several so called in every town, from custom, the origin of which is unknown), and the councillors. These two classes give their advice in relation to war, and are, in fact, the principal councillors.

"The division to the left is occupied by the E-ne-hau-ulgee (people second in command, the head of whom is called by the traders *second man*). These have the direction of the public
1798 works appertaining to the town, such as the public buildings, building houses in town for new settlers, or working in the fields. They are particularly charged with the ceremony of the ă-ce, (a decoction of the cassine yupon, called by the traders black drink,) under the direction of the Micco.

"2nd. Tus-tun-nug-ul-gee in-too-pau, the *warriors' cabin.* This fronts the south. The head warrior sits at the end of the cabin, and in his division the great warriors sit beside each other. The next in rank sit in the centre division, and the young warriors in the third. The rise is regular by merit from the third to the first division. The Great Warrior, for that is the title of the head warrior, is appointed by the Micco and councillors from among the greatest war characters.

"When a young man is trained up and appears well qualified for the fatigues and hardships of war, and is promising, the Micco appoints him a governor, or, as the name imports, a *leader* (Is-te-puc-cau-chau), and if he distinguishes himself they elevate him to the centre cabin. A man who distinguishes himself repeatedly in warlike enterprises, arrives to the
rank of the Great Leader (Is-te-puc-cau-chau-thlucco). This 1798
title, though greatly coveted, is seldom attained, as it requires a long course of years, and great and numerous successes in war.

"The second class of warriors is the *Tusse-ki-ul-gee.* All who go to war, and are in company when a scalp is taken, get a war-name. The leader reports their conduct, and they receive a name accordingly. This is the *Tus-se-o-chif-co* or war-name. The term, leader, as used by the Indians, is a proper one. The war parties all march in Indian file, with
the leader in front, until coming on hostile ground. He is 1798
then in the rear.

"3rd. Is-te-chaguc-ul-gee in-too-pau, the *cabin of the beloved men.* This fronts the north. There are a great many men who have been war leaders, and who, although of various ranks, have become estimable in a long course of public service. They sit themselves on the right division of the cabin of the Micco, and are his councillors. The family of the Mic-

CHAPTER II. Part 2.

co, and great men who have thus distinguished themselves, occupy this cabin of the Beloved Men.

"4th. Hut-te-mau-hug-gee, the *cabin of the young people and their associates.* This fronts the west.

"THE CONVENTION OF THE TOWN.

"The Micco, councillors and warriors meet every day in the public square, sit and drink of the black tea, talk of the news, the public and domestic concerns, smoke their pipes, and play Thla-chal-litch-cau (roll the bullet). Here all complaints are introduced, attended to and redressed.

"5th. Chooc-ofau-thluc-co, the *rotundo or assembly room,* called by the traders, "*hot house.*" This is near the square, and is constructed after the following manner: Eight posts are driven into the ground, forming an octagon of thirty feet in diameter. They are twelve feet high, and large enough to support the roof. On these five or six logs are placed, of a side, drawn in as they rise. On these long poles or rafters, to suit the height of the building, are laid, the upper ends forming a point, and the lower ends projecting out six feet from the octagon, and resting on the posts, five feet high, placed in a circle round the octagon, with plates on them, to which the rafters are tied with splits. The rafters are near together, and fastened with splits. These are covered with clay, and
1798 that with pine bark. The wall, six feet from the octagon, is clayed up. They have a small door, with a small portico curved round for five or six feet, then into the house.

"The space between the octagon and wall is one entire sofa, where the visitors lie or sit at pleasure. It is covered with reed, mat or splits.

"In the centre of the room, on a small rise, the fire is made of dry cane, or dry old pine slabs, split fine, and laid in a spiral line. This is the assembly room for all people, old and young. They assemble every night and amuse themselves with dancing, singing or conversation. And here, sometimes, in very cold weather, the old and naked sleep. CHAPTER II. Part 2.

"In all transactions which require secrecy, the rulers meet 1798
here, make their fire, deliberate and decide."*

A very interesting festival, common not only to the Creeks, but to many other tribes, will now be described. As Col. Hawkins was, in all respects, one of the most conscientious and reliable men that ever lived, his account, like the preceding, will be copied in his own style. Of the many descriptions of the Green Corn Dance, in our possession, that by the honest and indefatigable Creek Agent is the most minute and most readily understood.

"BOOS-KE-TAU.

"The Creeks celebrate this festival in the months of July and August. The precise time is fixed by the Micco and councillors, and is sooner or later, as the state of the affairs of the town or the early or lateness of their corn will suit. In
Cussetuh, this ceremony lasts for eight days. In some towns 1798
of less note it is but four days.

"FIRST DAY.

"In the morning the warriors clear the yard of the square,

* Sketch of the Creek Country in 1798-1799, by Benjamin Hawkins, pp. 68–72.

CHAPTER II. Part 2. and sprinkle white sand, when the black drink is made. The fire-maker makes the fire as early in the morning as he can, by friction. The warriors cut and bring into the square four logs, each as long as a man can cover by extending his two arms. These are placed in the centre of the square, end to end, forming a cross, the outer ends pointed to the cardinal points; in the centre of the cross the new fire is made. During the first four days they burn out these first four logs.

"The Pin-e-bun-gau (turkey dance) is danced by the women of the Turkey tribe, and while they are dancing the possau is brewed. This is a powerful emetic. It is drank from
1798 twelve o'clock to the middle of the afternoon. After this, Toc-co-yula-gau (tad-pole) is danced by four women and four men. In the evening the men dance E-ne-hou-bun-gau (the dance of the people second in command). This they dance till daylight.

"SECOND DAY.

"About ten o'clock the women dance Its-ho-bun-gau (gun dance). After twelve o'clock, the men go to the new fire, take some of the ashes, rub them on the chin, neck and abdomen, and jump head foremost into the river, and then return into the square. The women having prepared the new corn for the feast, the men take some of it and rub it between their hands, then on their face and breasts, and then they feast.

"THIRD DAY.

"The men sit in the square.

"FOURTH DAY.

"The women go early in the morning and get the new

CHAPTER II. Part 2. 1798

fire, clean out their hearths, sprinkle them with sand, and make their fires. The men finish burning out the first four logs, and they take ashes, rub them on their chin, neck and abdomen, and they go into the water. This day they eat salt, and they dance Obungauchapco (the long dance).

"FIFTH DAY.

"They get four new logs, and place them as on the first day, and they drink the black drink.

"SIXTH AND SEVENTH DAYS.

"They remain in the square.

"EIGHTH DAY.

"They get two large pots, and their physic plants, the names of which are:

Mic-ca-ho-you-e-juh, Co-hal-le-wau-gee, 1798
Toloh, Chofeinsack-cau-fuck-au,
A-che-nau, Cho-fe-mus-see,
Cap-pau-pos-cau, Hillis-hutke,
Chu-lis-sau (the roots), To-te-cuh-chooe-his-see,
Tuck-thlau-lus-te, Welau-nuh,
To-te-cul-hil-lis-so-wau, Oak-chon-utch-co.

These plants are put into pots and beat up with water. The chemists, E-lic-chul-gee, called by the traders physic-makers, blow into it through a small reed, and then it is drank by the men and rubbed over their joints till the afternoon.

"They collect old corn cobs and pine burs, put them into a pot and burn them to askes. Four very young virgins bring ashes from their houses and stir them up. The men take white clay and mix it with water in two pans. One pan

of the clay and one of the ashes are carried to the cabin of
the Micco, and the other two to that of the warriors. They
then rub themselves with the clay and ashes. Two men, appointed to that office, bring some flowers of tobacco of a small
kind, Itch-au-chee-le-pue-pug-gee, or, as the name imports, the
old man's tobacco, which was prepared on the first day and
1798 put in a pan in the cabin of the Micco, and they gave a little
of it to every one present.

"The Micco and councillors then go four times around the fire, and every time they face the east they throw some of the flowers into the fire. They then go and stand to the west. The warriors then repeat the same ceremony.

"A cane is stuck up at the cabin of the Micco, with two
white feathers at the end of it. One of the Fish tribe (Thlot-
logulgee) takes it, just as the sun goes down, and goes
off to the river, followed by all. When he gets half way
down the river he gives the death whoop, which he repeats
four times between the square and the water's edge. Here
they all place themselves as thick as they can stand near the
1798 edge of the water. He sticks up the cane at the water's edge,
and they all put a grain of the old man's tobacco on their
heads and in each ear. Then, at a signal given four different
times, they throw some into the river; and every man, at a
signal, plunges into the river and picks up four stones from
the bottom. With these they cross themselves on their breasts
four times, each time throwing a stone into the river and giving the death whoop. They then wash themselves, take up
the cane and feathers, return and stick it up in the square,

and visit through the town. At night they dance *O-bun-gau-hadjo* (mad dance), and this finishes the ceremony.

"This happy institution of the *Boos-ke-tau* restores man to himself, to his family, and to his nation. It is a general amnesty, which not only absolves the Indians from all crimes, 1 7
murder alone excepted, but seems to bring guilt itself into oblivion."*

With some slight variations, the Green Corn Dance was thus celebrated throughout the Creek confederacy. At the town of Tookabatcha, however, it will be recollected, that on the fourth day, the Indians introduced the "brass plates." At Coosawda, the principal town of the Alabamas, they celebrated a Boosketau of four days each, of mulberries and beans, when these fruits respectively ripened.†

James Adair, a man of learning and enterprise, lived more than thirty years among the Chickasaws, and had frequent intercourse with the nations of the Muscogees, Cherokees and Choctaws, commencing in 1735. He was an Englishman, and was connected with the extensive commerce carried on at
an early period with these tribes. While among the Chickasaws, with whom he first began to reside in 1744, he wrote a 1735
large work on aboriginal history. When he returned to his mother country, he published this work, the "American Indians," a ponderous volume of near five hundred pages, at London, in 1775. Well acquainted with the Hebrew language, and

* Hawkins' Sketch of the Creek Country, pp. 75–78.

† Adair's American Indians, p. 97.

CHAPTER II. Part 2. having, in his long residence with the Indians, acquired an accurate knowledge of their tongue, he devoted the larger portion of his work to prove that the latter were originally Hebrews, and were a portion of the lost tribes of Israel. He asserts, that at the Boosketaus of the Creeks and other tribes within the limits of Alabama, the warriors danced around the holy fire, during which the elder Priest invoked the Great Spirit, while the others responded *Halelu! Halelu!* then *Haleluiah! Haleluyah!* He is ingenious in his arguments, and introduces many strange things to prove, to his own satisfaction, that the Indians were descendants of the Jews—seeking, throughout two hundred pages, to assimilate their language, manners and customs. He formed his belief that they were originally the same people, upon their division into tribes—worship of Jehovah—notions of a theocracy—belief in the ministration of angels—language and dialects—manner of
1740 computing time—their Prophets and High Priests—festivals, fasts and religious rites—daily sacrifices—ablutions and anointings—laws of uncleanliness—abstinence from unclean things—marriages, divorces, and punishments for adultery—other punishments—their towns of refuge—purification and ceremony preparatory to war—their ornaments—manner of curing the sick—burial of the dead—mourning for the dead—raising seed to a deceased brother—choice of names adapted to their circumstances and times—their own traditions—and the accounts of our English writers, and the testimony which the Spanish and other authors have given concerning the primitive inhabitants of Peru and Mexico.

He insists that in nothing do they differ from the Jews except in the rite of circumcision, which, he contends, their ancestors dispensed with, after they became lost from the other tribes, on account of the danger and inconvenience of the execution of that rite, to those engaged in a hunting and roving life. That when the Israelites were forty years in the wilderness, even then they attempted to dispense with circumcision, but Joshua, by his stern authority, enforced its observance. The difference in food, mode of living and climate are relied upon by Adair, to account for the difference in the color, between the Jew and Indian, and also why the one has hair upon the body in profusion and the other has not.*

Adiar is by no means alone in his opinion of the descent of the American Indians. Other writers, who have lived among these people, have arrived at the same conclusion. Many of the old Indian countrymen with whom we have conversed, believe in their Jewish origin, while others are of a different opinion. Abram Mordecai, an intelligent Jew, who dwelt fifty years in the Creek nation, confidently believed that the Indians were originally of his people, and he asserted that in their Green Corn Dances he had heard them often utter in grateful tones, the word *yavoyaha! yavoyaha!* He was always informed by the Indians that this meant Jehovah, or the Great Spirit, and that they were then returning thanks for the abundant harvest with which they were blessed.†

* Adair's American Indians, pp. 15–220.

† Conversations with Abram Mordecai, a man of ninety two years of age, whom I found in Dudleyville, Tallapoosa county, in the fall of

CHAPTER II. Part 2. Col. Hawkins concludes his account of the religious and war ceremonies of the Creek Indians as follows:—

"At the age of from fifteen to seventeen, the ceremony of initiating youth to manhood, is performed. It is called the Boosketau, in like manner as the annual Boosketau of the nation. A youth of the proper age, gathers two handfuls of
1798 the Sou-watch-cau, a very bitter root, which he eats a whole day. Then he steeps the leaves in water and drinks it. In the dusk of the evening he eats two or three spoonfuls of boiled grits. This is repeated for four days, and during this time he remains in a house. The Sou-watch-cau has the effect of intoxicating and maddening. The fourth day he goes out, but must put on a pair of new moccasins (stilla-picas). For twelve moons he abstains from eating bucks, except old ones, and from turkey cocks, fowls, peas and salt. During this period he must not pick his ears or scratch his head with his fingers, but use a small stick. For four moons he must have a fire to himself to cook his food, and a little girl, a virgin, may cook for him. His food is boiled grits. The fifth moon any person may cook for him, but he must serve himself first, and use one pan and spoon. Every new moon he drinks for four days the possau (button snakeroot), an emetic, and abstains for three days from all food, except in the evening, a little boiled grits (humpetuh hutke). The
1798 twelfth moon he performs, for four days, what he commenced

1847. His mind was fresh in the recollection of early incidents. Of him I shall have occasion to speak in another portion of the work.

CHAPTER II. Part 2.

with on the first. The fifth day he comes out of his house, gathers corn cobs, burns them to ashes, and with these rubs his body all over. At the end of this moon he sweats under blankets, then goes into water, and thus ends the ceremony. This ceremony is sometimes extended to four, six or eight moons, or even to twelve days only, but the course is the same.

"During the whole of this ceremony the physic is administered by the Is-te-puc-cau-chau-thlucco (Great Leader), who, in speaking of the youth under initiation, says, "I am physicing him"—Boo-se-ji-jite saut li-to mise-cha. Or "I am teaching him all that it is proper for him to know"—(nauk o-mulgau e-muc-e-thli-jite saut litomise cha). The youth during this initiation does not touch any one except young persons, who are under a like course with himself. And if he dreams, he drinks the possau."*

Whenever Creeks were forced to take up arms, the Tustenuggee caused to be displayed in the public places a club, part of which was painted red. He sent it to each subordinate Chief, accompanied with a number of pieces of wood, equal to the number of days that it would take that Chief to present himself at the rendezvous. The War-Chief alone had the power 1778
of appointing that day. When this club had arrived, each Chief caused a drum to be beat before the grand cabin where he resided. All the inhabitants immediately presented themselves. He informed them of the day and place where he

* Hawkins', pp. 78–79.

CHAPTER II. Part 2. intended to kindle his fire. He repaired to that place before the appointed day, and rubbed two sticks together, which produced fire. He kindled it in the midst of a square, formed by four posts, sufficiently extended to contain the number of warriors he desired to assemble. As soon as the day dawned, the Chief placed himself between the two posts which fronted the east, and held in his hand a package of small sticks.
1778 When a warrior entered the enclosure, which was open only on one side, he threw down a stick and continued until they were all gone, the number of sticks being equal to the number of warriors he required. Those who presented themselves afterwards could not be admitted, and they returned home to hunt, indicating the place where they could be found if their services should be needed. Those who thus tardily presented themselves were badly received at home, and were reproached for the slight desire they had testified to defend their country.

The warriors who were in the enclosure remained there, and for three days took the medicine of war. Their wives brought them their arms and all things requisite for the campaign, and deposited them three hundred yards in front of the square, together with a little bag of parched corn-meal, an ounce of which would make a pint of broth.* It was only necessary to mix it with water, and in five minutes
1778 it became as thick as soup cooked by a fire. Two ounces would sustain a man for twenty-four hours. It was indispensable, for, during a war expedition, the party could not kill game.

* Called by the modern Creek traders "coal flour."

The three days of medicine having expired, the Chief de- CHAPTER
parted with his warriors to the rendezvous appointed by the II.
Grand Chief. Independently of this medicine, which was Part 2. 1778
taken by all, each subordinate Chief had his particular talisman, which he carefully carried about his person. It consisted
of a small bag, in which were a few stones and some pieces of
cloth which had been taken from the garments of the Grand
Chief, in the return from some former war. If the subordinate Chief forgot his bag, he was deprived of his rank, and
remained a common soldier during the whole expedition.
The Grand Chief presented himself at the rendezvous on the 1778
appointed day, and he was sure to find there the assembled
warriors. He then placed himself at the head of the army,
making all necessary arrangements, without being obliged to
rendezvous on account of any one. Being certain that his
discipline and orders would be punctually enforced, he
marched with confidence against the enemy. When they
were ready to march, each subordinate Chief was compelled
to be provided with the liquor which they called medicine of
war; and the Creeks placed in it such a degree of confidence,
that it was difficult for a War Chief to collect his army if they
were deprived of it. He would be exposed to great danger,
if he should be forced to do battle without having satisfied
this necessity. If he should suffer defeat—which would cer- 1778
tainly be the case, because the warriors would have no confidence in themselves, but be overcome by their own supersti-
tious fears,—he would be responsible for all misfortunes.

There were two medicines, the great and the little, and it

CHAPTER II. Part 2. remained for the Chief to designate which of these should be used. The warrior, when he had partaken of the great medicine, believed himself invulnerable. The little medicine served, in his eyes, to diminish danger. Full of confidence in the statements of his Chief, the latter easily persuaded him, that when
1778 he gave him only the little medicine, it was because circumstances did not require the other. These medicines being purgative in their nature, the warrior found himself less endangered by the wounds which he might receive. The Creeks had still another means of diminishing the danger of their wounds, which consisted in fighting almost naked, for it is well known that particles of cloth remaining in wounds render them more difficult to heal. They observed during war the most rigorous discipline, for they neither eat nor drank without an order
1778 from the Chief. They dispensed with drinking, even while passing along the bank of a river, because circumstances had obliged their Chief to forbid it, under pain of depriving them of their medicine of war, or, rather, of the influence of their talisman. When an enemy compelled them to take up arms, they never returned home without giving him battle, and at least taking a few scalps. These may be compared to the *colors* among civilized troops, for when a warrior had killed an enemy, he took his scalp, which was an honorable trophy
1778 for him to return with to his nation. They removed them from the head of an enemy with great skill and dexterity. They were not all of the same value, but were classed, and it was for the Chiefs, who were the judges of all achievements, to decide the value of each. It was in proportion to the num-

ber and value of these scalps that a Creek advanced in civil as well as military rank. It was necessary, in order to occupy a station of any importance, to have taken at least seven of them. If a young Creek, having been at war, returned without a single scalp, he continued to bear the name of his mother, and could not marry; but if he returned with a scalp, the principal men assembled at the grand cabin, to give him 1778 a name, that he might abandon that of his mother. They judged of the value of the scalp by the dangers experienced in the capture of it, and the greater these dangers, the more considerable were the titles and advancement derived from it, by its owner.

In time of battle, the great Chief commonly placed himself in the centre of the army, and sent reinforcements wherever danger appeared most pressing. When he perceived that his forces were repulsed and feared that they would yield entirely to the efforts of the enemy, he advanced in person, and combated hand to hand. A cry, repeated on all sides, 1778 informed the warriors of the danger to which a Chief was exposed. Immediately the *corps de reserve* came together, and advanced to the spot where the Grand Chief was, in order to force the enemy to abandon him. Should he be dead, they would all die rather than abandon his body to the enemy, without first securing his scalp. They attached such value to this relic, and so much disgrace to the loss of it, that when the danger was very great, and they were not able to prevent his body from falling into the hands of the enemy, the warrior who was nearest to the dead Chief, took his scalp and fled, at

CHAPTER II. Part 2.

the same time raising a cry, known only among the savages.
He then went to the spot which the deceased Chief had indicated, as the place of rendezvous, should his army be beaten.
All the subordinate Chiefs, being made aware of his death,
by this cry, made dispositions to retreat; and, this being
effected, they proceeded to the election of his successor, before
1778 taking any other measures. The Creeks were very warlike,
and were not rebuffed by a defeat. On the morrow, after an
unfortunate battle, they advanced with renewed intrepidity, to
encounter their enemy anew.

When they advanced towards an enemy, they marched
one after another, the Chief of the party being at the head.
They arranged themselves in such a manner as to place the
foot of every one in the track made by the first. The last one
concealed even that track with grass. By this means they
kept from the enemy any knowledge of their number. When
they made a halt, for the purpose of encamping, they formed
in a circle, leaving a passage only large enough to admit a
single man. They sat cross-legged, and each one had his
gun by his side. The Chief faced the entrance of the circle,
1778 and no warrior could go out without his permission. At the
time of sleeping he gave a signal, and after that no person
could stir. Rising was performed at the same signal. It
was ordinarily the Grand Chief who marked out positions,
and placed sentinels to watch for the security of the army.
He always had a great number of runners, both before and
behind, so that an army was rarely surprised. They, on the
contrary, conducted wars against the Europeans entirely by

sudden attacks, and they were very dangerous to those who were not aware of them.*

When the Creeks returned from war with captives, they marched into their town with shouts and the firing of guns. They stripped them naked and put on their feet bear-skin moccasins, with the hair exposed. The punishment was always left to the women, who examined their bodies for their war-marks. Sometimes the young warriors, who had none of these honorable inscriptions, were released and used as slaves. But the warrior of middle age, even those of advanced years, suffered death by fire. The victim's arms were pinioned, and one end of a strong grape vine tied around his neck, while the other was fastened to the top of a war-pole, so as to allow him to track around a circle of fifteen yards. To secure his scalp against fire, tough clay was placed upon his head. The immense throng of spectators were now filled with delight, and eager to witness the inhuman spectacle. The suffering warrior was not dismayed, but, with a manly and insulting voice, sang the war-song. The women then made a furious onset with flaming torches, dripping with hot, black pitch, and applied them to his back and all parts of his body. Suffering excruciating pain, he rushed from the pole with the fury of a wild beast, kicking, biting and trampling his cruel assailants under foot. But fresh numbers came on, and after a long time, and when he was nearly burned to his vitals, they ceased and poured water upon him to relieve him—only to prolong

* Sejour dans la nation Crëck, par Le Clerc Milfort, pp. 240, 252, 218, 219.

8

CHAPTER II. Part 2.

their sport. They renewed their tortures, when, with champing teeth and sparkling eye-balls, he once more broke through the demon throng to the extent of his rope, and acted every part that the deepest desperation could prompt. Then he died. His head was scalped, his body quartered, and the limbs carried over the town in triumph.*

An enumeration of the towns found in the Creek nation
1798 by Col. Hawkins, in 1798, will conclude the notice of the manners and customs of these remarkable people, though, hereafter, they will often be mentioned, in reference to their commerce and wars with the Americans.

TOWNS AMONG THE UPPER CREEKS.

Tal-e-se, derived from Tal-o-fau, *a town,* and e-se, *taken*—situated in the fork of the Eufaube, upon the left bank of the Tallapoosa.

Took-a-batcha, opposite Tallese.

Auttose, on the left side of Tallapoosa, a few miles below the latter.

Ho-ith-le-waule—from ho-ith-le, *war*, and waule, *divide*—right bank of the Tallapoosa, five miles below Auttose.

Foosce-hat-che—fooso-wau, *a bird*, and hat-che, *tail*—two miles below the latter, on the right bank.

Coo-loo-me was below and adjoining the latter.

E-cun-hut-ke—e-cun-nau, *earth,* and hut-ke, *white*—below Coo-loo-me, on the same side of the Tallapoosa.

Sou-van-no-gee, left bank of the river.

* Adair, pp. 390–391.

Mook-lau-sau, a mile below the latter, same side.

Coo-sau-dee, three miles below the confluence of the Coosa and Tallapoosa, on the west bank of the Alabama.

E-cun-chate—e-cun-na, *earth*, chate, *red*—(now a part of the city of Montgomery.) 1798

Too-was-sau, three miles below, same side of the Alabama.

Pau-woe-te, two miles below the latter, same side.

Au-tau-gee, right side of the Alabama, near the mouth of the creek of the same name.

Tus-ke-gee—in the fork of the Coosa and Tallapoosa, on the east bank of the former—the old site of Forts Toulouse and Jackson.

Hoochoice and Hookchoie-ooche, towns just above the latter.

O-che-a-po-fau, o-che-ub, *hickory tree*, and po-fau, *in* or *among*—east bank of the Coosa, on the plain just below the city of Wetumpka.

We-wo-cau—we-wau *water*, wo-cau *barking* or *roaring*—on a creek of that name, fifteen miles above the latter.

Puc-cun-tal-lau-has-see—epuc-cun-nau, *may-apple*, tal-lau-has-se, *old town*—in the fork of a creek of that name.

Coo-sau, on the left bank of that river, between the mouths of Eufaule and Nauche, (creeks now called Talladega and Kiamulgee.)

Au-be-cho-che, on Nauche creek, five miles from the Coosa.

Nau-che, on same creek, five miles above the latter. 1798

Eu-fau-lau-hat-che, fifteen miles still higher up on the same creek.

Woc-co-coie—woc-co, *blow horn*, coie, *a nest*—on Tote-paufcau creek.

CHAPTER II. Part 2.

Hill-au-bee, on col-luffa-de creek, which joins Hillaubee creek on the right side, one mile below the town.

Thla-noo-che-au-bau-lau—thlen-ne, *mountain*, ooche, *little*, au-bau-lau, *over*—on a branch of the Hillaubee.

1798 Au-net-te-chap-co—au-net-te, *swamp*, chap-co, *long*—on a branch of the Hillaubee.

E-chuse-is-li-gau, *where a young thing was found* (a child was found here), left side of Hillaubee creek.

Oak-tau-hau-zau-see—oak-tau-hau, *sand*, zau-see, *great deal*—on a creek of that name, a branch of the Hillaubee.

1778 Oc-fus-kee—oc, *in*, fus-kee, *a point*—right bank of the Tallapoosa.

New-yau-cau, named after *New York* when Gen. McGillivary returned from there in 1790, twenty miles above the latter, on the left side of the Tallapoosa.

Took-au-batche-tal-lau-has-se, four miles above the latter, right side of the river.

Im-mook-fau, *a gorget made of a conch*, on the creek of that name.

Too-to-cau-gee—too-to, *corn-house*, cau-gee, *standing*—twenty miles above New-yau-cau, right bank of the Tallapoosa.

Au-che-nau-ul-gau—auche-nau, *cedar*, ul-gau, *all*—forty miles above New-yau-cau, on a creek. It is the farthest north of all the Creek settlements.

E-pe-sau-gee, on a large creek of that name.

1798 Sooc-he-ah—sooc-cau—*hog* he-ah, *here*—right bank of the Tallapoosa, twelve miles above Oc-fus-kee.

Eu-fau-lau, five miles above Oc-fus-kee, right bank of the river.

Ki-a-li-jee, on the creek of that name, which joins the Tallapoosa on the right side.

Au-che-nau-hat-che—au-che, *cedar*, hat-che, *creek*.

Hat-che-chub-bau—hat-che, *creek*, chub-bau, *middle* or *half way*.

Sou-go-hat-che—sou-go, *cymbal*, (musical instrument) hatche, *creek*—joins the Tallapoosa on the left side.

Thlot-lo-gul-gau—thlot-lo, *fish*, ul-gau, *all*—called by traders "*Fish Ponds*," on a creek, a branch of the Ul-hau-hat-che. 1798

O-pil-thluc-co—O-pil-lo-wau, *swamp*, thlucco, *big*—twenty miles from the Coosa, a creek of that name.

Pin-e-hoo-te—pin-e-wau, *turkey*, choo-te, *house*—a branch of the E-pee-sau-gee.

Po-chuse-hat-che—po-chu-so-wau, *hatchet*, hat-che, *creek*—(in Coosa county.)

Oc-fus-coo-che, *little ocfuskee*, four miles above New-yau-cau.

TOWNS AMONG THE LOWER CREEKS.

Chat-to-ho-che—chat-to, *a stone*, ho-che *marked* or *flowered*. Such rocks are found in the bed of that river above Ho-ith-le-te-gau. This is the origin and meaning of the name of that beautiful river.

Cow-e-tough, on the right bank of the Chat-to-ho-che, three miles below the falls.

O-cow-ocuh-hat-che, *falls creek*, on the right side of the river at the termination of the falls. 1798

Hatche-canane, *crooked creek*.

Wac-coo-che, *calf creek*.

CHAPTER O-sun-nup-pau, *moss creek.*

II. Hat-che-thlucco, *big creek.*

Part 2.

1798 Cow-e-tuh Tal-lau-has-se—Cowetuh Tal-lo-fau, *a town*, hasse, *old*—three miles below Cowetuh, on the right bank of the Chattahoochie.

We-tum-cau—we-wau *water*, tum-cau *rumbling*,—a main branch of the Uchee creek.

Cus-se-tuh, five miles below Cow-e-tuh, on the left bank of the Chattahoochie.

Au-put-tau-e, a village of Cussetuh, on Hat-che-thluc-co, twenty miles from the river.

U-chee, on the right bank of the Chat-to-ho-che, ten miles below Cowetuh Tallauhassee, and just below the mouth of the Uchee creek.

In-tuch-cul-gau—in-tuch-ke, *dam across water*—ul-gau, *all;*
1798 a Uchee village, on Opil-thlacco, twenty-eight miles from its junction with Flint river.

Pad-gee-li-gau—pad-jee *a pigeon*—li-gau *sit*, *pigeon roost*—on the right bank of Flint river (a Uchee village).

Toc-co-qul-egau, *tadpole*, on Kit-cho-foone creek (a Uchee village).

Oose-oo-chee, two miles below Uchee, on the right bank of the Chattahoochie.

Che-au-hau, below and adjoining the latter.

Au-muc-cul-le, *pour upon me*, on a creek of that name, which joins on the right side of the Flint.

1798 O-tel-who-yau-nau, *hurricane town*, on the right bank of the Flint.

CHAPTER II. Part 2.

Hit-che-tee, on the left bank of the Chattahoochie, one mile below Che-au-hau.

Che-au-hoo-che, *Little Cheauhaw*, one mile and a half west from Hit-che-tee.

Hit-che-too-che, *Little Hitchetee*, on both sides of the Flint.

Tut-tal-lo-see, *fowl*, on a creek of that name.

Pala-chooc-le, on the right bank of the Chattahoochie.

O-co-nee, six miles below the latter, on the left bank of the Chattahoochie. 1798

Sou-woo-ge-lo, six miles below Oconee, on the right bank.

Sou-woog-e-loo-che, four miles below Oconee, on the left bank of the Chattahoochie.

Eu-fau-la, fifteen miles below the latter, on the left bank of the same river.

From this town settlements extended occasionally to the mouth of the Flint.*

* Hawkins' "Sketch of the Creek Country in 1798–99," pp. 26-66. In addition to the published copy of this interesting pamphlet, sent to me by I. K. Tefft, Esq., of Savannah, the Hon. F. W. Pickens, of South-Carolina, loaned me a manuscript copy of the same work, written by Col. Hawkins for his grandfather, Gen. Andrew Pickens, who was an intimate friend of Hawkins, and was associated with him in several important Indian treaties, and whose name will often be mentioned hereafter.

PART III.

MOBILIANS, CHATOTS, THOMEZ AND TENSAS.

CHAPTER In 1718, the French West India Company sent, from Ro-
II. chelle, eight hundred colonists to Louisiana. Among them
Part 3. was a Frenchman of intelligence and high standing, named
Le Page Du Pratz, who was appointed superintendent of the
public plantations. After a residence of sixteen years in this
country, he returned to France, and published an interesting
work upon Louisiana. Du Pratz was often at Mobile, and about
1721 the period of 1721 found living, in that vicinity, a few small
tribes of Indians, whom we will now describe.

The Chatots were a very small tribe, who composed a town
of about forty huts, adjoining the bay and river of Mobile.
They appear to have resided at or near the present city of
1721 Mobile. The Chatots were great friends of the French settlers, and most of them embraced the Catholic religion.
North from Mobile, and upon the first bluffs on the same side
of the river of that name, lived the Thomez, who were not
more numerous than the Chatots, and who, also, had been
taught to worship the true God. Opposite to them, upon the
Tensa river, lived a tribe of Tensas, whose settlement consisted of one hundred huts. They were a branch of the

Natchez, and, like them, kept a perpetual fire burning in their temple.

Further north, and near the confluence of the Tombigby and Alabama, and above there, the Mobilians still existed. It was from these people, a remnant of whom survived the invasion of De Soto, that the city, river and bay derive their names.* They, also, kept a fire in their temple, which was never suffered for a moment to expire. Indeed, they had some pre-eminence in this particular—for, formerly, the natives obtained this holy light from their temples.† These small tribes 1721
were all living in peace with each other, upon the discovery of their country by the French, and continued so. Gradually, however, they became merged in the larger nations of the Choctaws and Chickasaws. They were all, sometimes, called the Mobile Indians, by the early French settlers.

The Natchez once inhabited the south-western portion of
the Mexican empire, but on account of the wars with which 1721
they were continually harrassed by neighboring Indians, they began to wander north-east. Finally they settled upon the banks of the Mississippi, chiefly on the bluff where now stands the beautiful city which bears their name.‡ They retained, until they were broken up by the French, many of the religious rites and customs of the Mexicans. Their form of govern-

* Du Pratz's Louisiana, pp. 308–309.

† Charlevoix's "Voyage to North America," vol. 2, p. 273.

‡ Du Pratz's Louisiana.

CHAPTER II. Part 3. 1721

ment was distinguished from that of other tribes in Alabama and Mississippi, by its ultra despotism, and by the grandeur and haughtiness of its Chiefs. The Grand Chief of the Natchez bore the name of the Sun. Every morning, as soon as that bright luminary appeared, he stood at the door of his cabin, turned his face towards the east, and bowed three times, at the same time prostrating himself to the ground. A pipe, which was never used but upon this occasion, was then handed to him, from which he puffed smoke, first towards the Sun, and then towards the other three quarters of the world. He pretended that he derived his origin from the Sun, acknowledged no other master, and held absolute power over the lives and goods of his subjects. When he or his nearest female relation died, his body-guard was obliged to follow to the land of spirits. The death of a Chief sometimes resulted in that of an hundred persons, who considered
1721 it a great honor to be sacrificed upon his death. Indeed, few Natchez of note died without being attended to the other world by some of their relatives, friends or servants. So eager were persons to sacrifice themselves in this way, that sometimes it was ten years before their turn came; and those who obtained the favor, spun the cord with which they were to be strangled.*

The cabins of the Natchez were in the shape of pavilions,
1721 low, without windows, and covered with corn-stalks, leaves

* Charlevoix's "Voyage to North America," pp. 260–261.

and cane matting. That of the Great Chief, which stood upon an artificial mound, and fronted a large square, was handsomely rough-cast with clay, both inside and out. The temple was at the side of his cabin, facing the east, and at the extremity of the square. It was in an oblong form, forty feet in length and twenty in breadth. Within it were the bones of the deceased Chiefs, contained in boxes and baskets. Three logs of wood, joined at the ends, and placed in a triangle, occupied the middle part of the floor, and burned slowly away, night and day. Keepers attended and constantly renewed them.* The Great Sun informed Du Pratz, who had, in 1721
1820, taken up his abode among them, that their nation was once very formidable, extending over vast regions and governed by numerous Suns and nobility; that one of the keepers of the temple once left it on some business, and while he was absent, his associate keepers fell asleep; that the fire went out, and that, in the terror and dismay into which they were thrown, they substituted profane fire, with the hope that their shameful neglect would escape unnoticed. But a dreadful calamity was the consequence of this negligence. A horrible malady raged for years, during which many of the Suns, and an infinite number of people, died.† This fire was kept constantly burning in honor of the Sun, which they seemed to worship and adore above everything else. In the spring of 1700, Iben- 1721

* Charlevoix's Voyage to North America, p. 256.

† Du Pratz' Louisiana, p. 333.

CHAPTER II. Part 3. ville, in company with a few of his colonial people, visited the Natchez. While there, one of the temples was consumed by lightning. The Priests implored the women to cast their children in the flames to appease the anger of their divinity. Before the French, by prayers and entreaties, could arrest this horrible proceeding, some of the innocent babes were already
1700 roasting in the flames.* At this time, the Natchez, reduced by wars and by the death of the nobility, upon whose decease the existence of many others terminated, did not exceed a population of twelve hundred.

Fort Rosalie, erected by the French in 1716, upon the bluff which sustains the city of Natchez, had a garrison of soldiers
1729 November 28 and numerous citizens. On the morning of the 28th November, 1729, the Great Sun and his warriors suddenly fell upon them, and before noon the whole male population were in the sleep of death. The women, children and slaves were reserved as prisoners of war. The consternation was great throughout the colony when this horrible massacre became known. The French and Choctaws united, and drove the Natchez upon the lower Washita, just below the mouth of Little river. Here the latter erected mounds and embankments for defence, which covered an area of four hundred acres. In the meantime, having obtained assistance from
1733 January France, the colonists marched against this stronghold, and, in January, 1733, made a successful attack. They captured

* Gayarre's History of Louisiana, vol. 1, p. 73.

the Great Sun, several of the War Chiefs and four hundred and twenty-seven of the tribe, who were sent from New Orleans to St. Domingo, as slaves. The remainder of the tribe made their escape. Some of them sought asylums among the Chickasaws and Creeks, while others scattered in the far west.*

* The Natchez have been mentioned at length by a number of French authors, who were eye-witnesses of their bloody rites and ceremonies. See Bossu's Travels in Louisiana, vol. 1, pp. 32–67. Dumont's Louisiana, vol. 1, pp. 118–132. Charlevoix's Voyage to North America, vol. 2, pp. 252–274. Du Pratz' Louisiana, pp. 79–95–291-316. Les Natchez, par M. Le Vicompte de Chateaubriand—of this work 400 pages are taken up with the Natchez. Jesuits in America—a recent publication. Many other works in my possession, upon Louisiana and Florida, allude briefly to that tribe.

PART IV.

THE CHOCTAWS AND CHICKASAWS.

CHAPTER II. Part 4.

THE Choctaws and Chickasaws descended from a people called the Chickemicaws, who were among the first inhabitants of the Mexican empire. At an ancient period they began to wander towards the east, in company with the Choccomaws.

Period unknown

After a time they reached the Mississippi river and crossed it, arriving in this country with an aggregate force of ten thousand warriors. The Choccomaws established themselves upon the head-waters of the Yazoo, the Chickasaws upon the northwestern sources of the Tombigby, and the Choctaws upon the territory now embraced in southern Mississippi and south-western Alabama. They thus gradually became three distinct tribes; but the Chickasaws and Choccomaws were generally known by the name of the former, while the Choctaws spoke the same language, with the exception of a difference produced by the intonation of the voice.*

Upon the first settlement of Mobile by the French, they
1700 found that the Choctaws and the remnant of the Mobilians employed the same language. Indeed, we have seen that the

* Adair's American Indians, pp. 5, 66, 352.

great Mobilian Chief, in 1540, had a name which was derived CHAPTER
from two well-known Choctaw words—Tusca, *warrior*, and II.
lusa, *black*. The Indians who fought De Soto at Cabusto, Part 4. 1540
upon the Warrior, and who extended their lines six miles up
and down its western banks to oppose his crossing, were the
Pafallayas. They are believed to have been no other people
than the Choctaws. There is a word in the language of the
latter called fallaya—*long*.* It is scarcely necessary to remind
the reader that the Chickasaws were living in the upper part
of Mississippi when De Soto invaded it, and that they fought 1541
him with great courage. Now, as the Choctaws, according
to tradition, came with them to this country, and were a portion of the same family, it is reasonable to suppose that the
Pafallayas, the brave allies of Tuscaloosa, were the Choctaws—
especially when taken in connection with collateral evidence
in our possession. The tradition of the migration of the
Chickasaws and Choctaws from the Mexican empire has been Period unknown
preserved by the former alone; while the latter, with few exceptions, have lost it. On the road leading from St. Stephens,
in Alabama, to the city of Jackson, Mississippi, was, some
years ago, a large mound, embracing at the base about two
acres, and rising forty feet high in a conical form, and enclosed
by a ditch encompassing twenty acres. On the top of it was a
deep hole, ten feet in circumference, out of which the ignorant
portion of the Choctaws believed that their ancestors once

* Transactions of the American Antiquarian Society, vol. 2, p. 105. (A paper read before the society by Albert Gallatin.)

CHAPTER II. Part 4.

sprung as thick as bees, peopling the whole of that part of the
country. They had great regard for this artificial elevation, and
called it Nannawyah, the signification of which is, nanna,
hill, and wyah, *mother*. When hunting near this mound
they were accustomed to throw into the hole the leg of a
deer, thus feeding their mother. One day in 1810, Mr. Geo.
S. Gaines, the United States Choctaw Factor, in going to the
Agency, rode up on this mound, which lay near the road.
1810 Presently a good many warriors passed by, and, after he had
satisfied his curiosity, he rode on and overtook them. The
Chief, who was no less a personage than the celebrated Push-
matahaw, with a smile full of meaning and mischief, said—
"Well, Mr. '*Gainis*,' I suppose you have been to pay our
mother a visit; and what did she say?" Your mother,
said the Factor, observed that her children were poor, had
become too numerous to inhabit the country they were then
occupying, and desired very much that they would sell their
lands to the United States and move west of the Mississippi,
to better and more extensive hunting grounds.* The old
Chief laughed immoderately, vociferating "Holauba! holauba! feenah. (*It's a lie, it's a lie, it's a real lie.*) Our good
mother never could have made such remarks." On the jour-
1810 ney he conversed much with Mr. Gaines upon the Indian tradi-

* It was the policy of all the Indian Agents to encourage the emigration of the Indians further west, and they never let an opportunity slip of alluding to it.

tions, and said that the true account was that his ancestors came from the west.*

In 1771, the population of the Choctaw nation was considerable. Two thousand three hundred warriors were upon the superintendent's books at Mobile, while two thousand 1771
more were scattered over the country, engaged in hunting. At that period Capt. Roman passed through seventy of their towns.† The eastern district of the nation was known as Oy-pat-oo-coo-la, or the *small nation*. The western was called Oo-coo-la, Falaya. Oo-coola, Hanete and Chickasaha.

These people were more slender in their form than other tribes. The men were raw-boned and astonishingly active. None could excel them in the ball play, or run as fast upon 1745
level ground.‡ Both sexes were well made, and the features of the females were lively and agreeable. They had the habit of inscribing their faces and bodies with a blue indelible ink, which appears to have been the practice of all the tribes to which it has been our province to allude. The Choctaws formed the heads of the infants into different shapes by compression, but it was chiefly applied to the forehead, and hence they were called, by traders, "flat heads." The infant was placed in a cradle, with his feet elevated twelve inches above a horizontal position, while his head was bent back and rested in a hole made for the purpose. A small bag of sand was

* Conversations with Mr. George S. Gaines. See, also, Barnard Roman's Florida, pp. 71–90.

† Roman, pp. 70–90. ‡ Adair.

CHAPTER II. Part 4. 1745 fixed upon the forehead, and as the little fellow could not move, the shape required was soon attained, for at that age the skull is capable of receiving any impression.*

The dress of the male Choctaw was similar to that of the Creeks, and was influenced in its style by his wealth or poverty. But they all wore the buck-she-ah-ma, *flap*, made of woollen cloth or buckskin. The female had usually only a petti-
1745 coat reaching from the waist to the knees, while some of the richer classes wore a covering also upon the neck and shoulder, and little bells fastened to a buckskin garter, which clasped the leg just below the knee. They wore ornaments in their ears, noses and around the fingers, like the Creeks. They were not cleanly in their persons like the Creeks, who were eternally engaged in bathing; but, strange to relate of Indians, very few of the Choctaws could swim, a fact recorded by all
1759 early travellers among them. As they seldom bathed, the smoke of their lightwood fires made their bodies assume a soot color.† Peculiarly fond of the taste of horse flesh, they
1780 preferred it to beef, even if the animal had died a natural death; and it was not uncommon for them to devour snakes when hard pressed for food.‡ Yet, notwithstanding, they were, upon the whole, very agreeable Indians, being invariably cheerful, witty and cunning. The men, too, unlike the proud Chiefs of other nations, helped the women to work, and did not consider it a degradation to hire themselves for that pur-

* Adair, pp. 8–9.

† Bossu's Travels, p. 298.

‡ Milfort, p. 290; Adair, p. 133.

pose to their constant friends the French, and afterwards to the English.* No Indians, moreover, excelled them in hospitality, which they exhibited particularly in their hunting camps, where all travellers and visitors were received and entertained with a hearty welcome. In regard to their habits in the chase, it may here be observed, that they excelled in killing bears, wild-cats, and panthers, pursuing them through the immense cane swamps with which their country abounded; but that the Creeks and Chickasaws were superior to them in overcoming the fleet deer. While hunting, the liver of the game was divided into as many pieces as there were camp fires, and was carried around by a boy, who threw a piece into each fire, intended, it would seem, as a kind of sacrifice. 1771

The Choctaws were superior orators. They spoke with good sense, and used the most beautiful metaphors. They had the power of changing the same words into different significations, and even their common speech was full of these changes. Their orations were concise, strong and full of fire.† 1745
Excessive debauchery, and a constant practice of begging, constituted their most glaring faults; and it was amusing to witness the many ingenious devices and shifts to which they resorted, to obtain presents.

Timid in war against an enemy abroad, they fought like desperate veterans, when attacked at home. On account of their repugnance to invading the country of an enemy, in which they were unlike the Creeks and Chickasaws, they

* Roman, pp. 71-90. † Adair, p. 11.

CHAPTER II. Part 4. 1745 were often taunted by these latter nations with the charge of cowardice. Frequently, exasperated by these aspersions, they would boldly challenge the calumniators to mortal combat upon an open field. But the latter, feigning to believe that true Indian courage consisted in slyness and stratagem, rarely accepted the banter. However, in 1765, an opportunity
1765 offered in the streets of Mobile, when Hoopa, at the head of forty Choctaws, fell upon three hundred Creeks, and routed and drove them across the river, into the marsh. Hooma alone killed fifteen of them, and was then despatched himself, by a retreating Creek. They were pursued no further because the Choctaws could not swim.

They did not torture a prisoner, in a protracted manner, like other tribes. He was brought home, despatched with a bullet or hatchet, and cut up, and the parts burned. The scalp was suspended from the hot-house, around which the women danced until they were tired. They were more to be relied upon as allies, than most other American Indians. The
1765 August Creeks were their greatest enemies. In August, 1765, a war began between them, and raged severely for six years.* Artful in deceiving an enemy, they attached the paws or trotters of panthers, bears and buffaloes, to their own feet and hands, and wound about the woods, imitating the circlings of those animals. Sometimes a large bush was carried by the front warrior, concealing himself and those behind him, while the one in the
1745 extreme rear defaced all the tracks with grass. Most excel-

* Roman, pp. 70–91.

lent trackers themselves, they well understood how to deceive the enemy, which they, also, effected by astonishing powers in imitating every fowl and quadruped. Their leader could never directly assume the command, but had, rather, to conduct his operations by persuasion.*

Gambling was a common vice, and even boys engaged in it by shooting at marks for a wager. In addition to the great ball play, which was conducted like that of the Creeks, already described, they had an exciting game called Chunke, or, by
some of the traders, "running hard labor." An alley was 1745
made, two hundred feet long, with a hard clay surface, which was kept swept clean. Two men entered upon it to play. They stood six yards from the upper end, each with a pole twelve feet long, smooth and tapering at the end, and with the points flat. One of them took a stone in the shape of a grind-stone, which was two spans round, and two inches thick on the edges. He gave it a powerful hurl down the alley, when both set off after it, and running a few yards, the one who did not roll, cast his pole, which was anointed with bear's oil, with a
true aim at the stone in its flight. The other player, to defeat his 1745
object, immediately darted his pole, aiming to hit the pole of his antagonist. If the first one hit the stone he counted one, and if the other, by the dexterity of his cast, hit his pole and knocked it from its proper direction, he also counted one. If both of the players missed, the throw was renewed. Eleven was the game, and the winner had the privilege of casting the stone.

* Adair, p. 309—Bossu, p. 297.

CHAPTER II. Part 4. In this manner the greater part of the day was passed, at half speed; the players and bystanders staking their ornaments,
1771 wearing apparel, skins, pipes and arms upon the result. Some-
1745 1759 times, after a fellow had lost all, he went home, borrowed a gun, and shot himself. The women, also, had a game with sticks and balls, something like the game of battledoor.*

The funeral ceremonies of the Choctaws were singular, and, indeed, horrible, but like those of nearly all the aborigines at the time of the invasion of De Soto. As soon as the breath departed from the body of a Choctaw, a high scaffold was erected, thirty-six feet from the dwelling where the deceased died. It consisted of four forks set in the ground, across which poles were laid, and then a floor made of boards or cypress bark. It was stockaded with poles, to prevent the admission of beasts of prey. The posts of the scaffold were painted with a mixture of vermilion and bear's oil, if the deceased was an Indian of note. The body, enveloped in a large bear-skin, was hauled up on the scaffold by ropes or vines, and laid out at length. The relations assembled, and wept and howled with mournful voices, asking strange questions of the corpse, according to the sex to which it belonged. "Why did you
1782 leave us?" "Did your wife not serve you well?" Were
1771 you not contented with your children?" Did you not have
1745 corn enough?" "Did not your land produce?" "Were
1759 you afraid of your enemies?" To increase the solemnity and importance of the funeral of a noted Indian, persons were

* Roman, pp. 70–91.—Adair, p. 402.—Bossu, p. 306.

hired to cry—the males having their heads hung with black moss, and the females suffering their hair to flow loosely to the winds. These women came at all hours, for several weeks, to mourn around the scaffold; and, on account of the horrid stench, frequently fainted, and had to be borne away. When the body had thus lain three or four months, the BONE-PICKER made his appearance. In 1772, there were five of these hideous undertakers in the Choctaw nation, who travelled about in search of scaffolds, and the horrible work which will be described. The bone-picker apprised the relatives of the deceased that the time had arrived when dissection should
take place. Upon the day which he had appointed, the rela- 1745
tives, friends, and others hired to assist in mourning, sur- 1771
rounded the scaffold. The bone-picker mounted upon it, with 1782
horrid grimaces and groans, took off the skin, and commenced 1777
his disgusting work. He had very long and hard nails, growing on the thumb, fore and middle fingers of each hand. He tore off the flesh with his nails, and tied it up in a bundle. He cleaned the bones, and also tied up the scrapings. Leaving the latter on the scaffold, he descended with the bones upon his head. All this time the assembly moaned and howled most awfully. They then painted the head with vermilion, which, together with all the bones, was placed in a nice box with a loose lid. If the bones were those of a Chief, the coffin also was painted red. Next, fire was applied to the scaffold, around which the assembly danced and frightfully whooped until it was consumed by the flames. Then a long procession was formed and the bones were carried, amid weeping and

CHAPTER II. Part 4.

moaning, to the bone-house, of which every town of importance had several. These houses were made by four pitch-pine posts being placed in the ground, upon the top of which was a scaffold floor. On this a steep roof was erected, like that of some modern houses, with the gables left open. There the box was deposited, with other boxes containing bones.
1745 In the meantime a great feast had been prepared, and some-
1771 times three horses were cooked up, if the deceased was wealthy.
1782 But the infernal bone-picker still was master of ceremonies,
1777 and having only wiped his filthy, bloody hands with grass,
served out the food to the whole assembly.*

When the bone-house was full of chests, a general interment took place. The people assembled, bore off the chests in procession to a plain, with weeping, howling and ejaculations of Allelujah! Allelujah! The chests containing the bones were arranged upon the ground in order, forming a pyramid. They then covered all with earth, which raised a conical mound. Then returning home, the day was concluded with a feast.†

The Choctaws entertained a great veneration for their medicine men or doctors, who practiced upon them constant frauds. Their fees were exorbitant, and required to be satisfied in advance. When a doctor had attended a patient a
1745 long time, and the latter had nothing more to give as pay-
1771 ment, he usually assembled the relations in private, informed

* Adair, pp. 183–188. Roman, pp. 71–90. Milfort, pp. 293–298.

† Bartram, pp. 514–515.

them that he had done all in his power, and had exhausted CHAPTER
his skill in endeavoring to restore their friend; that he would II.
surely die, and it was best to terminate his sufferings. Re- Part 4. 1777
posing the blindest confidence in this inhuman declaration, 1782
two of them then jumped upon the poor fellow and strangled
him. In 1782, one of these doctors thus began to consult
with the relations upon the case of a poor fellow. While they
were out of the house, he suspected their intentions, and
making an unnatural effort, crawled to the woods which fortunately was near the house. It was night, and he succeeded
in getting beyond their reach. The doctor persuaded them
that he was certainly dead, and they erected a scaffold as
though he were upon it and wept around it. Fortunately, 1782
laying his hands upon an opossum, the poor fellow eat of it
from time to time, and gained strength, now that he had
escaped the clutches of the doctor, who had nearly smoked
and bled him into the other world. At length, after much suffering, he made his way to the Creek nation and threw himself
upon the compassion of Colonel McGillivray, who had him
restored to health by proper attention. Again going back to
his nation, at the expiration of three months, he arrived at 1782
the house from which he had escaped, at the very time that
the people were celebrating his funeral by burning the scaffold and dancing around it. His sudden appearance filled
them with horror and dismay. Some fled to the woods,
others fell upon the ground. Alarmed himself, he retreated
to the house of a neighbor, who instantly fell on his face, saying, "Why have you left the land of spirits if you were happy

CHAPTER II. Part 4. 1782

there? Why do you return among us? Is it to assist in the last feast which your family and your friends make for you? Go! return to the land of the dead for fear of renewing the sorrow which they have felt at your loss!" Shunned by all his people, the poor Choctaw went back to the Creek nation, married a Tuskegee women, and lived in that town the balance of his life. Before his door lay the four French cannon of old Fort Toulouse. When the Choctaws had become satisfied that he did not die, and was really alive, they killed the doctor who had deceived them. They often entreated the fellow to return home, but he preferred to remain among a people who would not strangle him when he was sick.*

The Choctaws had no other religion than that which attached to their funeral rites. The French, to whom they were warmly attached, sought in vain to convert them to Christianity. At Chickasaha, they erected a chapel and gave the control of it to a Jesuit missionary. When the English took possession of this country, the Choctaws of that place would, for the amusement of their new friends, enter the old chapel, and go through the Catholic ceremonies, mimicing the priest with surprising powers. In 1771, Capt. Roman saw the lightwood cross still standing, but the chapel had been destroyed.

The Chickasaws, although at the period of 1771 a small
1771 nation, were once numerous, and their language was spoken by many tribes in the Western States. They were the fiercest,

* Milfort, pp. 298–304.

most insolent, haughty and cruel people among the Southern Indians. They had proved their bravery and intrepidity in constant wars. In 1541, they attacked the camp of De Soto 1541 in a most furious midnight assault, threw his army into dismay, killed some of his soldiers, destroyed all his baggage, and burnt up the town in which he was quartered. In 1736, they whipped the French under Bienville, who had invaded their country, and forced them to retreat to Mobile. In 1753, 1753 MM. Bevist and Regio encountered defeat at their hands. They continually attacked the boats of the French voyagers upon the Mississippi and Tennessee. They were constantly at war with the Kickapoos and other tribes upon the Ohio, but were defeated in most of these engagements. But with the English, as their allies, they were eminently successful against the Choctaws and Creeks, with whom they were often at variance.

The Chickasaws were great robbers, and, like the Creeks, often invaded a country, killing the inhabitants and carrying off slaves and plunder. The men considered the cultivation of the earth beneath them; and, when not engaged in hunting or warfare, slept away their time or played upon flutes, while their women were at work. They were athletic, well-formed and graceful. The women were cleanly, industrious, and generally good-looking.

In 1771, they lived in the centre of a large and gently roll- 1771
ing prairie, three miles square. They obtained their water from holes, which dried up in summer. In this prairie was an assemblage of houses one mile and a half long, very nar-

CHAPTER II. Part 4.

row and irregular, which was divided into seven towns, as follows:

Mellattau—*hat and feather.*

Chatelau—*copper town.*

Chuckafalaya—*long town.*

Hickihaw—*stand still.*

Chucalissa—*great town.*

Tuckahaw—a certain *weed.*

Ash-wick-boo-ma—*red grass.*

The last was once well fortified with palisades, and there
they defeated D'Artaguette. The nearest running water was two
miles distant; the next was four miles off, to which point
canoes could ascend from the Tombigby in high tide. The
ford, which often proved difficult of crossing, was called Na-
1771 hoola Inalchubba—*the white man's hard labor.* Horses and
cattle increased rapidly in this country. The breed of the former descended from importations from Arabia to Spain, from
Spain to Mexico, and from thence to the Chickasaw nation.
Here they ran wild in immense droves, galloping over the
beautiful prairies, the sun glittering upon their various colors.
They were owned by the Indians and traders.

The Chickasaws were very imperious in their carriage towards females, and extremely jealous of their wives. Like the
Creeks, they punished adultery by beating with poles until
1771 the sufferer was senseless, and then concluded by cropping
the ears, and, for the second offence, the nose or a piece of the
upper lip. Notwithstanding they resided so far from large
streams, they were all excellent swimmers, and their children

were taught that art in clay holes and pools, which remained
filled with water unless the summer was remarkably dry.

Of all the Indians in America, they were the most expert in
tracking. They would follow their flying enemy on a long
gallop over any kind of ground without mistaking, where perhaps only a blade of grass bent down, told the footprint.
Again, when they were leisurely hunting over the woods, and
came upon an indistinct trail recently made by Indians, they 1782
knew at once of what nation they were by the footprints, the 1745
hatchet chops upon the trees, their camp-fires, and other dis- 1759
tinguishing marks. They were also esteemed to be admirable
hunters, and their extensive plains and unbroken forests afforded them the widest field for the display of their skill. In
1771, their grounds extended from Middle Mississippi to the
mouth of the Ohio and some distance into the territory
of the present State of Tennessee. But this extreme northern ground they visited with caution, and only in the
winter, when their northern enemies were close at home.
They were often surprised on the sources of the Yazoo, 1745
but below there, and as far east as the branches of the 1782
Tombigby to Oaktibbehaw, they hunted undisturbed. This 1759
last point they regarded as the boundary between them
and the Choctaws. With the latter they had no jealousies
in regard to the chase, and they sported upon each others'
grounds when not at war. Although the country of the
Chickasaws abounded with that valuable animal, the beaver, 1771
they left them for the traders to capture, saying, "Anybody
can kill a beaver." They pursued the more noble and diffi-

CHAPTER II. Part 4. cult sport of overcoming the fleet deer, and the equally swift and more formidable elk.

The summer habitations of the Chickasaws were cabins of an oblong shape, near which were corn-houses. In the yard stood also a winter-house, of a circular form. Having no chimneys, the smoke found its way out of this "hot-house" wherever it could. These they entered, and slept all night, stifled with
1745 smoke, and, no matter how cold the morning, they came forth naked and sweating as soon as the day dawned. These houses were used by the sick also, who, remaining in them until perspiration ensued, jumped suddenly into holes of cold water.

They dried and pounded their corn before it came to maturity, which they called Boota-capassa—*coal flour*. A small quantity of this thrown into water, swelled immediately, and made a fine beverage. They used hickory-nut and bear's oil; and the traders learned them to make the hams of
1771 the bear into bacon. In 1771, the whole number of gunmen in the Chickasaw nation only amounted to about two hundred and fifty. It is astonishing what a handful of warriors had so long kept neighboring nations of great strength from destroying them.

They buried their dead the moment vitality ceased, in the
1771 very spot where the bed stood upon which the deceased lay, and the nearest relatives mourned over it with woful lamentations. This mourning continued for twelve moons, the women practising it openly and vociferously, and the men silently.*

* Barnard Roman's Florida, pp. 59–71.

The modern reader may form some idea of the Chickasaw and Choctaw nations, as they once existed, by briefly tracing the route of Capt. Roman through their country. He began his tour at Mobile, encamped at Spring Hill, passed the head waters of Dog river, and again encamped at Bouge Hooma—*red creek*—the boundary between the English and the Choctaws. Pursuing his journey, the camp was pitched at Hoopa Ulla—*noisy owl*—where he saw the Creek painting described upon page 100. Then passing Okee Ulla—*noisy water*—and the towns of Coosa, Haanka Ulla—*bawling goose*—he crossed a branch of the Sookhan-Hatcha river. He reached a deserted town called Etuck Chukke—*blue wood*—passed through Abecka, an inhabited town, and there crossed another branch of the Sookhan-Hatcha, and arrived at Ebeetap Oocoola, where the Choctaws had erected a large stockade fort. A south-western direction was now assumed, and Capt. Roman passed through the following towns: Chooka, Hoola, Oka Hoola, Hoola Taffa, Ebeetap Ocoola Cho, Oka Attakkala, and crossing Bouge Fooka and Bouge Chitto, which runs into Bouge Aithe-Tanne, arrived at the house of Benjamin James, at Chickasaha.

1771 September 20 — September 30 — October 5 — October 23

He set out from this place for the Chickasaw nation, and crossed only two streams of importance—Nashooba and Oktibbehaw. Without accident, he arrived at the Chickasaw towns enumerated upon page 148, and lying within a few miles of Pontitoc. He proceeded east-by-south five miles and crossed Nahoola-Inal-chubba—*town creek*—and then assumed a south-east direction, and arrived at the Twenty-mile creek, a

November 10 — December 8

CHAPTER II. Part 4.

large branch of the Tombigby. At the mouth of Nahoola-Inal-chubba, Capt. Roman found a large canoe, in which he and his companions embarked and proceeded down the Tombigby. One mile below, on the west bank, they passed a bluff on
1771 December 26 which the French formerly had a fortified trading post. Capt.
1772 January 5 Roman next saw the mouth of the Oktibbehaw, the dividing line between the two nations, and passed the mouth of the
January 7 Nasheba, on the east. Floating with rapidity down the river, he next came to the Noxshubby, on the west side, and then to the mouth of a creek called Etomba-Igaby—*box maker's creek*—where the French had a fort.* From this creek, the name of which has been corrupted by the French to "Tombeckbe," and by the Americans to "Tombigby," the river takes its name. Upon it lived an Indian who made chests to hold the bones of the Choctaws.

January 10 Roman came to the confluence of the Tombigby and Warrior, and, a little below, passed some steep chalky bluffs, which the traders called the *Chickasaw Gallery*, because from this point they were accustomed to shoot at the French boats. On the top of this bluff was a vast plain, with some remains of huts standing upon it.† Three miles below the mouth of the Soukan-Hatcha, Roman came upon the old towns of the Coosawdas and Oahchois, commencing at Suctaloosa—*black bluff*—and extending from thence down the river for some distance.‡

* Now, Jones's Bluff.

† Now the site of Demopolis.

‡ Some of the Alabamas living at the town of that name below the confluence of the Coosa and Tallapoosa, and some Creeks of the town

CHAPTER II. Part 4. 1772 January 13

Next, passing a high bluff called Nanna Fallaya, he reached Batcha Chooka, a bluff on the east side, where he encountered a desperate band of thieves, belonging to the town of Okaloosa, of the Choctaws. He then came to some bluffs called Nanna Chahaws, where a gray flat rock, called Teeakhaily Ekutapa, rises out of the water. Here the people of Chickasaha once had a settlement. Lower down, the party saw a bluff upon the east side, called Yagna Hoolah—*beloved ground*—and encamped at the mouth of Sintabouge—*snake creek*—three miles below which was the English line separating them from the Choctaws. Having entered the British settlements, Capt. Roman continued his voyage until he reached Mobile.*

1772 January 20

of Oakchoy, to be nearer the French, who were their friends, moved upon the main Tombigby, and the deserted towns which Roman mentions were those in which they had formerly lived.

* Roman's Florida.

PART V.

THE CHEROKEES.

CHAPTER II. It has been seen that De Soto passed over a portion of the
Part 5. country of these Indians in the territory which embraces
1540 Northern Georgia. The name Cherokee is derived from Chera, *fire;* and the Prophets of this nation were called Chera-taghge, *men of divine fire.*

The first that we hear of the Cherokees, after the Spanish invasion, is their connection with the early British settlers of Virginia. A powerful and extensive nation, they even had settlements upon the Appomattox river, and were allied
1623 by blood with the Powhattan tribe. The Virginians drove them from that place, and they retreated to the head of the Holston river. Here, making temporary settlements, the Northern Indians compelled them to retire to the Little Tennessee river, where they established themselves permanently. About the same time, a large branch of the Cherokees came from the territory of South-Carolina, near Charleston, and formed towns upon the main Tennessee, extending as far as the Muscle Shoals. They found all that region unoccupied, except upon the Cumberland, where resided a roving band of Shawnees. But the whole country bore evidence of once having sustained a large Indian population.

Such is the origin of the first Cherokee settlements upon CHAPTER
the main Tennessee, but the great body of the nation appears II.
to have occupied Northern Georgia and North-western Carolina Part 5.
as far back as the earliest discoveries can trace them.

But very little was known of these natives until the Eng-
lished formed colonies in the two Carolinas. They are first 1693
mentioned when some of their Chiefs complained that the
Savannas and Congerees attacked their extreme eastern settlements, captured their people and sold them as slaves in
the town of Charleston. Two years afterwards, Governor
Archdale, of Carolina, arrested this practice, which induced
the Cherokees to become friends of the English. They joined 1712
the latter in a war against the Tuscaroras. But three years
afterwards they became allies of the Northern Indians, and
once more fought their European friends. At length Governor
Nichalson concluded a peace with them, which was con- 1730
firmed by Alexander Cummings, the British General Superintendent of Indian Affairs. The Cherokees assisted the Eng- 1758 November 24
lish in the capture of Fort Duquesne. When returning
home, however, they committed some depredations upon the
settlers of Virginia, which were resented. This, together with
the influence of French emissaries, had the effect again to
array them against the people of Georgia and the Carolinas.
Various expeditions marched against them, and their country
was finally invaded with success, by Colonel Grant. Having
sued for peace, articles of amity and alliance were signed at 1761 November 19
Long Island, upon the Holston. According to the traditions
preserved by Judge Haywood, who wrote the History of

Tennessee, the Cherokees originally came from the territory now embraced by the Eastern States of the Union, in which they differ from the other tribes of whom it has been our province to speak, all of whom came from the west.

When they began to be visited by the Carolina traders, their nation was powerful and warlike, and was divided into two parts. The Upper Cherokees lived upon the rivers Tellico, Great and Little Tennessee, the Holston and French Broad. The Lower Cherokees inhabited the country watered by the sources of the Oconee, the Ockmulgee and the Savannah. The great Unaka or Smoky mountain lay between and divided the two sections.* Their whole country was the most beautiful and romantic in the known world. Their springs of delicious water gushed out of every hill and mountain side. Their
1735 lovely rivers meandered, now smoothly and gently, through the most fertile vallies, and then, with the precipitancy and fleetness of the winds, rushed over cataracts and through mountain gaps. The forests were full of game, the rivers abounded with fish, the vales teemed with their various productions, and the mountains with fruit, while the pure atmosphere consummated the happiness of the blest Cherokees.

1700 About the period of 1700, the Cherokee nation consisted of sixty-four towns. But the inhabitants of those situated in the upper district, were continually engaged in wars with the

* Haywood's Aboriginal History of Tennesse, pp. 233–234. Transactions of the American Antiquarian Society, vol. 2, pp. 89–90 Adair's American Indians.

Northern Indians, while those below were harrassed by the Creeks. Then again, the Cherokees had to encounter, first the French, and then the English. From these causes, (added to which was the terrible scourge of the small pox, introduced 1738
into Charleston by a slave ship, and thence carried into their country,) the population had greatly decreased—so that, in 1740, the number of warriors was estimated at only five 1740
thousand. That year fully one thousand of these were destroyed by that disease.*

The Cherokees were so similar to the Creeks in their form, color, general habits and pursuits, that the reader is requested to refresh his recollection in relation to our description of the latter, and will not be required, tediously, to retrace the same ground. Their ball plays, green corn dances, constant habit of indulging in the purifying black drink, their manner of conducting wars and of punishing prisoners, their council-houses, 1735
their common apparel, and also their appearance during war, were all precisely like those of the Creeks. And, in addition, they played Chunke, like the Choctaws. However, a careful examination of several authorities, has unfolded a few peculiarities, which will now be introduced.

Unlike other Indian nations, who once trod our soil, the Cherokees had no laws against adultery. Both sexes were 1735
unrestrained in this particular, and marriage was usually of short duration.

On account of the pure air which they breathed, the exer-

* Historical Collections of Georgia, vol. 2, p. 72.

CHAPTER II. Part 5.

cise of the chase, the abundance of natural productions which the country afforded, and the delicious water which was always near, the Cherokees lived to an age much more advanced than the other tribes which have been noticed in this chapter.*

They observed some singular rules in relation to the burial of the dead. When a person was past recovery, (to prevent
1735 pollution,) they dug a grave, prepared a tomb, anointed the hair of the patient and painted his face; and when death ensued, interment was immediately performed. After the third day, the attendants at the funeral appeared at the council-house and engaged in their ordinary pursuits, but the relatives lived in retirement and moaned for some time.† Such ceremonies, practiced upon a poor fellow in his last moments, and while in his senses, was certainly a cooler and more cruel method than that of the Choctaws, who, as we have seen, suddenly jumped upon the patient and strangled him to death, after the doctor had pronounced his recovery impossible.

It was formerly the habit of the Cherokees to shoot all the stock belonging to the deceased, and they continued to bury, with the dead, their guns, bows and household utensils. If one died upon a journey, hunt or war expedition, his companions erected a stage, upon which was a notched log pen, in which the body was placed to secure it from wild beasts. When it was supposed that sufficient time had elapsed, so that nothing remained but the bones, they returned to the
1735 spot, collected these, carried them home, and buried them with

* Adair, pp. 226–228.

† Adair, p. 126.

great ceremony. Sometimes heaps of stones were raised as CHAPTER
monuments to the dead, whose bones they had not been able II.
to "gather to their fathers," and every one who passed by Part 5.
added a stone to the pile.*

Henry Timberlake, a Lieutenant in the British service, was
despatched with a small command from Long Island, upon 1761 November 28
the Holston, to the Cherokee towns upon the Tellico and the
Little Tennessee rivers. His object was to cultivate a good
understanding with these people, who had, indeed, invited
him to their country. He descended the Holston in canoes, to 1761
the mouth of the Little Tennessee, and thence passed up that
stream to their towns. Spending some weeks here, he returned to Charleston with three Cherokee Chiefs, and sailed
for England. Three years afterwards he published a book, 1762
from which we have been enabled to gain some information
respecting the Cherokees.†

The Cherokees were of middle stature, and of an olive color, but were generally painted, while their skins were stained with indelible ink, representing a variety of pretty figures. According to Bartram, the males were larger and more robust than any others of our natives, while the women were tall, slender, erect, and of delicate frame, with features of perfect
symmetry. With cheerful countenances, they moved about 1776
with becoming grace and dignity. Their feet and hands were small and exquisitely shaped. The hair of the male

* Adair—Bartram.

† Memoirs of Lieutenant Henry Timberlake. London: 1765.

CHAPTER II. Part 5.

was shaved, except a patch on the back part of the head, which was ornamented with beads and feathers, or with a colored deer's tail. Their ears were slit and stretched to an enormous size causing the persons who had the cutting performed to undergo incredible pain. They slit but one ear at a time, because the patient had to lay on one side forty days, for it to heal. As soon as he could bear the operation, wire was wound around them to expand them, and when they were entirely well, they were adorned with silver pendants and rings.

Many of them had genius, and spoke well, which paved the
1761 way to power in council. Their language was pleasant. It was very aspirited, and the accents so many and various, that one would often imagine them singing, in their common discourse.

They had a particular method of relieving the poor, which ought to be ranked among the most laudable of their religious ceremonies. The head men issued orders for a war dance, at which all the fighting men of the town assembled. But here, contrary to all their other dances, only one danced at a time, who, with a tomahawk in his hand, hopped and capered for a minute, and then gave a whoop. The music then stopped till he related the manner of his taking his first scalp. He concluded his narration, and cast a string of wampum, wire, plate, paint, lead, or any thing he could spare, upon a large bear-skin spread for the purpose. Then the music again began, and he continued in the same manner through all his warlike actions. Then another succeeded him, and the ceremony lasted until all the warriors had related their exploits and thrown presents upon the skin. The stock thus raised, after paying the musicians, was divided among the poor. The same ceremony was used to recompense any extraordinary merit. CHAPTER II. Part 5.

The Cherokees engaged oftener in dancing than any other 1761
Indian population; and when reposing in their towns, almost every night was spent in this agreeable amusement. They were likewise very dexterous at pantomimes. In one of these, two men dressed themselves in bear-skins, and came among the assembly, winding and pawing about with all the motions of that animal. Two hunters next entered, who, in dumb show, acted in all respects as if they had been in the woods. After many attempts to shoot the bears, the hunters fired, and one of them was killed and the other wounded. They attempted to cut the throat of the latter. A tremendous scuffle ensued between the wounded bruin and the hunters, affording the whole company a great deal of diversion. They 1761
also had other amusing pantomimic entertainments, among which was "taking the pigeons at roost."

They were extremely proud, despising the lower class of Europeans. Yet they were gentle and amiable to those whom they thought their friends. Implacable in their enmity, their revenge was only completed in the entire destruction of the enemy. They were hardy, and endured heat, cold, and hunger in a surprising manner. But when in their power to indulge, no people upon earth, except the Choctaws, carried debauchery to greater excess.*

* Timberlake's Memoirs, pp. 49–80; Bartram, pp. 368–369

CHAPTER II. Part 5. 1776 Spring season

William Bartram, who penetrated the Cherokee nation, mentions the following towns. We use his orthography.

ON THE LITTLE TENNESSEE RIVER, EAST OF THE SMOKY MOUNTAIN.

Echoe; Nucasse; Whataga; Cowe.

ON THE BRANCHES OF THAT RIVER.

Ticaloosa; Jore; Conisca; Nowe.

ON THE LITTLE TENNESSEE, NORTH OF THE SMOKY MOUNTAINS.

1776 Tomothle; Noewe; Tellico; Clennuse; Ocunnolufte; Chewe; Quanuse; Tellowe.

INLAND TOWNS ON THE BRANCHES OF THAT RIVER, AND OTHERS NORTH OF THE SMOKY MOUNTAIN.

Tellico; Chatuga; Hiwasse; Chewase; Nuanha.

OVERHILL TOWNS ON THE TENNESSEE OR CHEROKEE RIVER.

Tallasse; Chelowe; Sette; Chote-great; Ioco; Tahasse; Tamohle; Tuskege; Big Island; Nilaque; Niowe.

LOWER TOWNS, EAST OF THE MOUNTAINS.

Sinica; Keowe; Kulsage; Tugilo; Estotowe; Qualatche; Chote; Estotowe, great; Allagae; Iore; Nacooche.*

1792 March 5 Gov. Blount, of the Tennessee Territory, made a report to the Indian Department of the Federal Government, in which he described other towns of the Cherokee nation. It appears that a portion of the Cherokees established themselves upon Chicamauga Creek, one hundred miles below the mouth of the Holston, being averse to any terms of friendship with the English. But, believing these new settlements to be infested with witches, they abandoned them, moved forty miles lower

* Bartram, 371–372.

down the Tennessee, and there laid out the foundation of the "five towns" which they inhabited for many years afterwards, and until their final removal to Arkansas. These towns were: CHAPTER II. Part 5. 1782

Running Water—on the south bank of the main Tennessee, three miles above Nickajack, containing one hundred huts, the inhabitants of which were a mixed population of Cherokees and Shawnees. 1792

Nickajack—on the south bank of the Tennessee, containing forty houses.

Long Island Town—on the south side of the Tennessee, on an island of that name, containing several houses.

Crow Town—on the north side of the Tennessee, half a mile from the river up Crow creek. This was the largest of the towns.

Lookout Mountain Town—between two mountains, on Lookout Mountain creek, fifteen miles from its confluence with the Tennessee.

The first four of these towns were considerable Indian thoroughfares for a long period, being the crossing places of the Southern and Northern Indians during their wars with the Cumberland American settlements. Of these five towns, the sites of Nickajack and Long Island only are in Alabama, situated in the north-east part of De Kalb county. But still lower down, in the present State of Alabama, were Will's Town and Turkey Town—important Cherokee establishments. The former was named for a half breed called *Red-headed Will.* At these towns lived the British Superintendent, (the celebrated Col. Campbell,) before and during the Revolutionary War.*

* Indian Affairs, vol. 1, pp. 264-289.

CHAPTER III.

ANCIENT MOUNDS AND FORTIFICATIONS IN ALABAMA.

CHAPTER III. In the Southern and North-western States mounds of various dimensions and descriptions are yet to be seen, and continue to elicit no little speculation in regard to the race of people who formed them, and the objects which they had in view.

Mounds are most commonly heaps of earth, but in some instances they are made of fragments of rock. In Florida, Georgia, Alabama and Mississippi, they are of two classes. We will first treat of the large mounds, some of which are round, some eliptical, and others square. Many of them are flat on top, while others present conical forms. They ascend to the height of from forty to ninety feet, and some are eighteen hundred feet in circumference at the base. Especial contrivances appear to have been resorted to, to ascend these singular and imposing elevations, by means of steps cut in the sides, inclining at an easy angle, and reaching from the ground below
1540 low to their tops.* During the invasion of De Soto, they

* See Chapter 2, pp. 63-64.

were used as elevated platforms, sustaining the houses of the Chief, his family and attendants, while the common people lived around the base. The writers upon that expedition describe the manner in which the natives brought the earth to the spot and formed these elevations. Garcellasso de la Vega states that the erection of a mound was the first object in building a new town, which was generally located upon some low alluvial ground. When completed, the Chief's houses, from ten to twenty in number, were placed upon its top, and a public square laid out at the base, around which were the houses of the prominent Indians, while the humbler wigwams of the common people stood around the other side of the mound. CHAPTER III.

Such, then, three hundred and ten years ago, was found to be the use of these mounds. By the writers of De Soto, they are repeatedly mentioned as being almost daily seen in all the territory through which that remarkable adventurer passed. Yet, many very learned and wise antiquaries have contended, in various works which they have published, that these mounds must have been constructed at a very ancient period, by a race far advanced in civilization—that the aborigines who were first discovered by Europeans were incapable of erecting such works, on account of their ignorance of the arts and their want of sufficient population. Our readers have seen what a numerous population De Soto and other discoverers found here, and that they possessed much ingenuity in the building of boats, fortifications, temples, houses, &c. Of all people upon earth, the American Indians had most time to engage 1540 1540 1564

CHAPTER III. in such works, for they were never accustomed to regard their time as of the least importance. Indeed, the American citizen of the present day, who has lived upon the Indian frontiers, knows that they often assembled together in great numbers and performed public works of all kinds. But much later authority than that offered by the writers of De Soto
1730 will be presented. It will be recollected that when the French drove the Natchez tribe from the spot now occupied by the city of that name, that the latter established themselves upon
1731 the Lower Washita, where they "erected mounds and em-
1732 bankments for defence, which covered an area of four hundred acres." These mounds are still to be seen there, and some of them are very large. These Indians were driven from Natchez in 1730. Two years afterwards the French defeated them upon the Washita, where they were protected by their embankments and mounds, which they had only been a little over two years in constructing. Let it be borne in mind that this was about one hundred and ninety-one years after the invasion of De Soto; and the facts are attested by numerous Frenchmen and other authors, some of whom were eye-witnesses.*

Charlevoix and Tonti both mention that they found Indians a little south of Lake Michigan, who well understood the construction of mounds and fortifications. Even during the administration of Jefferson, Lewis and Clarke, who had been despatched upon an overland route to Oregon, discovered the

* See Chapter 2, Part 3, pp. 132–133.

Sioux and other Western Indians erecting earthen embankments around their camps and towns. Were it deemed necessary, other authorities could be adduced to overthrow the speculations of those antiquarians who endeavor to inculcate the belief that our country was once inhabited by an almost civilized race. We heartily concur in the opinion expressed by McCulloh, in his "Researches," that the "mounds were sites for the dwellings of the Chiefs, for council-halls and for temples, which fancy and conceit have constructed into various shapes and variously situated, one to the other." This author has reference, of course, to the larger mounds.*

Bartram found, in East Florida, many peculiar mounds. 1776
He saw groups of square mounds surrounded by walls of earth, and pyramidal mounds of great height. "From the river St. John, southwardly to the point of the peninsula of Florida, are to be seen high pyramidal mounds, with spacious and extensive avenues leading from them out of the town to an artificial lake or pond of water." In another place he says:—"At about fifty yards distance from the landing place stands a magnificent Indian mount. But what greatly contributed to the beauty of the scene, was a noble Indian highway, which led from the great mount, in a straight line three quarters of a mile, through a forest of live-oaks, to the verge of an oblong artificial lake, which was on the edge of an ex-

* Researches, Philosophical and Antiquarian, concerning the aboriginal history of America, by J. H. McCulloh, Jr., M.D. Baltimore: 1829. pp. 516.

10*

CHAPTER III. 1776 tensive level savannah. This grand highway was about fifty yards wide, sunk a little below the common level, and the earth thrown on each side, making a bank of about two feet high."

On the east side of the Ockmulgee, and a little below the city of Macon, in Georgia, are some large and interesting mounds. In the town of Florence, Lauderdale county, Alabama, is a very large and peculiar mound. Near Carthage, in the same State, there are many mounds of various sizes, some of which are large.

Dr. Charles A. Woodruff—a native of Savannah, but now a resident of Alabama—a man of letters and research, who has travelled over Georgia, Mississippi, Florida, Louisiana, Arkansas and Alabama, engaged in geological researches—has called our attention to a very remarkable group of mounds on the lands of Judge Messier, twenty-one miles in a south-eastern direction from Fort Gaines. A reference to the sketch which he has furnished us, and his description of it, which follows, will make the reader acquainted with these remarkable artificial elevations.

"No. 1. The large sacrificial mound, seventy feet in height and six hundred feet in circumference. This mound is cover-
1847 ed with large forest trees, from four to five hundred years old. A shaft has been sunk in the centre to the depth of sixty feet, and at its lower portion a bed of human bones, five feet in thickness, and in a perfectly decomposed state, was passed.

"No. 2, 2. Like the former, have hearth stones on the summit, with charred wood around them, which would show

Ancient Indian Fortifications and Mounds, in Early County, Georgia, from a sketch by the visitor, Dr. C, A, Woodruff.

that they, too, were used for sacrifices. They are thirty feet CHAPTER
high. III.

"No. 3. A wall of earth enclosing these mounds.

"No. 4, 4, 4, 4. Mounds outside of the enclosure, twenty feet high, and probably used as watch towers.

"No. 5. Entrance to the enclosure.

"In the rear of these mounds is a creek, No. 6, and from 1847
the large mound there has been constructed an arched passage, three hundred yards in length, leading to the creek, and probably intended to procure water for religious purposes."

The smaller mounds, to be found in almost every field upon the rivers Tennessee, Coosa, Tallapoosa, Alabama, Cahaba, Warrior and Tombigby, will next be considered.

Many of these elevations are cultivated in cotton and corn, the plough ascending and descending from year to year, with more ease, as they gradually wear away. They are usually from five to ten feet high, from fifteen to sixty feet in circumference at the base, and of conical forms, resembling haystacks. Where they have been excavated, they have, invariably, been found to contain human bones, various stone ornaments, weapons, pieces of pottery, and sometimes ornaments of copper and silver, but of a rude manufacture, clearly indicating Indian origin. Layers of ashes and charcoal are, also, found in these mounds.

It will be recollected that the Spaniards, during the inva- 1539
sion of De Soto, discovered temples in all the chief towns, in 1540
which the dead were deposited in baskets and wooden boxes. 1541
At a late day, this custom was found to exist only among the

CHAPTER III. Choctaws, Natchez, and a few other tribes. The Muscogees and Alabamas, who came into the country after it had been overrun by De Soto, had, as we have seen, simple modes of burial, and hence knew nothing about the construction of these mounds. The bone-houses of the Choctaws were miniature temples of the Indians of 1540. We have seen in
1735 what manner the Choctaws placed their dead upon scaffolds,
1777 and afterwards picked off all the flesh and fragments from
1759 the bones, and deposited the latter in bone-houses. It is posi-
1782 tively asserted by Bartram that every few years, when these houses became full of bones, the latter were carried out upon a plain, buried in a common grave, and a mound raised over them.* According to Charlevoix, another conscientious author, the Six Nations and the Wyandots, every eight or ten years, disinterred their dead, who had been deposited where they had died, and carried all the bones to a certain place, where they dug a pit, thirty feet in diameter and ten in depth, which was paved at the bottom with stones. In this the various skeletons, with the property which the deceased possessed, were thrown. Over the heap a mound was raised, by throwing in the earth they had dug out, together with rubbish of every kind. Much later authority will be adduced. Lewis and Clarke, whom, as we have said, Jefferson sent to explore Oregon, saw a mound twelve feet in diameter at the base, and six feet high, which had just been erected over the body of a Maha Chief. It appears to have always been the

* Bartram's Travels, p. 516. See also Bossu's Travels, vol. 1, p. 299

custom to erect a mound over a Chief or person of distinction, CHAPTER
and no other bodies were interred with him. Indeed, no prac- III.
tice has been more universal than that of erecting a mound or
tumulus over the dead, not only in America, but over the
world. Adair asserts that it was the practice of the Cherokees to collect the skeletons of those who had died far from
home, and erect over them stone mounds, and every person 1735
who passed by was required to add a stone to the heap.*
This, then, accounts for the heaps of stone to be found in the northern parts of Georgia and North-eastern Alabama, resembling mounds in form. In North Alabama and Tennessee, skeletons have been found in caves. In mountainous countries this may have been one of the modes of disposing of the dead, or, which is more probable, persons died there suddenly, and their bones were not afterwards gathered together, buried in a common grave, and a mound erected over them, as was the general custom of ancient times.

The small mounds in Alabama, which have been excavated, contain different stratas. Beginning to dig at the top, the operators first pass through a strata of earth about two feet thick, then they come to a bed of ashes and charcoal, and then a bed of human bones mixed with pieces of pottery, pipes, arrow-heads and various Indian ornaments. Muscle shells are often mixed with these. Continuing to dig downwards, the excavators pass through a strata of earth, which is succeeded by stratas of bones, charcoal, pottery, Indian orna-

* "Adair's American Indians."

CHAPTER ments and arrow-points. Now, from all we have read and
III. heard of the Choctaws, we are satisfied that it was their cus-
1735 1777 tom to take from the bone-houses the skeletons, with
1759 which they repaired in funeral procession to the suburbs of
1782 the town, where they placed them on the ground in one heap,
together with the property of the dead, such as pots, bows, arrows, ornaments, curious shaped stones for dressing deer-skins, and a variety of other things. Over this heap they first threw charcoal and ashes, probably to preserve the bones, and the next operation was to cover all with earth. This left a mound several feet high. In the course of eight or ten years, when the bone-house again became full of skeletons, the latter were carried in the same manner to the mound, placed upon top of it, and covered with ashes and earth. When the mound became high enough to excite a kind of veneration for it, by depositing upon it heaps of bones, from time to time, another was made not far from it, and then
1735 another, as time rolled on. This accounts for the different
1759 stratas of bones to be found in the same mound, and for the
1782 erection of several mounds, often found near each other.

As for the ancient ditches at Cahaba, and in other portions of Alabama, in which are now growing the largest trees of the forest, indicating the works to have been of very remote date, we have been unable, in our investigations, to ascribe them to European origin, as they are generally supposed to be. De Soto erected no forts, in passing through this country, and had no occasion to do so, for his army was competent to subdue the natives without such means of defence.

It is true, he cut some temporary ditches upon the Warrior, CHAPTER
near Erie, to repel the savages, who were charging him con- III.
stantly from the other side of the river. These were soon abandoned, and his journalists mention no other works of the kind which he made.* The French and Spaniards, who afterwards occupied Alabama, erected no forts, except those at Mobile, upon the Tensaw River, at St. Stephens, at Jones' Bluff upon the Tombigby, and four miles above the confluence of the Coosa and Tallapoosa, upon the east bank of the former.

The English, at an early period, constructed a fort at Ocfuskee upon the Tallapoosa. If any other forts or entrenchments were made by the Europeans who first established themselves upon our soil, we have not been so fortunate as to trace them. The conclusion, then, seems to us to be apparent, that these ancient entrenchments or fortifications were the works of the
aborigines of the country. It will be recollected that De Soto, 1540
and the French authors who succeeded him, nearly two centu- 1700
ries afterwards, discovered towns which were well fortified with 1792
immense breastworks of timber, around which were cut large ditches. It was easy,—within a short space of time,—for a few hundred Indians to have cut an immense ditch, or to have thrown up a great mound. The same tools employed in the

*"Had Hernando De Soto erected one-tenth of the works which have been ascribed to him, in the States bordering on the Gulf, in Tennessee, and even in Kentucky, he must have found ample demands on his time and exertions."—"Ancient Monuments of the Mississippi Valley," by E. G. Squier, A.M., p. 112.

CHAPTER III. erection of the latter, certainly the work of the ancient Indians, could well have been used in the cutting of these old entrenchments or ditches. Hence, we contend, that at the town of Cahaba there once existed a large Indian establishment, which was fortified with palisades, and that the ditch, which has produced so much modern speculation, among the good people of that place, was cut around these palisades, or rather around the town, having the Alabama river open on one side. There is a ditch near the Talladega Springs, which formerly had trees growing in it, and which surrounds an elevation, embracing a few acres and taking in a beautiful spring, which gushes out of the rocks at the side of the hill.* No doubt, this, and all other works like it, now frequently seen over the territories of Alabama and Mississippi, are the works of our ancients Indians, for they invariably erected their defences at those places which admitted of the encompassment of running water; while, on the other hand, the Europeans who came to this country at an early period, always dug wells within the fortifications which they made.

In the month of October, 1850, we visited a remarkable place at the Falls of Little River, situated in the north-eastern corner of Cherokee county, Alabama, and very near the line of De Kalb county, in the same State. [See picture at the beginning of volume II.] What is rather singular, Little River has its source on the top of Lookout Mountain, and runs
1850 October for many miles on the most elevated parts of it. In the winter

* Formerly the property of Henry G. Woodward.

and spring it is a stream of considerable size, affording a rapid and dangerous current of water; but when it was seen upon the present occasion, a very protracted drought had nearly dried it up. The river flows along the top of the mountain with very inconsiderable banks, until it reaches a precipice of solid rock, in the form of a half circle, over which it falls seventy feet, perpendicularly, into a basin. After being received in this rock basin, the river flows off without much interruption, and, in winding about, forms a peninsula about two or three hundred yards below the falls. The banks of the river bordering on this peninsula are the same unbroken rock walls which form the falls, and are equally high and bold. Across the neck of the peninsula are yet to be traced two ancient ditches, nearly parallel with each other, and about thirty feet apart in the middle of the curve which they form, though they commence within ten feet of each other upon the upper precipice, and when they have reached the lower precipice, are found to run into each other. These ditches have been almost filled up by the effects of time. On their inner sides are rocks piled up and mixed with the dirt which was thrown up in making these entrenchments, indicating them to be of the simplest and rudest Indian origin. The author has seen many such entrenchments in his travels over Alabama, Mississippi and Florida, and hesitates not to say that they are the works of the aborigines of the country.

1850 October

On one side of the bend of the peninsula, and about ten feet below the top of the rock precipice, are four or five small caves, large enough, if square, to form rooms twelve by fourteen feet.

CHAPTER III. 1850 October

They are separated from each other by strata of rock, two of which resemble pillars, roughly hewn out. Three of them communicate with each other by means of holes which can be crawled through. These caves open immediately upon the precipice, and from their floors it is at least seventy feet down to the surface of the river. Many persons who have visited this singular place, call these "De Soto's Rock Houses," and they have stretched their imaginations to such an extent, as to assert that they have distinctly traced his pickaxes in the face of the rocks. There can be no question, however, but that these caves have been improved, to a slight extent, in size and shape, by human labor. But it was the labor of the Red people. Occasionally we could see where they smoothed off a point, and leveled the floors by knocking off the uneven places. It was, doubtless, a strong Indian fortification, and long used as a safe retreat when the valleys below were overrun by a victorious enemy. The walls are black with smoke, and everything about them bears evidence of constant occupation for years. These caves or rock houses constituted a most admirable defence, especially with the assistance of the walls at the head of the peninsula. In order to get into the first cave, a person has to pass along a rock passage, wide enough for only one man. Below him, on his right, is the awful precipice, and on his left, the rock wall reaching ten feet above his head. A few persons in the first rock house, with swords or spears, could keep off an army of one thousand men; for, only one assailant being able to approach the cave at a time, could be instantly despatched and hurled down the abyss below. In regard to the inner walls of the ditches, the author saw no cement among the rocks, although he had heard that that ingredient (never used by Indians) was to be found there.

Upon creeks and rivers in Alabama, where they meander through mountainous regions, are occasionally seen cuttings upon rocks, which have also been improperly attributed to European discoverers. In the county of Tallapoosa, not far below the mouth of the Sougohatchie, and a few miles east from the Tallapoosa river, are cliffs of a singular kind of gray rock, rather soft, and having the appearance of of containing silver ore. The face of these cliffs is literally cut in pieces, by having round pieces taken out of them. The ancient Indians used to resort to this place to obtain materials for manufacturing pipes, of large and small sizes, and, more particularly, for bowls and other household vessels. They cut out the pieces with flint rocks fixed in wooden handles. After working around as deep as they desired, the piece was prized out of the rock. Then they formed it into whatever vessel, toy or implement, they pleased. Hence, bowls, small mortars, immense pipes, and various pieces resembling wedges* in shape, are often ploughed up in the fields in Macon, Tallapoosa and Montgomery, and other counties in Alabama, of precisely the same kind of rock of which these cliffs are com-

1847 April

* These wedges, in appearance, were used by the Indians in dressing their deer-skins. They were also used as clubs in war, having handles fixed to them.

posed. The author is also sustained in this position by unquestionable Indian testimony, which has been procured by him.

A few miles from Elyton, in the county of Jefferson, the author is informed that there stands a large quadrangular mound, about fifty feet high, and flat on the top; that, near its base, are to be seen cuttings in the rock something like mortars, some of which would hold over a gallon. These were done by the Indians, for the limestone rock could easily be worked into any shape by means of flint picks.

The reader has observed that we have often mentioned the published works of Bartram, the botanist, who was in our country just before the Revolutionary War. We now quote from his MS., never published entire, but occasionally intro-
1777 duced by Squier in his "Ancient Monuments of the Mississippi Valley." Squier embodies in his work the following account, from Bartram's MS., of the "CHUNK YARDS" of the Creeks or Muscogees: "They are rectangular areas, generally occupying the centre of the town. The public square and rotunda, or great winter council-house, stood at the two opposite corners of them. They are generally very extensive, especially in the large old towns. Some of them are from six hundred to nine hundred feet in length, and of proportionate breadth. The area is exactly level, and sunk two, and sometimes three, feet below the banks of terraces surrounding it, which are occasionally two in number, one behind and above the other, and composed of the earth taken from the area at the time of its formation. These banks or terraces serve the

purpose of seats for spectators. In the centre of this yard or area there is a low circular mound or eminence, in the middle of which stands the *Chunk Pole*, which is a high obelisk, or four-square pillar, declining upwards to an obtuse point. This is of wood, the heart of a sound pitch-pine, which is very durable. It is generally from thirty to forty feet in height, and to the top is fastened some object which serves as a mark to shoot at with arrows, or the rifle, at certain appointed times."

CHAPTER III.
1777

CHAPTER IV.

THE FRENCH IN ALABAMA AND MISSISSIPPI.

CHAPTER IV.

After the Spanish invasion of De Soto, to which allusion has so often been made, our soil remained untrodden by European feet for nearly a century and a half. At the end of that long and dark period, it became connected with the history of the distant French possessions of Canada, which were contemporaneous with the oldest English colonies in America. For more than fifty years, the French fur traders of Canada, associated with the enterprising Jesuit Fathers, had continued to advance south-westward upon the great lakes, discovering new regions, different races of Indians, more abundant game, and wider and brighter waters. At length, from the tribes upon the southern shore of Lake Superior, Father Allouez heard some vague reports of a great western river. Subsequently, Father Marquette was despatched from Quebec, with Joliet, a trader of that place, five other Frenchmen, and a large number of Indian guides, to seek the Mississippi, and thus add new regions to the dominion of France, and new missions to the empire of the Jesuits. Ascending Fox river to the head of navigation, and crossing the portage to the banks of the Wisconsin, with birch bark canoes, the adventurers again launched their tiny boats and floated down to the Mississippi river. Descending it to the mouth of the Arkansas, and encountering decided evidences of a southern climate, Marquette finally found himself among the Chickasaws, whose reports that hostile tribes thronged the banks from thence to the sea, served to arrest his progress. Reluctantly commencing his return up the stiff and turbid tide, he found the mouth of the Illinois river, ascended to its head, crossed the portage to Chicago, launched his canoes upon Lake Michigan, and paddled to Green Bay, where he resumed his missionary labors. Joliet proceeded to Quebec with the news of the discovery. 1673 June 17

The young and gifted La Salle, a native of Rouen, in France, educated as a Jesuit, went to Canada to acquire fortune and fame by finding an overland passage to China. Becoming fired at the discovery which Marquette had made, he returned to France and obtained a royal commission for perfecting the exploration of the Mississippi, for which he was granted a monopoly in the trade of the skins of the buffalo. Sailing back to Canada, with men and stores, and accompanied by 1678
the Chevalier Tonti, an Italian soldier, who acted as his lieutenant, La Salle proceeded, by way of the lakes, upon his important enterprise. Consuming over two years in exploring those vast sheets of water, in building forts and collecting furs, he at length rigged a small barge, in which he descended the Mississippi to its mouth. Here, upon a small marshy elevation, in full view of the sea, he took formal and ceremonious possession in the name of the King of France. The country 1682 April 9

CHAPTER IV. received the name of Louisiana, in honor of Louis XIV., who then occupied the French throne ; but the attempt to give the river the name of Colbert, in honor of his Minister of Finance, did not succeed, and it retained that by which the aborigines had designated it. Leaving the Chevalier Tonti in command of Fort St. Louis, which La Salle had established in the country of the Illinois, the latter returned to France, where the report of his discoveries had already given rise to much excitement and joy. The government immediately furnished him with a frigate and three other ships, upon which embarked two hundred and eighty persons, consisting of priests, gentlemen, soldiers, hired mechanics and agricultural emigrants, for the purpose of forming a colony at the mouth of the Mississippi. But the fearless adventurer, having crossed the Atlantic, and being unable to find, from the Gulf, the entrance to that river, was forced to disembark upon the coast (1685 February) of Texas. Here, erecting Fort St. Louis, and leaving the larger portion of the colonists, he explored the surrounding country, with the hope of finding the Mississippi, but returned unsuccessful. Death had hovered over the colony, which was now reduced to thirty-six persons ; and with sixteen of these, La Salle again departed, with the determination to cut his way to Canada by land. After three months' wanderings, he was murdered, by two of his companions, in the prairies (1687 March 19) of Texas, near the western branch of the Trinity river. In the meantime the Chevalier Tonti, with twenty Canadians and thirty Indians, descended from the Illinois to meet his old commander ; but, disappointed in not finding the French fleet at the Balize, he returned to the mouth of the Arkansas, where he established a little post. The few colonists left upon the coast of Texas all perished obscurely, except the brother of La Salle and six others, who made their way to Canada. Such was the melancholy termination of the first attempt to colonize Louisiana.*

Louis XIV. of France, the most splendid sovereign whom Europe had yet seen, had long been engaged in a war with William III. of England, which had extended to their respective colonies in North America. In consequence of these troubles, further efforts to colonize the Mississippi were not attempted, until after the peace of Ryswick. By the terms of the treaty; each party was to enjoy the territories in America which they possessed before the war. The attention of the French monarch was now once more turned to the new country which La Salle had discovered. A number of Canadians had been left upon the shores of France, upon the conclusion of the war, and among them was a distinguished naval officer, named Iberville, who had acquired great mili-

* Hildreth's History of the United States. New-York: 1849. Vol. 2, pp. 81–99. Historie de la Louisiane, par Charles Gayarre; vol. 1, pp. 23–61. Journal Historique du Dernier Voyage que feu M. de la Sale, fit dans le Galfe de Mexique, pour trouver l'embouchure, et le cours de la Riviere de Saint Louis, qui traverse la Louisiana. A Paris: 1713—386 pages. The History of Louisiana from the earliest period, by Francois Xavier Martin, vol. 1, pp. 59–121. New-Orleans: 1827. Also many other authorities.

CHAPTER IV. tary renown by his exploits against the English, on the shores of Hudson Bay and Newfoundland, and by the capture of Pemaquid. He was one of seven sons, all natives of Quebec, all men of ability and merit, and all engaged in the King's service.

1698 September 24 To Iberville was confided the project of peopling Louisiana. He sailed from Rochelle with the Badine, of thirty guns, of which he had the immediate command, and with the Marir, commanded by Count Sugeres, together with two harbor boats, each of forty tons. On board these vessels were his two young but gallant brothers, Bienville and Sauvolle, and two hundred colonists, mostly Canadians, who had gone to France to assist in her defence. Among them were some women and children. Arriving at Cape Francois, in the Island of St. Domingo, he was joined by the Marquis Chateau Morant, with a fifty-two gun ship. There he received on board a famous buccaneer named De Grace, who had pillaged
1699 January 20 Vera Cruz some years before. Leaving St. Domingo, Iberville sailed for the coast of Florida, and after a prosperous voyage, stood before the Island of St. Rosa, from which point he discovered two men-of-war, at anchor in the harbor of Pensacola, at whose mast-heads floated the colors of Spain. One month previous to this, Don Roalli, with three hundred Spaniards, from Vera Cruz, had established a battery upon the site of the present town of Pensacola.

A deputation sent by Iberville were received with much politeness, but the Don declined to permit the French vessels to enter the harbor, for fear of a treacherous surprise.* The French then made sail to the west, and presently cast anchor off an island, which, from the quantity of human bones discovered upon it by Midshipman Bienville, was called the Isle of Massacre. The small vessels passed through the channel between two elevations, to which they gave the name of Cat and Ship Islands. The fifty-two gun ship sailed for St. Domingo, while the frigates lay off a group of banks, which received the name of the Chandeliers. Iberville despatched two boats to the main land, the crews of which found seven recently abandoned canoes, and succeeded in capturing two sick old Indians, whom they left with presents. The next day, a woman being taken and likewise sent off with presents, returned with two of her people, who belonged to the Biloxi tribe, whose name was given by the French to the bay. Four savages of this nation were then carried on board of Iberville's ship, while his brother, Bienville, remained upon the beach, as a hostage. On the same evening, twenty-four Bayagolas arrived upon the shore, being on their way to fight the Mobilians, who, they said, lived on the banks of a great river which flowed into the sea, not far to the east.†

January 31

* The Spaniards, who still claimed the whole circuit of the Gulf, had hastened to occupy the Pensacola harbor, the best upon it. The barrier thus formed, made the dividing line between Florida and Louisiana.

† Journal Historique de l'Etablissement des Français a la Louisiane, par Bernard de la Harpe, pp. 4–8. La Harpe was one of the first French settlers in Mobile, and he kept a journal of all he witnessed in that place, at Dauphin, Biloxi, Ship Island, &c., &c.

CHAPTER IV. 1699 February 27 When Iberville had caused some huts to be erected upon Ship Island, he entered a boat with thirty men, accompanied by his brother Bienville, and Father Athanase, a Franciscan friar, the companion of the unfortunate La Salle in his descent of the Mississippi, and at the time when he was killed upon the plains of Texas. Upon the third day, Iberville made the Balize, and was the first to enter the great river from the sea. He ascended for the space of ten days, until he arrived at a town of the Bayagola nation. There he found, preserved by these Indians, a prayer book which belonged to the first expedition of La Salle, some cloaks which the discoverer had given them, a coat of mail which had belonged to the troop of De Soto, and a letter written by the Chevalier Tonti to La Salle, whom he had been disappointed in not meeting, as we have already seen. All these things combined to dispel the doubts which Iberville had entertained, that this was really the Mississippi, and re-assured the convictions of
1699 Father Athanase. Continuing the voyage to a point which he named Portage de la Croix, Iberville turned his boat down stream and touched at Bayou Manchac. Here Bienville, who was placed in command of the main boat, presently descended the river to the sea, while Iberville passed through the bayou, in birch-bark canoes, guided by a Bayagola Indian. Entering the river Amite, he soon fell into Lakes Maurepas and Pontchartrain, which he named in honor of the two principal Ministers of his King. Bienville joined him, soon after he reached his shipping.

At the eastern extremity of the bay of Biloxi and within

the limits of the present State of Mississippi, a fort, with four bastions and mounted with twelve pieces of artillery, was now erected, the command of which was given to Sauvolle, 1699 May 1
the elder of the two brothers of Iberville, while Bienville, the youngest of the three, was made lieutenant. After the colonists had built huts and houses around it, Iberville and the Count Sugeres sailed in the two frigates for France. Sauvolle despatched a vessel to St. Domingo for provisions, and Bienville, with a small command, to visit the neighboring tribes, with whom he desired to cultivate friendly relations. Visiting the Callapissas upon the northern shore of Lake Pontchartrain, and the Pascagoulas upon the river of that name, among whom he distributed presents, and going by land from Mobile Point to Pensacola to observe the movements of the Spaniards, he returned to Fort Biloxi; but in a few days set off in a boat, again to explore the Mississippi river. After having ascended it some distance, and while 1699 August 16
returning he met, not far below the site of New Orleans, an English captain named Bar, in charge of a vessel of sixteen guns, who asserted that there was another vessel of the same class belonging to him at the mouth of the river, and that his intention was to establish an English colony upon the banks of the Mississippi. The ingenious Bienville turned him towards the Gulf, by telling him that France had already taken possession of the river in which he then was, and above there had occupied it with a fort and garrison; and, furthermore, that the Mississippi river lay considerably to the west.

CHAPTER IV.

1699

In the meantime, Sauvolle received two Canadian missionaries, who had sometime before established themselves among the Yazoos. These holy men dropped down the Mississippi, entered the lakes by the Bayou Manchac, and paid their brethren an unexpected but most pleasing visit. Upon a bluff on the Mississippi, the site of old Fort Adams, lived one of these men, Father Davion, who erected a cross in the open air, and kept his holy relics in the hollow of a large tree. Here he told the Indians who the true God was, and baptized those who were converted, with the waters of the ancient Mississippi. Could a life so entirely solitary, and attended with so many dangers, have been influenced by any other motives than such as are prompted by the purest piety?

December 7

At length, the roar of distant cannon at sea announced the arrival of two large ships of war, commanded by Iberville and the Count Sugeres, direct from France, laden with provisions for the colony, and having on board thirty laborers and sixty Canadians, intended as military pioneers, with their commanders, St. Dennis and Malton, together with a person named Le Sueur, who had acquired some celebrity in his voyages to Canada. They brought the pleasing intelligence that Sauvolle had been appointed Governor of Louisiana, and Bienville Lieutenant Governor. Boisbriant, who also came with the ships, was commissioned to take the command of Fort Biloxi.

1700 January 15

Dreading the advance of the British, and determined to secure the banks of the Mississippi from their grasp, Iberville sailed, with fifty Canadians, to a point eighteen leagues above the Balize, which had been selected by the indefatigable young

Bienville, who had arrived for that purpose, a few days before, by way of Manchac, with some Bayagolas, who were acquainted with the inundations of the river. Here they immediately began the construction of a fort, and, after a short time, were joined by the aged Tonti, who came from Canada, down the Mississippi, with a few Frenchmen and Indians. This veteran pioneer was joyfully received by those who had so often heard of his intrepid and fearless adventures.

In the meantime Sauvolle wrote to the Minister, regretting that he was not allowed to accompany Iberville upon the Mississippi, where he could have learned so much of the country, condemned the location at Biloxi as too low, sterile and sick- 1700
ly, and gave it as his opinion that the country offered no inducement to enterprise, except in the solitary article of hides. He closed his letter by expressing the hope that some mines of precious metals would be discovered. About this time Governor Roalli, of Pensacola, advanced to Ship Island with a man-of-war and some smaller vessels, for the purpose of expelling the French; but, deterred by Iberville's fleet, he hastened back, leaving only a proclamation protesting against the settlement of any portion of the coast, the whole breadth of which, he contended, belonged to His Catholic Majesty's Mexican possessions.

Taking with them the Chevalier Tonti, Iberville and Bienville left their new fort and ascended the Mississippi, visiting March 11
the different tribes upon its shores, and finally resting at the site of the present city of Natchez, where lived the Indians who bore that name, and whose manners and customs have al-

CHAPTER IV. ready been described. Delighted with this place, and resolved to plant a settlement there, Iberville marked out a town, and called it Rosalie—the name of the Countess Pontchartrain. From this place the Chevalier Tonti went up the river, and Bienville and St. Dennis, with twenty-two Canadians, started to the west, by an overland route, to reconnoitre the Spanish settlements, while Iberville floated down the river to rejoin his fleet.

1700 Returning from the west to Biloxi, Bienville was sent to take the command of the new establishment upon the Missis-
May 28 sippi, and then Iberville once more spread the sails of his ships for beloved France. Meanwhile the colony languished; the earth was not cultivated, and, relying for supplies from St. Domingo, horrible famine and sickness reduced the num-
1701 August 22 ber of inhabitants to one hundred and fifty souls! Sauvolle himself died, leaving the cares of the colony to the more redoubtable Bienville. The latter, deploring the condition of his people, and seeing the necessity of tilling the earth, in a despatch to the French government urged them to send him laborers, rather than the vicious and the idle, who roamed the forests in search of mines and Indian mistresses.

A delegation of Choctaws and Mobilians visited Fort Biloxi, and requested assistance in their war with the Chicka-
September saws. These were succeeded by twenty other Mobilians, and the Chief of the Alabamas, all of whom were dismissed with presents and exhortations to remain at peace with each other. At this time, the Spaniards of Pensacola and the French colony were not only upon good terms, but of mutual assistance

to each other; so much so, that Bienville arrested eighteen Spanish deserters and sent them back to Don Martin, the Governor of Pensacola. CHAPTER IV.

1701 December 18

Iberville and his brother, Serigny, arriving at Pensacola, direct from France, on board two men-of-war, despatched supplies to the colonists in smaller vessels, which were joyfully received, as a meagre portion of corn had for a long time barely kept them alive. Having received orders to break up the colonial establishment at Biloxi, and to remove it upon the Mobile, Bienville left only twenty soldiers at the fort, under Boisbriant, and sailed with his people to Dauphin Island, to which, as we have seen, they first gave the name of Massacre. Here he met his brother, Serigny, and a person named La Salle. The latter had been sent out to perform the duties of Marine Commissary. With forty sailors and some ship-carpenters, Bienville began the construction of a warehouse on Dauphin Island. With a sufficient force of soldiers, artisans and laborers, he then sailed up the bay of Mobile, and at the mouth of Dog river commenced the erection of a fort, a warehouse and other public buildings. This place received the name of Mobile, from the spacious bay upon which it was situated, which was called after the tribe of Indians who had so resolutely fought De Soto upon the field of Maubila. The fort itself was long designated as Fort St. Louis de la Mobile.*

1702

1540 October 18

* In 1777, Bartram, being on a voyage from Mobile to Pearl river, in a French trading boat, touched at the mouth of Dog river and saw there the ruins of old Fort St. Louis de la Mobile, where lay some iron cannon and some immense iron kettles, formerly used by the French for boiling tar into pitch.—Bartram's Travels, pp. 416–417.

CHAPTER IV. Here was the seat of government for the space of nine years, when, in 1711, as we shall see, the French moved up to the mouth of Mobile river, where they founded the town of Mobile, which has since become the beautiful commercial emporium of the State of Alabama. A few days of activity and bustle had scarcely been passed at the new place, at the mouth of Dog river, before it was made sad by the meeting of Bienville and Iberville, who wept for the loss of Sauvolle while affectionately locked in each other's srms.

1702 February 18 Iberville had passed with his ship-of-war, the Palmier, over the bar of Mobile point, finding at least twenty feet of water. It was not long before La Salle and his family came up to Mobile, which now presented the appearance of a settlement, with houses and shelters. Bienville, anxious to obtain the friendship of all the tribes upon the Mobile river and its tributaries, and to institute friendly relations between the different savage nations themselves, had sent Tonti, with a small command, to the Choctaw and Chickasaw countries. They now returned, with seven Chiefs of those tribes. The Governor gave them handsome presents, and exhorted them to remain at peace with the French and with each other. Then Iberville and his retinue dropped down the bay of Mobile,
February 31 went to Pensacola, and from thence sailed for France.

Mobile being now the seat of government, various delegations of Chiefs, Spaniards from Vera Cruz, and Canadians from the northern lakes and rivers, constantly repaired there to see Governor Bienville upon business. Among others, a delegation of eight Chiefs of the Alabamas arrived, whom

his Excellency treated with kindness, and dissuaded from CHAPTER
making war upon the Mobilians, Tomez and Chickasaws. IV.
Don Robles came with a letter from the Governor of Pensa- June
cola, requesting the loan of provisions for his famishing garri- 1702
son, with which the generous Frenchman readily complied.
Midshipman Becaucourt, commanding the colonial marine,
made several trips to Vera Cruz and returned with provisions,
the King of Spain having granted the French free access to
his colonial ports. Father Davion, the missionary upon the
Mississippi, and Father Liomoge, a Jesuit, came by way of
the Bayou Manchac, and reported that one of their compan- Summer
ions and four other Frenchmen had been killed by the Indians
above the Yazoo river. News also reached Bienville, that
St. Dennis, at the head of his Canadian scouts, had wantonly
made war upon and killed some Indians with whom they
were at peace, for the purpose of obtaining slaves. Bienville,
grieved at his conduct, endeavored, unsuccessfully, to have
the slaves restored to their people. Governor Martin, of Pensacola, came to Mobile, with the information that France and
Spain had gone to war with England, and his request to be
furnished with arms and ammunition was granted by Bienville.
He was succeeded by two Spanish officers from St. Augustine, Autumn
with a letter from Serda, Governor of that place, requesting
military supplies, as he had been blockaded by the English
and Indians. Bienville sent to his assistance a liberal supply
of powder and ball.

The English of Carolina began to disturb the French 1703
colonies, by sending emissaries among the Muscogees and

CHAPTER IV. Alabamas. In a very short time, two artful Alabamas came down the river, to decoy the French into the country.
1703 Having assured the Governor that their homes abounded in corn, which would be furnished at the most reasonable price,
May 3 the latter forthwith despatched Labrie, with four Canadians in canoes, to procure some. They had not proceeded far, before they were all killed except one of the Canadians, who returned to Mobile with his arm nearly severed by a blow which he received from an axe. To avenge this outrage,
December 22 Bienville began the ascent of the Mobile in seven canoes, in which were forty soldiers and Canadians. In fourteen days he arrived in the vicinity of the Alabamas, upon the river of that name, where he discovered ten canoes without occupants, but saw smoke floating upon the air and rising over the forest trees and cane, upon the bluff. St. Dennis and Tonti advised him not to make the attack until night, to which he assented, contrary to his better judgment. The night was very dark, and the path which led to the Indian camp was full of weeds and briars. However, an engagement ensued, in which three Frenchmen were slain, and the savages dispersed. Capturing
1704 January 11 the canoes, which were laden with provisions, Bienville returned to Mobile. But he did not relax in his efforts to be revenged, for he presently engaged parties of Chickasaws and Choctaws to pursue the Alabamas, who brought some of their scalps to Mobile, for which they received rewards.*

* Journal Historique de l'Etablissement des Français a la Louisiane, par Bernard de la Harpe, pp. 35–83.

An official despatch represented the following to be the condition of the feeble colony of Louisiana at this period: CHAPTER IV. 1704 April 30

"180 men capable of bearing arms.

2 French families, with three little girls and seven little boys.

6 young Indian boys, slaves, from fifteen to twenty years of age.

A little of the territory around Fort Louis (Mobile) has been cultivated.

80 wooden houses, of one story high, covered with palm leaves and straw.

9 oxen, five of which belonged to the King.

14 cows.

4 bulls, one of which belonged to the King.

6 calves.

100 hogs.

3 kids.

400 hens."

This account did not, of course, include the officers.

The colonists, suffering from severe famine, were temporarily relieved by the Governor of Pensacola, but again became destitute of provisions; and, while forced to disperse themselves along the coast, procuring subsistence upon fish and oysters, a vessel of war from France, commanded by Chateaugné, another brother of Bienville, happily re-established abundance among them. This vessel was succeeded by the Pelican, July 24 another man-of-war, laden with provisions, and having on board seventy-five soldiers intended for the various posts, LaVente, of

CHAPTER IV. 1704 July 24 the foreign mission, sent as rector by the Bishop of Quebec, four Priests, and four Sisters of Charity, together with four families of laborers. But what created more novelty and excitement than all the rest of the arrival, were twenty-three girls, whom Bienville was informed, by the Minister's despatch, were all of spotless chastity, pious and industrious, and that his Majesty had enjoined upon the Bishop of Quebec to send no females to Mobile who did not bear characters as irreproachable as these. He was instructed to have them married to Canadians and others, who were competent to support them. Only a few days rolled round, before they all found

August husbands. These were the first marriages which were solemnized in old Mobile, or, indeed, upon any part of the soil of Alabama, by Christian marital rites.*

But sickness and disasters soon dispelled the joy which these arrivals had occasioned. Half the crew of the Pelican died. Tonti and Levassuer, invaluable officers—Father Dange, a Jesuit—and thirty of the soldiers lately arrived, soon followed

September them to the grave. The fort and out-houses at Pensacola were wrapped in flames. Lambert, with his Canadians, driven from the post of Washita by the Indians, had fled to Mobile, while the Chickasaws and Choctaws had began a war with

* "The first child born in the colony, and, consequently, the first "Creole," was named Claude Jousset, and was the son of a Canadian who carried on a small trading business at Mobile."—Louisiana, its Colonial History and Romance, by Charles Gayarre. New-York: 1851. pp. 464–465.

each other, which was exceedingly embarrassing to Bienville. More than seventy of the former, of both sexes, being in Mobile, and imploring Bienville to have them safely conducted to their nation, the route to which lay over the country of their enemies, he despatched twenty Canadians, under Boisbriant, with them. Arriving at one of the Choctaw towns, the inhabitants assembled in great numbers to put them to death, but Boisbriant interposing, they then fell upon a stratagem to accomplish their purposes. Pretending that they only desired to rebuke the Chickasaws for their conduct, while the Chief was accordingly making his speech to them, he let a feather fall, which was a signal for attack. The Chickasaw warriors were all instantly put to death, and the women and children reserved for slaves. Boisbriant was accidentally wounded by a ball, which was exceedingly regretted by the Choctaws, three hundred of whom carried him on a litter to Mobile, in mournful procession. Bienville was shocked and mortified at the ruthless massacre, and saw, at a glance, that the Chickasaws would suspect him of decoying these unhappy people there to meet the fate which they received.

1704 December

1705 February

When Boisbriant recovered from his wound, he was despatched up the Alabama river, with sixty Canadians, to fight the Alabamas and Muscogees. After a long absence he returned with only two scalps and an Indian slave. In the meanwhile, the Chickasaws and Choctaws continued their war, which raged with the most savage ferocity. The French unavoidably became implicated in these feuds. Being considered the exclusive friends of the Choctaws, on account of their

1706 February

CHAPTER IV. proximity, they were often suddenly slain by skulking Chickasaws. Iberville wrote to the Minister that famine again prevailed in the unhappy colony of Louisiana; that the Spaniards could afford them but little corn, which the men only had become accustomed to eat, the Parisian women eschewing it, and blaming the Bishop for not telling them what they had to
1706 encounter in the "promised land;" that fifty men had come to make a settlement at Mobile from the Upper Mississippi; and that the colonists would not unite to resist the savages and combat famine, but quarrelled among themselves. At this period, Commissary General La Salle had commenced a series of vindictive and unprincipled assaults upon the character of
September 7 Bienville, in his despatches to the Court. In one of these he said that "Iberville, Bienville and Chateaugné, the three brothers, are guilty of all kinds of malpractices, and are extortioners and knaves, who waste the property of his Majesty." Father La Vente, the rector of Mobile, a man of bad temper and sordid feelings, and unpopular with the priests over whom he was placed, became a willing coadjutor of La Salle in his indiscriminate abuse of the Governor. He, too,
October wrote letters to the Court, the burden of which was the corruption of Bienville's colonial government. He essayed to persuade the inhabitants that their sufferings were owing alone to the conduct of their Governor, who too tardily ordered supplies from France. He attempted to buy up the sick soldiers whom he visited by giving them (as his own) money which had been placed in his hands for charitable purposes. The Lady Superior also vented her spleen against

Bienville, by writing to the Minister that Boisbriant had intended to have *married* her, but had been prevented by the Governor. Hence, she adds, "Bienville does not possess the qualities necessary for a Governor." CHAPTER IV.

The colonists continued to lead unpleasant lives; the Muscogees and Alabamas threatened their existence; their hearts were troubled with the Chickasaw and Choctaw war; while the quarrels among the authorities continued to increase. Father Gravier, a Jesuit, took up the cudgels for Bienville, and defended him in a letter which he addressed to the Minister. But Bienville, disdaining these cabals, continued to discharge his duty faithfully to the government, as far as it could be done with his means and ability, and in his despatches refrained from alluding to the animosities of the commissary and rector, except casually to mention that he had encountered much opposition from the former. Iberville, the indefatigable founder of Louisiania and the devoted friend of the colonists, died of the yellow fever at Havana, where he had touched with his fleet while on his way to attack Charleston and Jamaica. This was a severe blow, added to the general sufferings of the colony, and seriously retarded its advance. About the same time, Berguier, Grand Vicar of the Lord of Quebec, came from the Illinois country to Mobile, and reported that St. Come, a missionary among the Natchez, with three other Frenchmen, had been murdered, while descending the Mississippi, by the Chaumachas. This induced Bienville to send presents to all the nations of the Lower Mississippi, which would cause them to

1706 December

1707 February 27

January 1

CHAPTER IV. 1706 make war upon those savages. The English from Carolina, aided by troops from Great Britain, had continued to advance upon the Spanish settlements of the Floridas, assisted by large bands of Muscogee Indians, and had overrun the greater portion of Middle and East Florida, laying waste the Spanish settlements, and forcing the inhabitants and friendly Indians almost to abandon the country. News reaching Bienville that they had beseiged the fort of Pensacola, which had recently
1707 November 24 been rebuilt, he advanced from Mobile with one hundred and twenty Canadians; but, on reaching that place, he found that the thirteen Englishmen and three hundred and fifty Muscogees, who for two days had lain around the fort to attack it, becoming destitute of provisions, had already retired.

In the meanwhile, Bienville, in a despatch to the Minister, urged the necessity of sending out more colonial supplies, as the inhabitants had not yet made plantations ample enough, from which to derive a support. He stated that the lands were fertile up the Mobile river, but too unhealthy during the period of cultivating the crops. The want of negroes, horses and oxen, also contributed its share in embarrassing the feeble efforts of the Louisiana planter, and failures were often made. He informed the Minister, further, that he had intended establishing a fort upon the "Tombecbe," in the vicinity of the Chickasaws, in order to secure the friendship of those Indians, who were the most warlike of all, and who were daily tampered with by the English of Carolina, but that the distance to that point, and the general distress of the colony, had prevented it; that all the Indians were treacherous, and often assassinated the French, for whose strength they had begun to entertain a most contemptible opinion; that three-fourths of the soldiers were too young to prosecute a war, and constantly deserted, while the Canadians, whom he had declined to discharge, contrary to the orders of Begar, Intendant of Rochefort, were the sole pillars of the colony. In consequence of these things, he had been compelled to abandon the establishment upon the Mississippi. In addition, he stated that La Salle had refused to pay the colonists their just dues, and had withheld payment from those who had been sent to a distance upon important duties.

CHAPTER IV. 1707

The continued reports of the malpractices of Bienville, which reached the ears of the Minister, induced the French government to order his arrest. DeMuys was appointed Governor of Louisiana, "to prove the facts charged against this person, to arrest him if they were true, and to send him a prisoner to France." Thus the unjust and singular position was assumed, of leaving to Bienville's *successor* to decide whether he was guilty or innocent! In the meantime, Bienville, hearing of his disgrace at Court, demanded to be dismissed from his post, to enable him to return to France. This startled the inhabitants of Mobile, who were warmly attached to him, and who immediately petitioned the government that, if Bienville's request should be allowed, that he should immediately be sent back to them as their Governor. But DeMuys, his successor and his judge, died at Havana on his passage out. Diron D'Artaguette was appointed commissary general in the place of the growling La Salle, whom the government

July 23

CHAPTER IV. had also removed. D'Artaguette, more fortunate than his companion, had reached Mobile in safety, and was directed to investigate the charges against Bienville, without letting him know what they were. However, fortunately for the cause of justice, and perhaps the future welfare of the colony, D'Arta-
1708 February 26 guette, in the report of his investigations to the Minister, was enabled to close by saying, that "all the accusations brought against Bienville were most miserable calumnies." Subjoined to this statement was the attestation of Boisbriant, now Major of the fort at Mobile. But the disappointed and vindictive La Salle renewed his accusations, in which he assured the Minister that an understanding existed between Bienville and the new commissary, and that the report of the latter was not to be believed. At the same time he denounced Barrot, the surgeon of the colony, as "an ignorant man—a drunkard and a rogue, who sold, for his own profit, the medicines belonging to the King."

1708 August The following is a statement of the condition of the colony of Louisiana at this period:

GARRISON.

14 superior officers, comprising a midshipman attending on the commandant.

76 soldiers, comprising four military officers.

13 sailors, comprising four naval officers.

2 Canadians, serving as clerks in the warehouses, by order of Bienville.

1 superintendent of the warehouses.

3 priests, comprising one rector.

6 workmen.

1 Canadian, serving as interpreter.

6 cabin boys, learning the Indian language, and intended to serve by land and sea as workmen.

INHABITANTS.

1708 August

24 inhabitants who have no grants of land, which prevents the majority from working plantations.

28 women.

25 children.

80 slaves, men and women, of various Indian nations.

157

TOTAL.

279, of whom six are sick.

In addition to these there are more than 60 Canadians who live in the Indian villages on the Mississippi, without the permission of the Governor, and who destroy, by their evil and libertine life with the Indian women, all that the missionaries and others have instructed them in the mysteries of religion.

ANIMALS.

50 cows.

40 calves.

4 bulls.

8 oxen, four of which belong to the King.

1400 hogs and sows.

2000 hens or thereabouts.

In consequence of the death of the recently appointed

CHAPTER IV. Governor of Louisiana, and the complete overthrow of the charges brought against the old one, the French government permitted the latter to continue at his responsible and thankless post. Knowing that the colony could not prosper unless the earth was cultivated, Governor Bienville endeavored in vain to make the whites under him labor in the fields. On the other hand, the savages, whom the French had endeavored to enslave, would escape to their native woods, at the slightest appearance of coercion. 1708 October 12 In a despatch to the Minister, Bienville recommended that the colonists be allowed to send Indians to the West India Islands, and there to exchange them for negroes, asserting that these Islanders would give two Africans for three savages. His proposition was laid before M. Robert, one of the heads of the Bureau of the Minister of November 26 Marine, who pronounced against it, upon the ground that the inhabitants of the West Indies would not part with their good negroes, and that the only way to obtain such was by purchases from Guinea. Another idea of Bienville's seemed still more unreasonable. He had given orders to watch several inhabitants of Mobile, to prevent them from leaving the country. As they had "amassed considerable property in the colony, by keeping public-houses, it was but just," said he to the Minister, "to compel them to remain."

Although discharged from office, La Salle, far from remaining quiet, continued to complain of the administration of the colony. 1709 May 12 He urged the Minister to send thirty females to Mobile, to prevent, by marriage, the debauchery which was committed with Indian women. He said that such an importation would serve to keep at home a number of Canadians who roamed the country in search of female slaves. He agreed in opinion with Bienville that negroes were indispensable to the prosperity of the colony; and in this he was right, for experience has proved that neither South-Carolina, Louisiana, nor any other Southern State, with such low rich lands, and with a humid atmosphere so destructive to the constitutions of the whites, could ever have been successfully brought into cultivation without African labor.

CHAPTER IV.

Commissary D'Artaguette, visiting the country lying between Lake Pontchartrain and the Mississippi river, now a portion of New Orleans, found there seven Frenchmen, who 1709
had each planted an acre of Indian corn, brought from the Illinois, and which grew most luxuriantly. He wrote to the Minister, as Iberville and Bienville had often done before, urging the establishment of colonies upon that river, and for their protection against the floods, the erection of embankments along the margin.

Although La Salle had died at Mobile early in the year 1710
1710, a short time after the death of his second wife, who, like the first, had been reared in the hospitals, yet Bienville failed not to find those who were equally willing to comment, in the most illiberal manner, upon his administration. Marigny, an officer of the garrison, in a despatch to the Minister, accused him with disregarding the interests of the colony. La Vente, the curate, who appeared officiously desirous to attend to the temporal as well as the spiritual affairs of Louisiana, also abused him without measure, attributing to him every

CHAPTER IV. misfortune which attended the inhabitants of Mobile. He assured the Minister, that if the permission of the government could be obtained, they had determined to form a colony upon

1710 Dauphin Island, where there were twenty fortified houses, for the purpose of catching fish, and being more convenient to the supplies which might be sent to them from Pensacola and France. Under these repeated assaults, Bienville lost the dignity and patience which had formerly characterized his conduct, and now retorted upon his adversaries with considerable acrimony. In one of his despatches, he said, that "the curate, La Vente, endeavored to excite everybody against him;" that the curate was "not ashamed to keep an open shop and sell like an avaricious Jew." Verily, this father must have been a man who possessed too much malignity, avarice and bad temper, to have been a successful missionary in the holy cause in which he was ostensibly engaged.

December Thus the year 1710 closed with such controversies, while Bienville had been obliged to distribute his men among the Indian towns to procure something to eat.* How unfortunate that the colonists, like mere children, should have depended upon the mother country for every thing which went into their mouths, when moderate industry, bestowed higher up the Tombigby and Alabama rivers, upon the more elevated and less sickly lands, would have ensured them an abundance.

* Histoire de la Louisiane, par Charles Gayarre, vol. 1, pp. 78–91.

CHAPTER V.

THE COLONY OF LOUISIANA GRANTED TO CROZAT.

CHAPTER V.

THE high floods having inundated the settlements around Fort St. Louis de la Mobile, Bienville determined to place his people upon more elevated ground. All the inhabitants, except the garrison of the fort, removed upon the Mobile river, where, upon the site of the present beautiful and wealthy commer- 1711 March
cial emporium of Alabama, they established themselves. Here Bienville built a new wooden fort, which, in a few years, was destroyed to give place to an extensive fortress of brick, called, in French times, Fort Conde, and, in English and Spanish times, Fort Charlotte. The seat of government was permanantly fixed here, and the leading characters of the colony made Mobile their head-quarters. Only a small garrison was left at the old settlement at the mouth of Dog river, which, however, continued to guard that point for several years after this period.

The Chickasaws having again engaged in a war with the Choctaws, at the instance of the English, and thirty of the former tribe being at Mobile at the time, they implored Bienville to have them safely conducted home, through the coun-

12*

CHAPTER V. try of their enemies. Desiring to acquire the confidence of the Chickasaws by acts of kindness that would induce them to break up their alliance with the Carolinians, Bienville readily granted their request, and despatched his brother, Chateaugné, with thirty soldiers, to escort them. He was successful in his mission, and returned to Mobile without having met with any serious adventures.

The colony of Louisiana still remained in a precarious situ-
1711 October 27 ation. It is true, the inhabitants had to some extent begun the cultivation of tobacco, the first samples of which were supposed to be superior to the quality raised in Virginia. Wheat came up most luxuriantly, but the damp atmosphere destroyed it when it commenced maturing. Notwithstanding the long war which had existed between France and England, no attacks of the enemy had been directed against any part of the Louisiana colony, until about this time, when a pirate ship from Jamaica disembarked on Dauphin Island, and plundered the inhabitants of nearly all which they possessed. Not long afterwards, this first and last act of hostility during the present war, was succeeded by the arrival of a ship which came upon a more agreeable mission. She brought large
1711 supplies for the colony, and when she hoisted her sails to return to France, D'Artaguette, the commissary general, an accomplished man, who well understood his business, became a passenger on board of her, to the regret of all the inhabitants, who ardently desired him to remain longer with them.

The following is a statement of the colonial disbursements of the year 1711 :

PAYMENTS.

To 12 workmen on the fortification, -	4,480 *livres.*
" 23 naval officers, soldiers and cabin boys,	4,572
" superior officers, - - - -	19,988
" medicine chest, - - - -	506
" wax candles in the chapel, - -	270
" presents to the Indians, - - -	4,000
" maintenance of military companies, -	27,688
	61,504 *livres.*

1711

D'Artaguette, the colonial commissary, had a prosperous voyage to France, and arrived there "at the time," to use the eloquent language of Gayarre, "when the star of Louis XIV., which had shed such brilliant glory around for half a century, was almost extinguished, and the doors of the old cathedral of St. Dennis had already opened in expectation of receiving the great monarch, whom age and misfortune urged rapidly towards the tomb." The country, too, over which he had so long reigned, was then groaning under the effects of the long, bloody and expensive wars which he had waged. The report which D'Artaguette now made of the unhappy condition of the colony of Louisiana, induced the French government to number that fruitless and extravagant bantling among its other misfortunes. It determined to hand the colony over to the care of a company, or to some rich merchant, with a grant of its exclusive commerce and other important privileges. Accordingly, an opulent merchant, named Antione Crozat, entered into a contract with the King of France. The King

CHAPTER V. 1712 September 14 granted to him, for the term of fifteen years, the exclusive commerce of all the country known as the colony of Louisiana, embracing the country upon the Alabama and Tombigby, with their various tributary streams; of all the islands at and near their entrance to the sea; of all the lakes, rivers and islands connected with the lakes Pontchartrain, Mauripas, Borne, &c.; of all the country upon the Mississippi and its numerous tributaries, from the sea as high up as the Illinois river, together with that of Texas. He also ceded to him "*forever*," all the lands which he could establish himself upon, all the manufactures which he could put into operation, and all the structures which he should erect. The King also granted to him the proceeds of all the mines which he might find and work, and agreed to appropriate fifty thousand livres annually to-
September 14 ward the payment of his officers and troops in Louisiana.

For all these privileges, Crozat obligated, on his part, to appropriate one-fourth of the proceeds of the mines of precious metals to the King's use; to forfeit the lands which were granted to him "*forever*," if the improvements or manufactures which he placed upon them should be abandoned by him or should cease to exist; to send a vessel annually to Guinea for slaves for the colony, and to send every year two ships from France, with a certain number of emigrants to Lou-
September 14 isiana; and, at the expiration of nine years, to pay the salaries of the King's officers in the colony during the remainder of his time, with the privilege of nominating those officers for his majesty's appointment.

All this country was to be a dependency upon the government of New France. The ordinances and usages of the Provost and Viscount of Paris were to rule the colony, in connection with a council similar to that which then existed in St. Domingo.

About the time that France thus abandoned our soil and the few white inhabitants upon it, to the wealthy Parisian merchant, the King, by the treaty of Utrecht, ceded to England the country of Nova Scotia, with its ancient boundaries.

The population of Louisiana, now turned over to Crozat, consisted of twenty-eight families, twenty negroes, seventy-five Canadians, and two companies of infantry of fifty men each, the whole numbering three hundred and twenty-four souls. They were scattered over the colony, and separated by large rivers and expansive lakes, protected by only six forts of miserable construction, built of stakes, trees and earth, and portions of them covered with palm leaves. These forts were situated as follows: one upon the Mississippi, one upon Ship Island, one upon Dauphin Island, one at Biloxi, one at the old and the other at the new settlement of Mobile.

1712 September 14

At length, a vessel of fifty guns disembarked, on Dauphin Island, the officers intended for the government of Louisiana under Crozat's charter. Among them were Lamotte Cadillac, the new Governor; Duclos, the Commissary General; Lebas, the Comptroller; and Dirigoin and Laloire de Ursins, directors of the affairs of Crozat in the colony. Governor Cadillac had served with distinction in the wars of Canada, and brought with him to the colony of Louisiana his daughter,

1713 May 17

CHAPTER V. whom he attempted, as we shall see, to marry to Bienville. He was a man of poor judgment, of week feelings, and much selfishness. To interest him in the deepest manner, in accomplishing his various schemes of colonial aggrandizement, Crozat had promised him a portion of his profits. But Cadillac, in his first despatch to the Minister, began to complain of every-
1713 May 17 body and of every thing appertaining to the colony; and all his other documents to that high functionary were, likewise, filled with carping epithets, which could only emanate from a selfish and childish mind like his. Dauphin Island, which, he said, had been represented to him as a terrestrial paradise, he assured the Minister, was a poor and miserable spot, supporting but a few improvements, with a few fig trees and sapless vines of the grape and lemon. Wheat did not grow upon the whole continent, having been abandoned upon the borders of Lake Pontchartrain and at Natchez, where one Larigne had endeavored to raise it. Other colonial officers,
July 15 also, hastened to complain. Duclos wrote to the Minister that twelve girls had lately arrived from France, who were too ugly and badly formed to secure the affections of the men, and that but two of them had yet found husbands. He was afraid that the other ten would remain on hand a long time. He thought proper to suggest, that those who sent girls to the colony in future, should attach more importance to beauty than to virtue, as the Canadians were not scrupulous as to the lives which their spouses may have formerly led. But if they were only to be offered girls as ugly as these, they would

rather attach themselves to Indian females, particularly in the Illinois country, where the Jesuit priests sanctioned such alliances by the marital ceremony. CHAPTER V.

Duclos again wrote to the Minister, accusing Cadillac with having appropriated the presents intended for the Indians, to his own use, and recommended that the Governor should, in future, be required to confer with Bienville in relation to the distribution of those presents; the latter, he remarked, having for so many years, by justice, honor and good advice, so happily conciliated the different tribes. On the same day Cadillac wrote to the Minister, the Count Pontchartrain, that the inhabitants knew nothing of the culture of silk, tobacco and indigo, but confined their attention to the production of Indian corn and vegetables. That the commerce of the colony consisted merely in skins of deer, bear, and other animals, and lumber. That the *coureurs de bois* hunted for peltry and slaves, which they brought to Mobile and sold, and that the peltry was then re-sold, together with vegetables and poultry, to the Spaniards at Pensacola, or to ships which touched upon the coast, while the Indian slaves were employed to saw out lumber and till the earth. But the very next day Cadillac made another despatch, in which he pronounced the country to be good for nothing, and the inhabitants "a mass of rapscallions from Canada, a cut-throat set, without subordination, with no respect for religion, and abandoned in vice with Indian women, whom they prefer to French girls." He complained that upon arriving at Mobile he found the garrisons dispersed in the woods and Indian villages, where they

1713 October 25

October 25

CHAPTER V. went in search of bread; that Bienville, his brother Chateaugné, and their cousin Boisbriant, the Major of Mobile, came to the colony too young to know how to drill soldiers, and had not since learned any thing of proper discipline; and that the soldiers all had Indian wives, who cooked for them and waited upon them—all of which he pronounced to be intolerable. He believed that the colony presented but two objects of commerce—trade with the Spaniards of Mexico and
1713 the working of precious mines, if the latter could be discovered; but that, unfortunately, Dirigoin, one of Crozat's directors, was a man of no capacity, while Lebas, the comptroller, was extremely dissipated. He desired more trade's-people, sailors, Canadians and artizans to be sent out, and a church to be erected at Mobile. But the latter the inhabitants would be delighted not to have. Indeed, a majority of the gentlemen, priests and missionaries, had not taken sacrament for eight years, the soldiers had not kept Palm Sunday, but followed the example of Bienville and his adherents; that the sea captain who brought out the twelve girls had seduced more than half of them upon the passage, which was the cause of their not having married respectable persons in the colony, and he contended that it was best, under the circumstances, that the *soldiers* should be allowed to marry them, for fear that their poverty would drive them to prostitution. In relation to the council which was to co-operate in the government of the colony, Cadillac said that it had not convened for the want of suitable members. To this string of complaints were added many others in a subsequent despatch, among which

CHAPTER V. 1714 February 20

were the following: That Bienville had governed the colony for years without having discovered any mines, which he (Cadillac) could have done in a short time; that Duclos was guilty of great impudence and presumption in censuring his official acts; that the French government was entirely too lenient to its colonial officers and soldiers, who threatened to revolt and burn up Crozat's establishment; and that libertinism was carried to such an extent, that even the boys had Indian mistresses! In again alluding to the council, he stated that Duclos had nominated for Attorney-General a store-keeper; for Councillor, the chief surgeon; for Secretary, Door-keeper and Notary, one Roquet, a low soldier; and that the Assembly, which for the present was to meet at his house, wanted nothing but the bonnet and robe to make it perfect! He said that if the Minister did not crush the cabals formed against him by Bienville and his clan, who kept up an intercourse with the inhabitants of Pensacola, to whom they sold and from whom they bought, that Crozat would be compelled to abandon his colonial project. He denied that he had withheld grants of land to the inhabitants, but admitted that his requirement that such grants as he had given should be subject to the ratification of the King, gave great dissatisfaction. He concluded this remarkable despatch with the assertion that none of the lands were worth granting!

In the meantime, a ship had arrived from the mother country with a large supply of provisions and considerable merchandize. She was followed by the Louisiana, owned by

CHAPTER V. Crozat, also laden with provisions for the colony. Delegations
of Chiefs of different tribes visited Mobile and smoked the pipe
1714 with Cadillac and Bienville, who received them with friendship,
gratified them with presents, and dismissed them under pledges
that they would abandon the interests of the English of Carolina
and Virginia. But even after this, twelve Englishmen came
among the Choctaws with a large number of Creeks or Muscogees,
and were graciously received by the inhabitants of all save
two towns, who fortified themselves, and while besieged by the
Creeks, one night made their escape to Cadillac at Mobile.*

1630 During the reign of Charles I. of England, the region
south of the Chesapeake Bay was granted by that monarch
to Sir Robert Heath, but the projected colony was neglected,
1663 and the grant was forfeited. Charles II. decreed that this
territory should assume the name of Carolina, and embrace
the region from Albemarle Sound southward to the River St.
Johns and westward to the Pacific, forming a province vast in
extent, which was conveyed to eight joint proprietors. In
the meantime some adventurers from New England had planted
a little colony at the mouth of the Cape Fear river. From
that time emigrants gradually settled upon the coast now
1670 known as that of North-Carolina, and extended their enterprises
to South-Carolina, where they formed a settlement

* Historie de la Louisiane, par Charles Gayarre, vol. 1, pp. 91–112. Journal Historique de l'Etablissement des Français a la Louisiane, par Bernard de la Harpe, 78–115.

several miles above the mouths of the Ashley and Cooper rivers, and at length established themselves upon the site of the present city of Charleston.* CHAPTER V. 1680

From the time that South-Carolina was thus colonized, down to the period of 1714, to which we have brought the history of the French colony of Louisiana, forty-four years had passed. During much of that time, Carolina and Virginia traders had penetrated portions of the great Muscogee nation, which extended from the Savannah nearly to the Warrior, in Alabama. They also carried their merchandize further west, into the heart of the Chickasaw nation, among whom they established trading shops, in defiance of the French settlements upon the Mobile. Notwithstanding that the French 1700 to 1714 were the first, since the invasion of De Soto, to discover and occupy the country where the Tombigby and Alabama lose themselves in the sea—and although the indefatigable Bienville had explored those rivers to their highest navigable points, at a very early period, freely interchanging friendly assurances with the Chickasaws living upon the one, and the Muscogees and Alabamas upon the other—yet the grasping English government attempted, through its enterprising traders and special emissaries, to occupy this region, and to induce

* Hildreth's History of the United States, vol. 2, pp. 25–36. Coxe's Carolana, 2; London, 1741. Stevens' History of Georgia, vol. 1, pp. 140, 141, 58, 59. Simms' History of South Carolina, pp. 56–57. Carroll's Historical Collections of South-Carolina, vol. 1, pp. 42–52. Ramsay's History of South-Carolina, vol. 1, pp. 2–3. Hewett's History of South-Carolina.

CHAPTER V.

1700 to 1714

the inhabitants to expel the French, not only from the head waters of those streams, but from their very mouths. These fearless British traders conveyed, upon the backs of pack-horses, such goods as suited these Indians, from distant Charleston to the remote Chickasaw nation, over creeks without bridges, rivers without ferries, and woods pathless and pregnant with many dangers. They did not, however, establish any permanent trading shops upon the Coosa, Tallapoosa or Alabama, at the period under review, but occasionally traded with the Indians upon those streams, dwelling in their towns no longer than sufficed to dispose of their goods, and receive, in return, valuable peltries, which they conveyed back to Charleston. But their intercourse with these tribes was vastly pernicious to the French below, and to the Spaniards inhabiting the provinces of Florida. The Creeks, in conjunction with their British allies, invaded the latter provinces, as we have already seen.

1702 to 1714

Bienville had repeatedly suggested to the French government the necessity of establishing a fort and trading post upon the Alabama river, in the immediate strong-hold of the powerful Creeks, to counteract the influence of the Carolinians; but a war ensued between him and the Creeks, with whom he had an engagement, as we have seen, and against whom he found it imperative, for the preservation of his colony, to incite the Choctaws and other tribes. About the commencement of the year 1714, and when Crozat's charter had been in operation for near a twelve-month, Bienville, who was still retained high in authority as royal lieutenant, only second to the Governor, was most fortunate in making peace with the Creeks. Having obtained from them their consent for the erection of a fort high up in their country, he was authorized, by the colonial council at Mobile, to immediately establish it. Crozat's directors deemed the location a most suitable one for the advancement of his commerce, besides the barrier it would interpose to the enemies of that commerce.

Accordingly Bienville embarked at Mobile, with eight iron cannon, many fire-arms, a large supply of ammunition, merchandize suitable for the Indians, and a liberal supply of provisions, on board two small sailing vessels. With these vessels also went a number of canoes of various descriptions. The expedition was composed of soldiers, Canadians, and Mobile and Choctaw Indians. Bienville sailed up the Mobile 1714 April 5
river to the confluence of the Tombigby and Alabama. Here, passing with his singular fleet into the latter stream, he slowly ascended it. After a long and tedious voyage, he arrived at one of the Alabama villages, not far above the site of the modern town of Selma. Continuing the voyage up the river, he successively passed the towns of Autauga,* Powacte and Ecuncharte; † and at length moored his boats at the beautiful June 21
Indian town of Coosawda. These towns were inhabited by the Alabamas, who, as we have seen, were members of the great Creek nation, which was composed of several different tribes, whom they had conquered and incorporated into their confederacy. Many of these people joined the fleet on its

* Now the site of Washington. † Now the site of Montgomery.

CHAPTER V.

passage up the Alabama, and joyfully greeted Bienville, who was popular with all the savages, and who, with wonderful facility, acquired a perfect knowledge of their different dialects. He was met at Coosawda by some of the most prominent Chiefs; and here leaving his fleet, he embarked in a canoe, and explored the Coosa and Tallapoosa rivers for several miles up. He then resolved to erect his fort at the town of Tuskegee, which was then situated on the east bank of the Coosa, four miles above the junction of that stream with the Tallapoosa. Bienville displayed much judgment in the selection of this place. It was at the head of a peninsula formed by the windings of these rivers, which here approached within

1714 June 22

six hundred yards of each other; after which they diverged considerably before they finally came together. It was in the neighborhood of some of the most populous towns,—the inhabitants of which could easily bring down to the fort their articles of commerce by either river. Returning to Coosawda, Bienville now advanced his fleet from thence to the junction, where, entering the Coosa, he arrived at Tuskegee, where the voyage terminated. The crew left the boats—ascended the bluff—formed themselves in religious order, and surrounded a cross which had been hastily constructed. Two priests, who accompanied the expedition, chanted praises to the MOST HIGH, and went through other solemn ceremonies, in presence of a number of the natives, who contemplated the scene with calmness and respect, and who preserved the most profound silence. With the assistance of the natives, Bienville began the erection of a wooden fort with four bastions, in each one of which he mounted two of the cannon. As the history of these cannon is rather singular, and may interest some of our readers, we must be allowed to digress a little from the main narrative, by a brief reference to it. These cannon remained upon the entrenchments of Fort Toulouse from 1714 to 1763. Then the French commandant spiked them, broke off the trunions, evacuated the fort, and left the cannon there in that situation. The English, who, in 1763, succeeded to the possession of this country, threw a garrison into Fort Toulouse, but in a very short time also evacuated it, and it fell into rapid decay; but still the French cannon remained there. A few years after Col. Hawkins had been stationed among the Creeks, as their agent, he induced the government, as a means of encouraging agriculture, to send some blacksmiths to the nation. One of these men succeeded in filing away the spikes from two of the cannon. These the Indians used to fire with powder, for amusement. Afterwards, the army of Jackson occupied the site of the old fort. In due time they marched away, and still these French pieces remained there.

Finally, the town of Montgomery, now our capital, began to be settled, and the inhabitants went up to old Fort Toulouse, then Fort Jackson, and brought down two of these cannon, which they fired at 4th July festivals, and upon other extraordinary occasions. When it was known that John Quincy Adams had been elected President of the United States, his warm friends in Montgomery determined to make the forests resound with the noise of powder. One of the cannon was

CHAPTER V. over-charged, and when touched off by Ebenezer Pond, burst into pieces and mangled that gentleman in such a horrid manner, that he was a long time in recovering. The breech of the other cannon was, some years afterwards, burst off by heavy charges, and the portion which remains now stands at Pollard's corner, in Montgomery, being there planted in the ground, the muzzle up, for the purpose of protecting the corner of the side-walk. About the year 1820, another of these cannon was carried to the town of Washington, the then county seat of Autauga, where the inhabitants used to fire it upon the celebration of the 4th July, and whenever a steamboat arrived, but at length it was also burst, by a party rejoicing one night at the result of a county election. Another of these old French pieces was carried to Wetumpka when that town was first established, and was fired upon like occasions. It is now at Rockford, in Coosa county, in the possession of the same Ebenezer Pond who was so badly wounded at Montgomery by the explosion of one of its mates. What became of the other four cannon we do not know, but have understood that they, together with a fine brass piece, are in the river opposite Fort Jackson.

1714 August But to return to Bienville and his romantic expedition. Around the stockading the governor cut intrenchments, and one hundred years afterwards, Jackson placed an American fort upon the ruins, which assumed his name. Bienville occupied the summer and fall in completing the fort and
November out-houses, and in exploring the surrounding country. He visited Tookabatcha, upon the Tallapoosa, and extended his

journey among the Lower Muscogees, upon the Chattahooche,—even crossing that river, and conferring with the Chiefs in the towns of Coweta and Cusseta, within the present limits of Georgia. Upon all these dangerous excursions he was accompanied by only a few faithful Canadians, and always performed his journeys on foot. Was not this whole expedition most interesting,—nay, romantic? Here was the former governor of Louisiana, and now the lieutenant-governor, in the centre of Alabama, in the deepest depths of her forests, among people with whom he had been at war, and who were yet tampered with by the English, visiting their towns, distributing presents, and exhorting them to form alliances with the French colony of Louisiana, and to expel the English who should attempt to form posts among them. Yes! citizens of the counties of Montgomery, Coosa, Tallapoosa, Macon and Russell, reflect that one hundred and thirty-seven years ago* the French governor of Louisiana,—the great and good Bienville,—*walked* over your soil and instituted friendly relations with its rude inhabitants,—among whom not a solitary white man had a permanent abode,—and established a small colony upon the east bank of the Coosa!

CHAPTER V.

1714

Giving the fort the name of "Toulouse," in honor of a distinguished French Count of that name, who had much to do with the government of France and her colonies, and leaving in command Marigny de Mandaville with thirty soldiers, and one of the priests, Bienville turned his boats down the river, and,

December 27

* This being now 1851.

CHAPTER V. after a prosperous voyage, arrived at Mobile with the Indians and Canadians who had accompanied him.*

Thus, we see, that although the French had been residing upon the Mobile river since 1702, and the Canadians had several times explored Central Alabama, yet no attempt was made to form permanent settlements in this region, until twelve years afterwards, when it was so successfully accomplished by Bienville.

Governor Cadillac, in a despatch to the Minister, attempted to acquire all the credit for the peace which had been made with the Creek nation, and boasted, generally, of the important services which, he contended, he had rendered the colony. But he was the same inefficient, selfish and fault-finding officer. A large majority of the inhabitants relied solely upon Bienville, whose most prominent friends were Duclos, Boisbriant, Chateaugné, Richebourg, and du Tisne, and the larger number of the priesthood. The friends of Cadillac were Marigny de Mandaville, Bagot, Bloundel, Latour, Villiers and Terrine. Thus this handful of men were at daggers' points with each other, instead of uniting for their own preservation and prosperity, and that of the feeble settlements over which they had

1714 December 27 charge. A tyrannical ordinance was issued in France, upon the petition of Crozat, which further embarrassed affairs. All persons were forbidden to bring any merchandize into Louisiana, or to carry any out of it, under penalty of confiscation to the profit of Crozat. No person in the colony was allowed

* MS. letters obtained from Paris.

to have a vessel fit to go to sea, and all subjects of the King were prohibited from sending vessels to the colony to carry on commerce. Crozat was determined to avail himself of the monopoly which had been granted him, and this ordinance was based upon the representations of Cadillac, who had, more than once, complained to the Minister, that the inhabitants of the colony were *making a little for themselves*, in a commerce with the Spaniards, which was deemed a very unwarrantable thing by that illiberal man. Cadillac hated Bienville for 1714
several reasons, the most prominent of which were, that he was too popular with the Canadians and Indians, too much respected and obeyed by the inhabitants generally, and had absolutely refused to become his son-in-law. Cadillac's daughter, who had been educated in France, and who, like her father, thought much of the blood and honor of the family, fell in love with Bienville, soon after her arrival in Mobile. The proud governor could not, at first, brook the idea of an alliance with a *Canadian*, but he saw, as he supposed, the strong attachment of his daughter, who now began, like many other hypocritical girls, to pine away and sicken in consequence of his refusal. Believing that Bienville's great influence with the inhabitants, as well as with the various Indian tribes, would materially strengthen his administration and advance the commerce of Crozat, the profits of which he was to share, if he could but once secure his friendship and obedience, he resolved to sacrifice his family dignity by gratifying the wishes of his daughter. One day he accosted Bienville, with much respect and suavity of manner, and invited him

CHAPTER V. into his closet. He there disclosed to him his entire willingness to sanction the contemplated match between him and his daughter, charged him to treat her with affection, and concluded his conversation with a very patronizing air. Bienville, much surprised at the whole affair, as he had never alluded to marriage, in the few visits which he had paid the daughter, gravely assured Cadillac that he had "determined never to marry." This was too bad; and, from that moment, Bienville found, in the persons of the Governor and his daughter, two most cordial haters.

1714 December The redoubtable Curate de la Vente continued to declaim, not only against the colonial government, but against every body except his friend Cadillac. In his despatches to the Minister, he said that the Canadians particularly "did not wish to connect themselves with any women by marriage, much preferring to carry on scandalous concubinage with the young Indian squaws, who were hurried by their nature into all kinds of irregularities." That they scarcely ever saw a church, never performed mass, and never partook of the sacraments; that, while a few of the inhabitants did celebrate Sundays and festival days, the large majority resorted to taverns and to public games—"whence it is easy to comprehend that they are almost all drunkards, gamesters, blasphemers of the holy name of God, and declared enemies of all good, making a matter of ridicule of our holy religion and of the persons who perform its exercises." They corrupted the soldiers by such horrid examples; and even officers, who wore the sword and plume, had children by Indian females. The missionaries found themselves useless to a people who were led away by such vices, and to the Indians, who were corrupted by the sins of the latter, and consequently they would be forced to leave a land so accursed. La Vente suggested to the Minister two plans "to rectify the affairs of the past and those of the future:"—either to solely colonize Louisiana with Christian families, or permit the French to marry the Indian women by religious rites. Or, if these plans could not be carried into effect, that a large number of girls, "better chosen than the last, and especially some who will be sufficiently pleasing and well-formed to suit the officers of the garrisons and the principal inhabitants," should be sent over from France as a partial remedy. Verily, the worthy curate's head appeared to run much upon women of various grades!

CHAPTER V.

1714 December

1715

According to the orders which he had received, De la Loire des Ursins made a settlement at Natchez, to promote the commerce of Crozat. Cadillac set off on an expedition to discover mines of gold and silver in the Illinois country, and did not return from his chimerical excursion until October, when he wrote to the Minister that he had everywhere set the Indians upon the English, but, in truth, he had aroused the anger of the savages against himself wherever he had appeared among them; and, in descending the Mississippi, upon his way to Mobile, he had refused to smoke with the powerful and warlike Natchez Chiefs, which was highly resented on their part, and afterwards led to a war with the French.

An English officer from Carolina, named Hutchey, who had passed through the Creek and Chickasaw nations, came into

CHAPTER V. the territory of the Natchez. From thence he began the descent of the Mississippi, to form alliances with the tribes below. But Des Ursins, who had gained intelligence of his movements, pursued him in a boat, captured him near Manchac, and carried him to Mobile. From thence Bienville sent him to Pensacola; but having determined to reach Carolina by land, he was killed upon the route by a Thomez Indian.
1715 July A large canoe, containing seven Alabamas, an Englishman and a Canadian named Boutin, arrived at Mobile. They reported that the Indians, bordering upon Carolina, had risen in war against the inhabitants of that province, had killed those upon the frontiers, and that even Port Royal and several other towns had been destroyed. The war extended to the distant Chickasaw nation. There, fifteen English traders, who had taken shelter in one cabin, were instantly slain in the presence of De St. Helene, a Frenchman, who was then among the tribe, and who, a few minutes after the massacre, was killed himself, through mistake, by two young Chicka-
1715 saws, engaged in the bloody scene, they supposing him to be one of the enemy. His death was regretted by all the Chickasaws who were present.

To profit by this intelligence, so agreeable to the French colony, Bienville immediately despatched emissaries among the Alabamas and Muscogees, to renew the alliances which he had formed with them, and to engage them to turn their whole commerce into French channels. He sent messengers to the Choctaws, demanding the head of Outactachito, who had introduced the English into their nation, and who had driven off the inhabitants of the two Choctaw towns that were faithful to the French and who still lay around Mobile, anxious to return home. The messengers returned to Mobile with the head of this warrior, which had been reluctantly stricken off by the Chiefs, who were afraid to disobey Bienville. They bore an invitation to those Choctaws whom they had forced to leave their homes, to return in peace. CHAPTER V.

1715 August

The store-ship Dauphin came to anchor in Mobile bay, where she landed two companies of infantry, commanded by Mandaville and Bagot, which increased the expenditures of the colony to the amount of thirty-two thousand livres a year. One of the passengers, named Rogeon, came to fill the place of Dirigoin, one of the directors of Crozat, who had been removed from office. At the same time, a frigate from Rochelle, and a brigantine from Martinique, arriving in the bay, requested permission to dispose of their cargoes to the inhabitants; but the authorities, anxious to perfect the monopoly of Crozat, refused them the privilege.

In the meantime, Cadillac had not forgotten how to fill the sheets, which he sent to Count Pontchartrain, with gloomy pictures of the colony, and the licentiousness of its inhabitants. In one of these despatches he denominated Louisiana "a monster which had neither head nor tail." He complained of the manner in which the council unscrupulously altered the decrees of the French government. He said that the whole country was the poorest and most miserable upon the globe, the people of which would much sooner believe a lie than the truth. He recommended that a stone fort be erected at Mo- 1715

CHAPTER V. bile, but immediately interposed an obstacle to the project by saying that the topographical engineer was a man without firmness and judgment, and was always drunk. He was violently opposed to the establishment of a colony upon the Mississippi, on the ground which sustains New-Orleans, a measure now contemplated by Crozat, through the recommendation of Bienville. He asserted that the Mississippi river was too crooked, too rapid in high tides, and too low in the dry season, for the navigation of canoes!

At length Cadillac went to reside on Dauphin Island, where he had formerly spent much of his time. It was fortified with four barracks of palisades, covered with rushes, and a guard-house, with a prison of the same style—the whole surrounded
1716 July 20 with palisades very irregularly arranged. From this island he immediately issued the following singular ordinance:

ORDINANCE OF M. DE LAMOTTE CADILLAC.

"As we have obtained certain knowledge of several cabals and conspiracies which tend to revolt and sedition, and on account of some disturbances from which evil consequences may ensue, in order to abolish and obviate the misconduct caused by drunkenness and also all disturbances fomented by women of irregular life, or by the instigation of other persons who excite to vengeance those who are so unfortunate as to expose themselves by evil discourse, and as every one takes it upon himself to carry a sword and other weapons without having any right to do so, we most positively prohibit to all persons of low birth, to all clerks of M. Crozat, sailors and strangers lately arrived from France, if they are not provided with his majesty's commission, from carrying a sword or any other weapons, either by day or night, on Dauphin Island, or at any other settlements where there is an actual garrison, under the penalty of three hundred *livres* fine, to be applied to the erection of a church on Dauphin Island; and in default of payment the offender shall be confined in prison for the space of one month, and the penalty shall be greater for each repetition of the offence. We grant to all gentlemen the privilege of wearing a sword after having proved their nobility, and presented their titles to the secretary of the council for examination, and not otherwise, under the same penalties. We grant, also, to all civil and military officers, actually serving in the country, permission to wear a sword, &c."

Thus, while this ridiculous governor was establishing himself in a court of heraldry, in a miserable cabin of palm logs on Dauphin Island, and pronouncing upon titles of nobility, Bienville was in the interior of the immense wilds of Louisiana, establishing trading posts and advancing the interests of the colony. Cadillac, whom the excellent commissary, Duclos, pronounced to be "an avaricious, cunning and obstinate man, who kept for himself everything which the court sent to the savages," was fast losing ground with the authorities in France. Crozat, in one of his last communications to him, used this language: "It is my opinion that all the disorders of which M. Cadillac complains in the colony proceed from the mal-administration of M. Cadillac himself." The Minister added this postscript: "Messrs. Cadillac and Duclos, whose characters are utterly incompatible with each other, and who,

CHAPTER V. 1716

at the same time, lack the intelligence necessary to the performance of their duties, are recalled, and their places are filled by others." It was unjust that Duclos should have been made to lose his station because his views of colonial policy clashed with those of the Governor.

The King of France had ordered Bienville to form several establishments upon the Mississippi, and to commence with that among the Natchez, with eighty soldiers. As soon as possible he began the construction of large canoes to be used as transports. Cadillac refused to place at his disposal the number of soldiers designated by his majesty, and Bienville, when all things were ready, departed with only thirty-four soldiers under the command of Richebourg. To these

April 23

were added fifteen sailors. Bienville advanced to a town of the Tonicas, eighteen leagues below Natchez, and there learning from Father Davion, still a missionary among those people, that they were not to be trusted and would probably become allies of the Natchez, he established himself temporarily upon an island in the Mississippi, where he erected three barracks, which he enclosed with piles. His object was to obtain possession of the persons of those Chiefs and prominent warriors of the Natchez, who had recently murdered some Frenchmen, in consequence of the refusal of Cadillac to smoke with them, which they viewed as a declaration of war. He intended, after he had made an example of a few Chiefs, and had intimidated the common people, to proceed to their towns and there construct a fortification in obedience to the orders of his King. Father Davion further informed Bienville that the Natchez Chiefs did not suspect that the murders which they had committed were known to the French authorities, and were anxious to keep them concealed. Bienville then despatched messengers up the river, who were instructed to pass by the Natchez during the night, and proceed towards the Wabash settlements, and inform all Frenchmen, whom they met descending, to be upon their guard, for that he was stationed at the Tonicas, and that he was preparing to be revenged upon the murderers of the Frenchmen, which would possibly produce a serious war with that tribe.

1716 April 27

Three Natchez, who were sent by their Chiefs to Bienville, arrived with the pipe of peace, but the latter declined to receive it, and stated that the messengers might smoke with his soldiers, but that he would only smoke with the Great Sun Chiefs, for he was the Great Chief of the French. He affected indifference about establishing a trading post among them, and intimated an intention to give the Tonicas the benefit of his merchandize, as the Natchez Chiefs had exhibited such a want of respect and friendship, in not coming themselves to greet him.

May 8

The three savages speedily returned home with this startling message, and with a French interpreter, who could further explain the reply of Bienville. One morning, Bienville saw four magnificent canoes descending the river, and bearing towards the island. Eight warriors stood erect and sung the pipe-song, while three Chiefs, in each canoe, sat under immense umbrellas. They were the Natchez Chiefs, allured thither by the snare which the royal lieutenant had laid for

CHAPTER V. them. Concealing one half of his soldiers, and advancing, with apparent friendship, he conducted them within his rude military works, which they entered singing the song of peace, and holding the pipe over his head. Afterwards, they passed their hands over his stomach without rubbing, and then over themselves. Bienville refused the pipe with contempt, and desired, first, to know the nature of their visit. Much disconcerted, the Chiefs went out and presented their pipes to the Sun. The High Priest, with his arms extended and his eyes fixed upon the bright luminary which he daily worshipped, invoked it to soften the temper and change the resolution of
1716 the stern Bienville. Again entering the works, he presented the pipe to Bienville, who scornfully refused it. At that moment the Chiefs were seized, ironed, and placed in the prison. At night, Bienville informed the Grand Sun, and his brothers, the Angry Serpent and the Little Sun, whom he had caused to be separated from the others and brought into his presence, that nothing would satisfy him but to be placed in possession of the heads of the Chiefs who advised the murder of the five Frenchmen, and of those who executed the horrid deed; that he knew that *they* were not concerned in the transaction themselves, and, consequently, he did not desire to take their lives, unless they failed to comply with his demands. He
May 9 gave them until morning to determine upon his requisition, and by daylight the three brothers appeared before him, and implored him to remember that no one now remained in their town of sufficient authority to chop off the heads of the men whom he demanded, and requested that the Angry Serpent

might be permitted to return home to accomplish the dangerous mission. Bienville refused, but sent the Little Sun in his place, with an officer and twelve soldiers, who conveyed him in a canoe within six miles of Natchez, where he was placed on shore. The Little Sun returned to Bienville, with three heads, two of which the French commander recognized as those which he had demanded. The other head was that of an innocent person, the brother of one of the murderers, who had fled to the forests. Bienville expressed his deep regret to the Chiefs, that they had thus caused an innocent person to suffer, and assured them that nothing would compromise his resentment but the possession of the head of the Chief, White Earth. Notwithstanding the Little Sun had acted with so much promptness, and had brought with him a Frenchman and two Illinois Indians, whom he found tied to stakes in one of the Natchez towns, ready to be burned to death, yet Bienville caused him to be ironed and remanded to prison with the others. The next day he despatched to the Natchez, the High Priest of the Temple, and two Chiefs of War, for the head of White Earth. They were conducted by a detachment, almost to their villages. In the meantime, by a confession of the imprisoned Chiefs, Bienville ascertained that the English had been encouraged, and the Frenchmen had been killed, at the instance of White Earth, Grigars, and two Chiefs and two warriors then in his custody. The Indians whom he had sent to the Natchez, having returned without the head of White Earth, who had made his escape, and the inundations of the Mississippi having caused much sickness on

1716 May 14

May 15

CHAPTER V. the island, Bienville determined to end the affair by a treaty with the Chiefs, who willingly acceded to his terms, and were grateful that he had spared their lives. They bound themselves to kill White Earth whenever he could be captured—to restore all the goods which they had seized—to cut two thousand five hundred piles of acacia wood, thirty feet long and ten inches in diameter, and to deposit them at the spot, at Natchez, where it was contemplated to erect a fort—and to furnish the bark of three thousand cypress trees, for covering the houses, by the end of July.*

1716 June 3 Adjutant Pailloux departed, with two soldiers, to the town of the Natchez, with the Chiefs and other warriors; Bienville, however, retained the Angry Serpent and his brother, the Little Sun, as hostages, and also kept the four murderers, who now rent the prison with their doleful death-songs and loud speeches of defiance. Pailloux, upon arriving among the Natchez, found them assembled in council, and learned, with pleasure, that they were satisfied with the compact which their Chiefs had made with Bienville. He selected an eminence, near the Mississippi, advantageously situated for that purpose, for the site of a fort. In the meantime, Bienville had been visited, at the island, by nine old Natchez men, who came with much show of solemnity, and invited him to
June 8 smoke the pipe of peace with them, which he now no longer

* Histoire de la Louisiane, par Charles Gayarre, vol. 1, pp. 114–144. Journal Historique de l'Etablissement des Français a la Louisiane, par Bernard de la Harpe, pp. 115–128.

refused to do. He sent them home with the Little Sun and four soldiers, who conveyed, in a large canoe, axes, spades, pickaxes, nails and other irons, to construct the fort. The next day, the soldiers, at the island, struck off the heads of the two warriors. Afterwards Captain Richebourg was obliged to depart for Mobile, on account of sickness. A number of Canadian *voyageurs*, whom Bienville detained at the island, while on their way from the Illinois country, with peltries and supplies for the people of the lower part of Louisiana, now that the difficulties with the Natchez had ended, were permitted to proceed down the Mississippi; the royal lieutenant caused them to take with them the two Chiefs, whose heads he ordered to be struck off twelve leagues below, which was faithfully executed.

CHAPTER V. 1716 June 9 June 11 June 12

The Natchez, directed by the French officer and assisted by a few soldiers, labored upon the fort and ditches with great assiduity, and soon brought the works to a state of completion. Bienville had arrived a few days before, in company with the Angry Serpent, whom he had retained about his person until every seeming obstacle was overcome. Before the gate of the fort, six hundred Natchez warriors appeared, unarmed, and joined three hundred women in a dance in honor of Bienville; afterwards the Chiefs crossed the threshold and smoked the pipe of peace with him. Such was the end of the first Natchez war.

August 2 August 25

Leaving Pailloux in command of the post at Natchez, Bienville descended the Mississippi, and sailed to Mobile for the purpose of reporting to Governor Cadillac. Here he

October 4

CHAPTER V. received a packet from the Marine Council, in which he was ordered by the King of France to govern as chief of the colony, until L'Epinay, the successor of Cadillac, should arrive. He was thus saved the disagreeable necessity of reporting to his old enemy, who had, in advance, denounced his conduct to the Minister, as fraught with cruelty and the deepest treachery towards the Natchez Chiefs. We are not prepared to defend Bienville from these charges, although his course was approved by the government and by all the colonial authorities, with the exception of Cadillac and his junto.

The King of France, acceding to the request of Crozat, allowed one hundred salt-makers to be sent annually to Louisiana, who, after laboring there for three years, were to receive land. He also consented to send thither eight companies of soldiers, with permission to two, out of each company, to settle in the country, together with a hundred hospital girls, annually, to increase the colonial population. The King refused to adopt the suggestion of the Curate La Vente, of permitting Frenchmen to marry Indian women.

For the payment of the colonial expenses, for the year 1716, now nearly brought to a close, Duclos, the commissary-general, required of the French government an appropriation of the following amounts:

A governor, - - -	6000 *livres.*
A commissary, - -	6000 "
A royal lieutenant, - -	2000 "
An adjutant, - - -	900 "

Four captains of companies,	4800	*livres.*
Four lieutenants, - -	3600	"
Ensigns, - - -	2400	"
A secretary, - - -	1000	"
A store-keeper, - -	800	"
A surgeon, - - -	800	"
A chaplain, - - -	800	"
Incidental expenses, -	80,992	"
	110,092	*livres.* *

* Histoire de la Louisiane, par Charles Gayarre, vol. 1, pp. 148–152.

CHAPTER VI.

THE INDIA OR MISSISSIPPI COMPANY.

CHAPTER VI.

1717 March 9

L'EPINAY, the new governor, and the fourth which had been placed over the colony of Louisiana, Hubert, the new commissary-general, three companies of infantry and fifty colonists, arrived from France, on board three vessels, which belonged to Crozat. Among the colonists were Roi Dubreuil, Guennot, Trefontaine and Massy, men of worth and intelligence, who had formed themselves into an association to settle some portion of the almost boundless country of Louisiana.

To prevent the struggle for power which had never failed to display itself between the former governors, commissaries and officers of the colony, the King of France, by written instructions, defined the duties of each. He declared that all military regulations, and the "dignity of command," should pertain to the governor alone; but in the building of public houses and fortifications, the marching of expeditions, and the means of raising funds, he was to confer with the commissary, whose joint views were to be presented for the ratification of his majesty. The administration of the funds, provisions, merchandize and everything which related to the ware-houses was confided to the commissary, who, however, could make no bargain or sale without the consent of the governor. The administration of the hospitals was also confided to the commissary, with the supervision of the governor. The administration of justice was committed to the commissary in his function of first councillor and chief judge. The affairs of the police, and the power of conferring grants of land were given jointly to these officers. Letters patent established a Supreme Council of Louisiana, the meetings of which, his majesty authorized to be held, either at Fort St. Louis, of Mobile, or upon Dauphin Island. The King granted to Bienville, for his numerous services, the Island of Come, not as a fief, but in villanage, and instructed L'Epinay to present him with the cross of St. Louis. These marks of favor did not reconcile Bienville, who considered himself, beyond all others, entitled to the government of Louisiana. Consequently jealousies and disputes soon created a disagreeable and unhappy state of things, arraying the friends of Bienville on one side, and those of the governor and commissary, on the other. As Crozat attempted to bribe Cadillac, in order to attain his most vigorous and successful exertions in advancing his commerce, so, for the same end, he entered into a contract with L'Epinay, engaging to give him two thousand livres a year, and divers other advantages. The great monopolist had designed to establish a large contraband trade, with the Spanish possessions, if he could not carry on a legitimate one. But, he succeeded in neither, and next, turning his attention to a

CHAPTER VI. commerce with the various Indian tribes upon the Mississippi, Alabama, Tombigby and their tributaries, he found that so far from being remunerated, he had to encounter the heaviest 1717 August losses. At length, aware that he had assumed a burthen beyond his strength, he humbly offered to return to the King that charter, the extensive privileges of which he had once imagined would make him the richest man in the world! October 27 The proposition was accepted, and the Council of State transmitted orders to L'Epinay to transfer the colonial government to Bienville, and to return to France. The gubernatorial career of the former gentleman was of short duration, and remarkable for nothing, except a proclamation, in which he forbade the sale of brandy to the Indians—at that period, a very unpopular measure.

During the five years of the existence of the colony, under the charter of Crozat, commerce and agriculture had not prospered, yet the population had slowly increased, and now numbered about seven hundred souls. The colonists, also, possessed some four hundred horned cattle. The inhabitants had devoted themselves to a trade in provisions and Indian slaves, and to a commerce with the Spaniards, who, despite of the watchfulness of Crozat's agents, had managed to carry off, annually, about twelve thousand piastres.

The Marine Cabinet of France, composed of De Bourbon and D'Estrees, came to the conclusion, that as the enterprise which Crozat had assumed, had proved itself of too gigantic a character for any one man, and as it would not be proper for the King to take charge of Louisiana, and embarrass himself by entering into its thousand cares and commercial details, it would better comport with the welfare of France and her colony, to turn the latter over to the management of an association of men. Accordingly, the Western or India Company, with a capital of one hundred thousand livres, was allowed to take the unhappy people of Louisiana under their charge, and to expose them, once more, to an arbitrary and grinding monopoly. The members of this company were not required to be solely subjects of the King of France, but might be foreigners. The charter, which was registered in the Parliament, at Paris, gave this company the exclusive privilege of carrying on all commerce in Louisiana, for the long period of twenty-five years. It also gave them the exclusive privilege, extending from the 1st January, 1718, to the 31st December, 1742, of purchasing beaver skins from Canada—the King reserving the right of regulating their price, and of determining the quantity to be sold. The company possessed the power of conferring grants, making war or peace with the Indians, establishing forts, levying troops, appointing governors, or other officers for the colony, upon the recommendation of the directors of the company; building vessels of war, casting pieces of artillery, and of nominating the inferior judges, and all the other officers of justice, the King reserving to himself only the right of appointing the members of the Supreme Council.

CHAPTER VI.

1717 — September 6

It was further provided by the charter that the military officers could enter into the service of the company without losing their rank in the army or navy, but they were not allow-

CHAPTER VI.

ed to seize, either in the hands of the directors, or in those of its cashier or its agents, the effects, shares, or profits of the stockholders, except in case of failure or open bankruptcy or death of said stockholders. The merchandize of the company was to be free from all charges either of entry or departure, and to those portions of the territory where they made permanent improvements, the company was to have durable rights, which were to extend also to the mines, which they might discover and work. The only thing which savored of

1717 September 6

liberality towards the inhabitants, was their exemption from taxation during the existence of the charter. The ecclesiastical jurisdiction was still to form a part of the diocese of Quebec, while the company was to build churches and pay the clergy. It was to transport to the colony, during the term of its charter, six thousand whites, and three thousand negroes; but it was prohibited from sending negroes or whites to the other French colonies, without the permission of the Governor of Louisiana. The directors were to be appointed by the King, for the first two years, and afterwards they were to be elected every three years, by the stockholders, each of whom had a vote for every fifty shares. In short, the India Company was granted all manner of powers and privileges.

A celebrated Scotchman, named Law, who was now director of the Bank of France; D'Artaguette, receiver-general of the finances of Auch; Duché, receiver of those of Rochelle; Moreau, commercial deputy of the city of St. Malo; Piou, deputy of the city of Nantes; and Costaignes and Mauchard, merchants of Rochelle—were nominated by the King of France as the first directors for the colony of Louisiana, under the new charter. The company then sent over three companies of infantry, and sixty-nine colonists. The three vessels, which bore them, arrived at Dauphin Island, and the inhabitants were revived with pleasing anticipations of better times, especially as the great and good Bienville, whom they almost idolized, was made governor, with a salary of six thousand livres. He, who had been twenty years in this wild and inhospitable country, and who, amidst the deepest gloom and the greatest suffering of the colonists, had never once left them, but had sustained them with his fearless spirit, mighty arm and benevolent heart,—was eminently deserving the high post to which he was now elevated. The first thing he did was to seek a suitable place for the location of the principal settlement of the colony. He selected the site of New-Orleans, which had long been a favorite point with him, as we have seen. He proceeded there with fifty persons, carpenters and galley-slaves, whom he set to work to clear away the woods and erect houses. He next sent a detachment of fifty soldiers, under Chateaugné, to build a fort upon the bay of St. Joseph, situated between Pensacola and St. Marks,—which being completed, De Gousy was left there in command. From him, Captain Roka, a Spaniard, induced twenty-five soldiers to desert and flee to St. Augustine. The post of St. Joseph was soon abandoned by the French, who had no right to settle any part of Florida, and it was immediately occupied by the Spaniards.

CHAPTER VI.

1718 February 9

March

CHAPTER VI.

In the vessels which arrived on the 9th of February, came Major Boisbriant, who had paid a visit to France, and who was now commissioned a royal lieutenant, with a salary of three thousand livres. D'Hubert was retained as commissary-general with a salary of five thousand livres. These vessels were succeeded by another, having on board sixty passengers for the grant belonging to Paris Duvernet, which embraced the old Indian village of Pascagoula, where they were presently located. Three more ships arrived at Dauphin Island, which brought out Richebourg, now Chevalier of the order of St. Louis; Grandval, intended to act as major of Mobile; Lieutenants Noyan and Meleque, and Daniel, major of New-Orleans. At the same time there arrived forty commissioners, with Le Gac, sub-director; seventy persons for the grant of Houssays, and sixty for that of La Harpe.

1718 April 28

August 25

It was wisely determined to encourage agriculture, as the best means of increasing the wealth and importance of Louisiana; and for that purpose, extensive grants of land were made to the richest and most powerful persons of the kingdom of France. Four leagues square were ceded to the Scotch financier, Law, on the Arkansas river, where he was to settle fifteen hundred Germans, whom he was to protect by a small body of cavalry and infantry. The other persons to whom grants were made, likewise bound themselves to furnish a certain number of emigrants. But the experiment did not succeed. These great proprietors did send to Louisiana a few colonists, but a majority of them fell victims to the climate, and those who survived did not devote themselves to any useful occupation. Among the grants were several upon the Yazoo river, near Natchez, upon Red river, at Baton Rouge, and at other points upon the Mississippi river. Failing in the scheme to make the colony an agricultural country, by the importation of colonists who were to have settled upon these grants, the company next turned its attention to SLAVERY, as a means of effecting that which was so much desired.* CHAPTER VI.

The following regulation of the company fixed the price the colonists were to pay for the negroes, which they imported from Africa: "The company considers every negro of seventeen years of age, and over, without bodily defect, also every negress from fifteen to thirty years of age, as worth 'piece d'Inde.'†

Three little negroes, from eight to ten years old, are valued at two of the same coins.

Two negro children, over ten years of age, are valued at one 'piece d'Inde.'

One year's credit will be given to the old inhabitants for half the price. The other half must be paid immediately.

Those colonists who have been settled here two years are called old inhabitants.

The new settlers shall be entitled to one and two years credit."

In a despatch to the Minister, Bienville complained that 1718 September 25

* Histoire de la Louisiane, par Charles Gayarre, vol. 1, pp. 148-166. Journal Historique de l' Etablissement des Français a la Louisiaue, par Bernard de la Harpe, pp. 131–144.

† Piece d'Inde was 660 livres.

CHAPTER VI. the colonists recently sent to Louisiana, were not the kind desirable; that among them were to be found scarcely any carpenters or laborers, "notwithstanding laboring people employed in the country are paid ten or fifteen livres per day, which delays improvement and causes great expense to the company."

1719 April 19 Two vessels arrived from the mother country, and brought the startling intelligence that Spain and France had gone to war with each other. A council, composed of Bienville, D'Hubert, Larchebault and Le Gac, determined upon the necessity of immediately possessing the important post of Pensacola. None of the military officers were consulted in this movement, as they should have been, especially upon the plan of attack. Bienville assembled, at Mobile, some Canadians and four hundred Indians. His brother, Serigny,
May 13 sailed from Dauphin Island, with three men-of-war, on board of which he had embarked one hundred and fifty soldiers. Bienville embarked in a sloop, with twenty men, made the mouth of the Perdido, and went up that river to meet the Canadians and Indians, whom he had instructed to march across the country from Mobile, and whom he found already at the place of rendezvous. Placing himself at their head,
May 14 he marched to Pensacola. In the meantime, the fleet stood before that place, and at four o'clock, in the evening, Governor Matamora surrendered to the French, when he found that he was invested both by sea and land. According to the terms of the capitulation, Bienville embarked the Spanish garrison on board two of the men-of-war, with directions to

convey them safely to Havana. Arriving at that place, the governor of Cuba ordered all the French forces to be landed and imprisoned, seized the two men-of-war, manned them with sailors and soldiers, and sent them back to attack Pensacola. This was a most shameful disregard of the terms of the capitulation. The Spanish fleet, comprising the two French vessels and a Spanish man-of-war, with nine brigatines and eighteen hundred men, invested Pensacola, and the next day made their attack. Bienville had returned to Mobile, and had left his brother, Chateaugné, in command. Seeing the superior force of the enemy, fifty soldiers deserted from the fort and joined the Spaniards, which forced Chateaugné to capitulate. He was allowed to march out of the fort, with the honors of war and to be carried to old Spain. The store ship Dauphin was accidentally destroyed by fire, and the St. Louis was captured by the Spaniards. The commander of the Spanish squadron next turned his eyes to Dauphin Island, and presently sent thither two well manned brigantines. To the captain of the French ship, Phillippe, which lay at anchor at Dauphin Island, he sent a summons to surrender, but the captain referred the messenger to Serigny, who commanded the fort; the latter declined to surrender the island. During the night the two brigantines entered the bay of Mobile, and half way between Dauphin Island and the town of Mobile, landed thirty-five men to burn and plunder the inhabitants. While they were here destroying the improvements of a settler, they were suddenly attacked by a detachment of Canadians and Indians, whom

1719 August 6

CHAPTER VI. Bienville had hastened to send from Mobile, to support his brother, Serigny. Five Spaniards were slain, whose scalps the Indians immediately secured; six were drowned in the endeavour to reach the brigantines, while eighteen were made prisoners; among the latter were some of the French soldiers, who had deserted from Chateaugné, and who were now promptly beheaded for their treason.* Two days afterwards the remainder of the Spanish squadron stood before
1719 August 19 Dauphin Island, and continued for four days to cannonade the Philippe and the town. Serigny, with one hundred and sixty soldiers and two hundred Indians, aided by the gallant officers and men of the Philippe, which was anchored within pistol shot of the fort, succeeded in repulsing the Spaniards,
August 26 who sustained considerable loss. The ships of the enemy then set sail for Pensacola.

Three ships of the French line, under the command of
September 2 Champmeslin, convoying two of the company's ships, arrived off Dauphin Island, direct from France. The two Spanish brigantines, which were cruising in the bay, between this island and Mobile, escaped to sea and sailed to Pensacola, as soon as the French fleet was discovered. Bienville and Serigny repaired on board of the ship of Champmeslin, where was presently convened a council, composed of all the sea captains

* La Harpe states (page 155,) that eighteen French deserters, who were made prisoners, were bound by the Indians and carried to Bienville, at Mobile, who caused seventeen of them to be decapitated, and that the remaining one was hung on Dauphin Island.

CHAPTER VI.

in port, who decided to capture the Spanish squadron and to take the Fort of Pensacola. Time was allowed the vessels to discharge their freight and to take in wood and water, and Bienville to assemble the savages and prepare them for the expedition. When all things were ready, the Philippe and the Union, vessels belonging to the company, were joined to the squadron, together with two hundred and fifty of the new troops, lately arrived, while Bienville, with the soldiers and volunteers, sailed in sloops to the river Perdido, where he was joined by five hundred Indians, under the command of Langueville, who had marched with them from Mobile. From this point Bienville sent a detachment of French and Indians to invest the principal fort at Pensacola, to prevent all egress from it, and to harrass the enemy as much as possible. In the meantime, Champmeslin entered the harbor of Pensacola, and, after a conflict of two hours duration, captured four ships and six brigantines, which were anchored before St. Rosa, and reduced the small fort, situated at the point of that island. Bienville, having marched across the country from the Perdido, had advanced in the rear of the town with his whole force. He made a resolute attack upon the fort, which was surrendered two hours after the victory at St. Rosa's Island. The Indians fought with great courage, often attempting to pull up the palisades of the fort. The plunder was divided among them, but they were prohibited, by Bienville, from taking any scalps. The pillage being ended, Champmeslin returned the sword which Don Alphonzo, commander of the Spanish fleet, had presented to him as his conqueror, assuring him that he

1719 September 17

CHAPTER VI. was worthy of wearing it. But Matamora, the governor of Pensacola, who had acted with so much perfidy towards the French victors who conveyed him to Havana, was suffered to be disarmed by a common sailor, and was severely reproached for his conduct. The loss of the French in these engagements was only six men; that of the Spaniards was much greater. Champmeslin despatched the St. Louis, one of the Spanish vessels, to Havana, with three hundred and sixty of the prisoners. The commander was instructed to demand an exchange of the French prisoners, at the head of whom was Chateaugné, who had not been carried to Spain, according to the capitulation, but had been closely confined in Moro Castle.

1719 September 18 A Spanish brigantine from Havana, laden with corn flour, and brandy for the garrison, entered the bay of Pensacola, supposing the fleet to belong to Spain, into whose hands, it was now believed, the whole of Louisiana had fallen, and was immediately captured by the French squadron. On the same day, forty-seven French deserters were tried, twelve of whom were hung at the yard-arms of the Count de Toulouse, and the remainder condemned to serve the company as galley-slaves. Thus ended the expedition against Pensacola, the command of which was given to DeLisle, a lieutenant of the navy.

1719 Since the commencement of this year, vessels from France had constantly brought over to Louisiana liberal supplies of provisions, merchandise, and not unfrequently distinguished persons and emigrants, thus adding to the number and giving character to her population, and causing her slowly to emerge from the supineness and insignificance of former times. For this reason, and also on account of the war with Spain, it became necessary to re-organize the colonial government in several respects. A royal ordinance decreed that a Supreme Council should be composed of those directors who were residents in the colony, the governor, the two royal lieutenants, four councillors, an attorney-general, and a secretary. Three members for civil affairs, and five for criminal cases, could constitute a quorum. Its jurisdiction was to be the highest in the colony, and its sessions were to be monthly. The former council had been the only tribunal in the colony, but now it was decided to establish inferior courts, of which the directors of the company, or their agents, were to be judges, in the places where they resided. These, with two respectable citizens of the neighborhood, were to have cognizance of civil business. They were required, in criminal cases, to add four more citizens to their number. An appeal from their decisions could be had to the Supreme Council,—the members of which were not allowed to charge for their final opinions.

Bienville, the governor, D'Hubert, commissary-general and first councillor, Boisbriant and Chateaugné, royal lieutenants, L'Archambault, Villardo and Legas, other councillors, Cartier de Baune, the attorney general, and Couture, secretary, composed the first Supreme Council, which met under the auspices of the Western or India Company. Although the governor occupied the place of honor in this body, D'Hubert, the first councillor, was the real president, who took the vote, pro-

CHAPTER VI. nounced judgment, affixed the public seals, and filled the station of chief judge.

1719 Bienville was opposed in his long cherished desire of removing the government to the site of New-Orleans, by D'Hubert and the Directors, who dreaded the inundations of the Mississippi, and who contended that the colony was not in a situation to oppose levees to the floods at that point. D'Hubert suggested the location of Natchez; but as he owned large grants there, his motives were suspected. It was decided to adopt the views of L'Archambault, Villardo and Legas, who inclined more towards commerce than agriculture, and who recommended that a new establishment should be formed east of the bay of Biloxi, which should be called New Biloxi. A detachment was sent there to build barracks and houses.

The cultivation of rice, indigo and tobacco had already occupied the attention of the colonists to some extent, who found the lands extremely productive for those profitable plants. But the climate was too warm and unhealthy for European labor, and hence one thousand of the *Children of the Sun*, from Africa, had been introduced into the colony, and from that moment Louisiana began to prosper. But many things yet impeded its advancement. Among other impediments, the company, to secure the exclusive com-
November 26 merce of Louisiana, issued an edict forbiding any vessel to enter the colony under penalty of confiscation. This was
1720 January followed up by a proclamation, regulating the price of merchandize, which the colonists were compelled to buy at the company's ware-houses, and *no where else*. It also arbitrarily

fixed the price which the colonists were to receive for their products, skins, and for every thing which they had for sale.* Gayarre says—" At the present day, we can hardly discover how the whites, whom the company transported from Europe, differed from the blacks, who were bought from Africa, at least as to their relation to the company; for these two classes of men belonged both to one master—the all-powerful company!"

The Royal Squadron intended to protect the commerce of Louisiana, arrived with two hundred and thirty passengers, 1720 February 28
among whom were several girls, and a considerable quantity of provisions and merchandize. Several months elapsed when two vessels of the Royal Navy bore the intelligence, June 8
that a treaty of peace had been concluded with Spain. These were succeeded by three other vessels of war, which July 1
anchored at Dauphin Island, and which brought with them a contagious malady, contracted at St. Domingo, which killed many of the crew, and filled their bodies, as it was ascertained by *post mortem* examination, with horrible worms! At the same time, the ship Hercules came with one hundred and twenty negroes from Guinea, and a brigantine from Havana,

* Goods were to be obtained in the company's stores at Mobile, Dauphin Island, and Pensacola. To these prices, an advance of five per cent. was to be added on goods delivered at New-Orleans, ten at Natchez, thirteen at the Yazoos, twenty at Natchitoches, and fifty at the Illinois and on the Missouri. The produce of the country was to be received in the company's ware-houses in New-Orleans, Biloxi, Ship Island and Mobile.—Martin's Louisiana, vol. 1, pp. 218-219.

CHAPTER VI. arrived at Mobile with Chateaugné and others, who had been made prisoners at Pensacola, and who were now released in pursuance of the treaty of peace.

So long as the French colony of Louisiana remained in a feeble and thriftless condition, the English of Carolina were content only to annoy it occasionally; but now that it gave signs of durable vitality, under the auspices of a powerful company, they began to oppose it with the fiercest hostility. Rivalry in trade, together with national jealousy, fomented quarrels, and caused blood to flow between the *Coureurs de bois* and the English. The French traders also met the latter in all parts of the Indian nations, within the limits of the present states of Alabama and Mississippi. Each contended for the patronage of the savages, and each endeavored to expell the other from those situations, where they had established themselves. The Carolina traders, many of whom had quartered themselves in the Chickasaw towns, arrayed that tribe in war against the French, and they committed the first act of hostility, by the murder of Serigny, a French officer, whom Bienville had posted among them to cultivate their friendship. This war greatly embarrassed Bienville, who, with difficulty, brought to his assistance the
1720 July larger body of the Choctaws. At this time, the forces of the colony had been augmented to twenty companies, of fifty men each, who were required to defend the province of Louisiana, the inhabitants of which were scattered from Fort Toulouse, upon the Coosa, to La Harpe's station, upon Red river. The Alabamas could barely be kept neutral, for they

complained that their peltries brought lower prices at the French ports, than at those of the English, and that the goods which they received for them, were also held at a dearer rate. CHAPTER VI.

Vessels with emigrants and provisions, continued to cast their anchors upon the sands of Mobile Bay. A store ship brought out two hundred and sixty persons for the grant of St. Catherine, in the vicinity of Natchez. Another arrived at Ship Island with two hundred and forty emigrants, for the grant of Louvre, and was succeeded by still another, on board of which was de L'Orme, new director-general, with a salary of five thousaud livres, together with other vessels laden with provisions, laborers and merchandize. 1720 August September

In the meantime, the public houses had been completed at New Biloxi, and thither the government of Louisiana was, unwisely, transferred. It had remained at old and new Mobile, since January, 1702, but during this trying period, of eighteen years, the governors occasionally resided at Dauphin Island. December 20

A vessel, belonging to the company, furled her sails in the splendid bay of Mobile, and disembarked three hundred colonists, for the grant of Madame Chaumont, at Pascagoula, whom the colonial government soon placed there, but whom they forbade to enter into any branch of trade, such as that which would result from the culture of hemp, flax, and the vine, or which would compete with the commerce of the company. A ship arrived with twenty-five girls, taken from a house of correction, in Paris, called the Saltpetriere. They 1721 January 3 January 9 January 5

CHAPTER VI. had been sent over in consequence of the great complaints made to the Minister, by various officers of the colony, on account of the want of wives, and they had been confided, by the directors in France, to sister Gertrude, and, under her, to sisters Louise and Bergere, who were authorised to conduct to Louisiana, "such girls as were willing to go thither and remain under the care of sister Gertrude, until they shall marry, which they must not do without her consent." The directors or the Minister in sending these prostitutes to Mobile, where they soon took up their abode, did not act consistently with a previous ordinance, which they had passed, that "hereafter, no more vagabonds shall be sent to Louisiana, but that any French and foreign families and laborers might go." Much contention now arose between the stockholders and the directors. The latter were reproached for their enormous outlays, and for the appointment of persons to govern the colonies, who appeared to have their exclusive interest to subserve; and Bienville was written to, and informed that the Regent complained that his services were not effectual. But to arouse all his exertions, the same letter promised the governor the rank of Brigadier, with the ribbon of St. Louis, if his future conduct should merit them.

1721 March 17 The Africaine, a ship of war, arrived at Mobile, with one hundred and twenty negroes, out of the number of two hundred and twenty-four, who had embarked at Guinea. She

March 23 was succeeded by the Maire, with three hundred and thirty-eight more, who were, for the present, all quartered at Mobile, and where they remained in a state bordering upcn starvation, from the famine which now universally prevailed in the colony. The Neride also came with two hundred and thirty-eight Africans, the remainder of three hundred and fifty, who sailed from Angola. She had put to sea, with the frigate Charles, laden with negroes, which took fire and was consumed, more than sixty leagues from land, a large majority of her crew perishing in the flames. The whites escaped in the boats, with a few of the Africans, but tossed for many days at the mercy of the waves, and suffering for subsistance, the unhappy negroes were killed, one after another, for food! The present population of France are *abolitionists*, and denounce the Southern States for their mild and beneficial system of domestic slavery, and yet their ancestors, in the manner we have described, put these slaves into our possession. So did England with her men-of-war, at the same period, plant her American colonies with slaves, also captured in Africa. The Puritan fathers of New England received them, paid for them, put them to hard labor, sold and re-sold them for many years, and yet their descendants profess to be shocked at the sight of a Southern slaveholder, and denounce Southern slavery as a "damning sin before God!"

With two hundred German emigrants, who were sent over to occupy the grant of Law upon the Arkansas river, came also a woman, whose adventures in Europe and America are related in the histories of that period. She was believed to be the wife of the Czarowitz Alexis Petrowitz, son of Peter the Great, Emperor of all the Russias. Her resemblance to that Princess was so striking, as to deceive those who knew the

1721 March

CHAPTER VI.

latter intimately. The story ran, that to escape the brutal treatment of the Prince, her husband, she pretended to die, and was actually entombed, but when taken from the tomb in a few hours afterwards, put herself beyond the reach of persecution, by flying to a foreign land. The Chevalier d'Aubont, one of the officers of the Mobile garrison, who had been at St. Petersburg, had seen the Princess, and had heard of her strange escape, now believed that this woman who was then in Mobile, was the beautiful and accomplished lady herself. He was sure he recognized her beneath the incognito which she had assumed, and which she appeared desirous to retain.

The Chevalier married her, and after a long residence in Louisiana, most of which was passed in Mobile, she followed him to France, and thence to the Island of Bourbon, whither he was sent with the rank of Major. In 1765, she became a widow, and went to Paris with a daughter born in Mobile. In 1771, her mysterious and romantic life was terminated in the midst of the most abject poverty !*

* Judge Martin, in his history of Louisiana. vol. 1, pp. 231–232, states, that this woman was an impostor, and that she imposed on the credulity of the Chevalier d'Aubout and many others; that she had once been attached to the wardrobe of the Princess whom she assumed to represent; and that a few years before the declaration of American Independence, a similar imposition was practiced upon the people of the Southern British Provinces, by a female, driven by her misconduct from the post of maid of honor, to Princess Matilda, sister of George III. She was convicted at Old Baily, and transported to Maryland. Before the expiration of her time, she effected her escape, travelled

An ordinance decreed that the council should meet daily at New Biloxi; that merchandize should be sold at that place, Mobile, and New-Orleans, at fifty per cent. profit on the manufacture of France, seventy per cent. among the Natchez and Yazoos, one hundred per cent. among the Arkansas, and fifty per cent. among the Alabamas and Muscogees, on account of the proximity of Fort Toulouse to the English influence, with which the French company were anxious successfully to compete. Another ordinance declared that negroes should be sold to the inhabitants at the price of the "piece de Inde," or six hundred and sixty livres,* in three annual instalments, to be paid in tobacco or rice. If, after the second year, the debtor failed to pay, the company could take the negro if not paid for during the third year. If the effects of the debtor failed to discharge the whole debt, the company could then take his body. It also declared that leaf tobacco delivered at the warehouses of New Biloxi, New-Orleans and Mobile, should command the price of twenty livres per quintal; rice, twelve livres per quintal; wine, one hundred and twenty livres a hogshead; and a quarter of brandy, the same price. It also declared that Louisiana should, hereafter, be formed into nine divisions: New-Orleans,

CHAPTER VI. 1721 September 5

September 27

through the provinces of Virginia and the Carolinas, personating the princess, and levying contributions upon the credulity of the inhabitants. She was at length arrested in Charleston, prosecuted and publicly whipped.

* Equal to one hundred and seventy-six dollars.

CHAPTER VI. Biloxi, Mobile, Alabama, Yazoo, Natchitoches, Arkansas, and Illinois; that in the chief town of each there should be a commandant and a judge, from whose decisions an appeal could be had to the supreme council of New Biloxi.

STATE OF THE COLONY AT THE CLOSE OF 1721.

"In the vessels which the India Company has sent thither from the 25th October, 1717, to May, 1721, there have emigrated, on the forty-three belonging to it, and in the squadron of M. de Saunjor, - - - - - - 7020
These, with the 400 who were already there, - 400

7420

Of this number those who have died, deserted, or returned to France, - - - - - - 2000

5420

To them the number of colonists is added, to which may be set down about 600 negroes."

From this statement it appears that the colony of Louisiana had really begun to prosper, but many impediments still retarded its more rapid advance, among which may be enumerated its expenses, which, for the year 1721, amounted to four hundred and seventy-four thousand, two hundred and seventy-four livres.
1722 March 12 The company, too, issued an ordinance prohibiting the inhabitants from selling their negroes to the Spaniards, or to other foreigners, or taking them out of the colony, under a severe penalty, besides their confiscation.

April 20 Bienville, writing from Mobile, acquainted the Minister with the difficulty of discharging the cargoes of vessels upon the low shores of New Biloxi, and again brought to his consideration the superior advantages of New-Orleans, for the capital of the colony. One more councillor was added to the supreme council, which, now, consisted of Brusle, Fazende, Perry, Guilhet and Masclary. Two hundred and fifty Germans, commanded by the Chevalier D'Arensbourg, a Swedish officer, arrived at Mobile, with whom came Marigny de Mandaville, who had obtained, in France, the Cross of St. Louis and the command of Fort Conde, in Mobile. This was by far the best fort in the colony, and was now rapidly drawing to a state of completion; it was built of brick, with four bastions, and a great many casements for soldiers.* The vessel which brought over these Germans, bore the distressing news that the great royal bank, which Law, the Scotch financier, under the auspices of the Duke of Orleans, had established in France, had utterly failed; that Law had left the country in disgrace, and that the people whom he had induced to take stock, found it worthless and themselves ruined. All Paris was in a ferment, and no one could anticipate an end to the long train of commercial evils which the scheming ability of this Scotchman had engendered.

CHAPTER VI.

1722 June 4

* Mr. E. T. Wood, of Mobile, who wrote a history of that place, embodied in a directory, which he published, says that when Fort Conde (which was also called Fort Charlotte by the British after they took possession of it,) was pulled down by the Americans some years after the place fell into their hands, that the corner-stone was found with the date of 1717, distinctly engraved upon it.

CHAPTER VI. The company which had charge of Louisiana, and indeed the chief inhabitants of the province, were soon made to feel the explosion of this once powerful and popular institution. Louisiana, herself, was deeply involved in the failure, and her inhabitants now feared that the government of France would abandon them. But some supplies continued to arrive, in spite of the panic which pervaded the mother country. Duvergier, who had been appointed director-gene-
1722 July 15 ral and commander of the marine, disembarked at Pensacola, bearing the Cross of St. Louis for Boisbriant, St. Dennis and Chateaugné.

The failure of the Royal Bank of France, and the distress which it produced in all parts of that kingdom, caused Louisiana, for a time, to be so neglected, that the inhabitants became destitute of provisions. The officers were obliged to dismiss the garrisons of Mobile and Biloxi, and send them to the Choctaw nation to procure subsistence among the Indians, while many of the colonists abandoned their homes and betook themselves to the sea-side to procure a scanty living upon fish and oysters. It was even worse at some of the more distant posts, particularly at Fort Toulouse, upon the Coosa, now in Alabama. There, the soldiers were tortured by famine, and corrupted by some British traders, who induced them to desert and fly to Charleston. The command consisted of a captain, a lieutenant, an ensign, a corporal and twenty-six soldiers. When the latter had perfected their mutiny, the
August planning of which had occupied several days, they rose upon the officers, one morning, about breakfast. Capt. Marchand was

instantly slain. Lieutenant Villemont and Ensign Paque made their escape through a port-hole of one of the bastions, and fled to the Hickory Ground, a town of Creek Indians, three miles above, on the east bank of the Coosa, and embracing the lower suburbs of the modern city of Wetumpka. Here Villemont made irresistible appeals to the warriors to march against the mutineers. He, at the same time, despatched Paque across the river to the town of Coosawda, where then lived the great Chief, Big Morter, whom the ensign succeeded in enlisting in the cause of the King. In the meantime, the mutineers, having killed the captain, intimidated the corporal, who now joined them in a general pillage of the fort. They appropriated to themselves the money and clothing of the officers, leaving only the sacred wardrobe of the priest, a Jesuit father, whom they did not molest. The magazine, constructed of brick, was forced open, and arms and ammunition taken from it.* The store-room was plundered of its contents, consisting of a very limited supply of flour and meat. The mutineers, after partaking of a hearty repast, marched off to the Red Warrior's Bluff,† where they crossed the Tallapoosa and took up the line of march for Charleston. Villemont, with the Indian force which he had speedily raised, marched against them. A battle ensued at the ford of Line

* Some of the brick of this magazine are yet to be seen lying about the ruins of old Fort Toulouse, now called old Fort Jackson, and I have several of them in my house, taken from that place.

† The Red Warrior's Bluff of that day, is the present Grey's Ferry.

CHAPTER VI. 1722 August Creek, which now divides the modern counties of Montgomery and Macon. Sixteen of the deserters were slain. They all fought with the desperation of tigers.* The others, except two who escaped, were taken prisoners, and Villemont, who was wounded in the action, marched with them back to Fort Toulouse. Here, the fort was found to be in a very solitary condition, being inhabited only by the Jesuit father, who had resolved to remain until he could get a favorable opportunity of going to Mobile, not believing that the brave and indefatigable Villemont could subdue the deserters; the body of the unfortunate Captain Marchand had been already interred by him and some Indians. Villemont, the next day, obtained some canoes and placed the deserters in them, in charge of an Indian guard, at the head of which was Ensign Paque, who conveyed them to Mobile, where September they were, shortly afterwards, executed. Villemont and the priest were solitary inmates of Fort Toulouse for several months, until another garrison was sent up the river. The lieutenant had, however, many Indian warriors lying around the fort, who were ready to aid him, if he had been attacked by the English, who were anxious to occupy this post.†

* The bones of these sixteen Frenchmen lay, for many years, very near the house which Walter B. Lucas afterwards erected, and where he, for a long time, kept entertainment.

† The revolt of the garrison of Fort Toulouse, upon the Coosa, is mentioned by Gayarre, in his History of Louisiana, vol. 1, p. 190; by La Harpe, p. 261; by Judge Martin, vol. 2, p. 239; but I have derived the chief facts from Indian traditions handed down by General Alexander

Fortunately, a vessel arrived with provisions for the King's troops. She brought the news that the Regent had entrusted the affairs of the colony to the management of three commissioners: Ferrand, Faget and Machinet. A detailed account of a great hurricane which swept along the coast of Louisiana, of the desertion of soldiers, sailors and workmen, and a recommendation to allow free passage to all who might choose to return to France, as a remedy for desertions generally, formed the subjects of a communication addressed by De l'Orme to the Minister. While the distressing situation of the colony rendered the offices of the three commissioners by no means sinecures, embarrassments were further produced by a war which the Natchez had begun, and the worthlessness of the paper money hitherto used in the colony, to remedy which, *cards* were substituted, after the notes were suppressed. One Michel, of Mobile, was the person appointed to engrave these cards.

CHAPTER VI. 1722 September 28 ... October 30

The new commissioners who had succeeded to the directorship of the company, readily acceded to the long cherished wish of Bienville, to remove the seat of government to New-Orleans, and it was accordingly established at that place.*

1723

McGillivray, a very great Indian Chief of mixed blood, who was the grandson of the unfortunate Captain Marchand, who was killed upon this occasion.

* Histoire de la Louisiane, par Charles Gayarre, vol. 1, pp. 166–193. Journal Historique de l'Etablissement des Français a la Louisiane, par Bernard de la Harpe, pp. 144–289.—Martin's History of Louisiana, vol. 1, pp. 218–244.

CHAPTER VI. The population of New-Orleans at that period, numbered only two hundred souls, who occupied a hundred huts and cabins!

The commissioners of the company, in a new code of regulations, declared that negroes should hereafter be sold at six hundred and seventy-six livres,* payable in one, two or three years, either in rice or tobacco. The province was divided into nine districts, civil and military, as follows: Alabama, Mobile, Biloxi, New-Orleans, Natchez, Yazoo, Illinois, Wabash, Arkansas, and Natchitoches. There was a commandant and a judge appointed for each of these districts. Three great ecclesiastical districts were also formed. The first was entrusted to the Capuchins, and extended from the mouth of the Mississippi river to Illinois. The bare-footed Carmelites were stationed at Fort Toulouse, upon the Coosa river, at Mobile and at Biloxi, while the Jesuits labored upon the Wabash and Illinois. Churches and chapels were ordered to be constructed, for many of the colonists had been forced to worship in the open air, around crosses, the bottom parts of which were buried in the ground!

Bienville restored Pensacola to the Spaniards in pursuance of orders from his government; for Spain and France had
1723 January 1. concluded a peace. In a despatch to the Minister, he stated that his allies,—the Choctaws,—had destroyed three towns of the Chickasaws, and had brought to him one hundred prisoners and four hundred scalps! Bienville communicated this intelligence with much apparent *gusto*, accompanied with the

* Equal to one hundred and sixty-nine dollars.

remark that "this important result was obtained without risking the life of a single Frenchman." CHAPTER VI.

Although the colonists often existed in a state of penury and want, they did not abandon their passion for *gambling*, which was carried to such an extent that the government issued an ordinance against all games of chance. An ordinance was also promulgated against the trade which many of the colonists were illicitly conducting with the Natchez Indians. The month of September terminated with a dreadful tornado, which prostrated the church, the hospital, and thirty houses in New-Orleans; destroyed the crops upon the Mobile and Pearl rivers; dismantled the shipping in the different ports, and left the whole colony in a condition of wretchedness and famine. Added to all this, a whole company of Swiss infantry, which had embarked at Biloxi for New-Orleans, rose upon the captain of the vessel and compelled him to carry them to Charleston. Yet, in the midst of all these calamities, the indefatigable Bienville departed from New-Orleans with seven 1723 October
hundred men to punish the Natchez, who had recently killed several Frenchmen. He returned after having terminated the second war with them, by procuring the heads of the principal offenders. Notwithstanding the important services which this great man was continuing to render the colony, his relentless enemies sought every opportunity to make him odious to the ruling powers of France. Aspersed in despatches, which were speedily borne across the ocean, he was at the same moment insulted at home by libellous placards in the streets. At 1724 February 16
length he received orders to sail for France, to answer the

CHAPTER VI. charges against him, leaving the command to Boisbriant until his return.

1724 March But before Bienville embarked upon the broad Atlantic, he issued the celebrated "BLACK CODE," in the name of the King. It declared that all Jews should leave the colony; that all slaves should be instructed in the Roman Catholic religion; that no other religion should be tolerated in the colony; that if the owners of negroes were not true Catholics, their slaves should be confiscated; and that the white inhabitants should not enter into marital relations with negroes, nor live with them in a state of concubinage.

The "Black Code" contained many other articles in relation to the government of slaves,—some of which were precisely like those now in force in the South-western States of the present confederacy. The year 1724 was remarkable for arbitrary edicts; but there was one which was beneficial. The inhabitants had become so accustomed to rely upon France for all the necessaries of subsistence, that valuable cattle, sent to Louisiana for purposes of propagation, were always killed and devoured. An ordinance was issued by the King, at the request of the Superior Council, punishing with *death* every person who should intentionally kill or severely wound any horse or horned animal which did not belong to him.

De la Chaise, nephew of the famous father of that name,
1725 who was the confessor of Louis XIV., presided over the council, which was now held monthly in the town of New-Orleans.

But to return to Bienville. That brave man appeared at

Paris, after a prosperous voyage, and submitted an eloquent memoir to the King, in justification of his official conduct. It also contained a history of the services to which he had, from the commencement of the colonial establishment, devoted a period of twenty-five years. But, in despite of this true exposition of his arduous labors spent in the insalubrious forests of America, among savages and reptiles, and in spite of the exertions made by his friends, both in France and Louisiana, to re-establish him in the confidence of the King, he was removed from office, and Perrier nominated Governor of Louisiana. The government did not stop here. Chateaugné, the brother of Bienville, lost the post of royal lieutenant, while two nephews of Bienville, named Noyan, one a captain and the other an ensign, were cashiered without any just cause. Thus the influence of Bienville was overthrown in Louisiana. In the meantime, the new governor arrived at New-Orleans.

1726 August 9

Governor Perrier, in a despatch to the Minister, employed this language in reference to the encroachments of the English of South-Carolina:—"The English continue to urge their commerce into the very heart of the province. Sixty or seventy horses, laden with merchandize, have passed into the country of the Chickasaws, to which nation I have given orders to plunder the English of their goods, promising to recompense them by a present. As yet I have heard nothing from that quarter. It appears that a league was formed among all the Indian nations of their neighborhood, to attack the Spanish settlements. Whereupon the Governor of Pensacola requested assistance from me. Having no news from

1727

CHAPTER VI. Europe, I thought it was for our interest not to have the English so near us, and, in consequence, informed the Tallapoosas,* who were before Pensacola, that if they did not immediately retire, I should attack them with those nations who were friendly to us. I also gave notice to the Alabamas, that if they attacked the Spaniards, who were our friends, I should be compelled to assist the latter. But I should have taken care not to have interfered with the natives who were friendly to us, in order that I might not commit myself with regard to the English. This had a good effect. The governor thanked me, informing me that war was declared in Europe. Notwithstanding, I shall indirectly assist the Spanish until I receive other orders from your highness, at the same time taking the liberty to represent that our sole effort should be to prevent the English from approaching us.

"I have caused all the nations, from the Arkansas to the mouth of the river, to make peace with each other. There remain at variance only the Choctaws and Chickasaws, who
1727 have a discussion concerning a Chief of the latter nation, who was killed by the former. I shall go to Mobile to settle their affairs, and shall take measures, with them, to prevent the English from entering our territory during the ensuing year, and by degrees to abolish the custom which they have formed, of trading for all the deer-skins obtained by the Indians, in order that the latter may not be obliged to trade with the English to get rid of them."

* Meaning the Creeks, who lived upon the Tallapoosa river.

CHAPTER VI. 1728 February

A vessel belonging to the company arrived with quite a number of young girls, who, unlike many others who had been sent to Louisiana, had not been taken from the houses of correction. They were each provided with a little chest, containing articles of apparel, and from this circumstance they were called girls *de la cassette*—girls of the chest. They were placed under the surveillance of the Ursuline nuns until they could be disposed of by marriage.*

* Histoire de la Louisiane, par Charles Gayarre, vol. 1, pp. 193–235.

CHAPTER VII.

TERRIBLE MASSACRE AT NATCHEZ.

CHAPTER VII. THE colony of Louisiana was now in a flourishing condition; its fields were cultivated by more than two thousand
1728 negroes; cotton, indigo, tobacco and grain were produced; skins and furs of all descriptions were obtained in a traffic
1729 with the Indians; and lumber was extensively exported to the West India islands. The province was protected by eight hundred troops of the line; but the bloody massacre of the French population of Fort Rosalie, at the Natchez, arrested these rapid strides of prosperity, and shrouded all things in sadness and gloom. Our library contains many accounts of this horrible affair, which harmonize very well with each other; but in reference to the causes which led to it, more particularly, we propose to introduce the statement of Le Page DuPratz, who was residing in Louisiana at the time. We give his account, in his own faithful style:

"Chopart had been commandant of the post of the Natchez, from which he was removed on account of some act of injustice. Governor Perrier, but lately arrived, suffered himself to be prepossessed in his favor, on his telling him that he had commanded that post with applause, and thus he obtained the command from Pèrrier, who was unacquainted with his character. This new commandant, on taking possession of his post, projected the forming of one of the most eminent settlements of the whole colony. For this purpose he examined all the grounds unoccupied by the French, but could not find any thing that came up to the grandeur of his views. Nothing but the village of the White Apple, a square league, at least, in extent, could give him satisfaction, and there he resolved immediately to settle. This ground was distant from the fort about two leagues.* Conceited with the beauty of his project, the commandant sent for the Sun of that village, to come to the fort; upon his arrival, he told him, without ceremony, that he must look out for another ground to build his village on, as he, himself, resolved, as soon as possible, to build on the village of the Apple, and that he must directly close the huts and retire somewhere else. The better to cover his design, he gave out that it was necessary for the French to settle on the banks of the rivulet, where stood the great village and the abode of the Grand Sun. The commandant, doubtless,

*"The site of the White Apple village was about twelve miles south of the present city of Natchez, near the mouth of second creek, and three miles east of the Mississippi. The site was occupied by the plantation of Col. Anthony Hutchens, an early emigrant to Florida. All vestiges of Indian industry have disappeared, except some mounds in the vicinity."—Monette's History of the Valley of the Mississippi, vol. 1, p. 258.

CHAPTER VII. supposed that he was speaking to a slave, whom we may command in a tone of absolute authority. But he knew not that the natives of Louisiana are such enemies to a state of slavery, that they prefer death itself; above all, the Suns, accustomed to govern despotically, have still a greater aversion to it.

* * * * * *

Spring of 1729 "The Sun of the Apple made answer, that his ancestors had lived in that village for as many years as there were hairs in his double cue, and, therefore, it was good they should continue there. Scarce had the interpreter explained this answer to the commandant, when the latter fell into a passion and, threateningly, told the Sun, that if he did not quit his village, in a few days, he might repent it. The Sun replied: 'When the French came to ask us for land, to settle on, they told us there was land enough still unoccupied for them, and that the same sun would enlighten them all, and all would walk in the same path.' He wanted to proceed further, in justification of what he alleged, but the commandant, in a passion, said he was resolved to be obeyed. The Sun, without discovering any emotion or passion, then withdrew, only observing that he was going to assemble the old men of his village to hold a council upon the affair.

* * * * * *

"In this council it was resolved to represent to the commandant, that the corn of all the people of their village was already shot a little out of the earth, and that all the hens were laying their eggs. That if they quitted their village

CHAPTER VII.

now, the chickens and corn would be lost both to the French and to themselves. * * * * The commandant turned a deaf ear to these views, and threatened to chastise the Chiefs if they did not comply with his orders, in a very short time, which he named. The Sun reported this answer to his council, who debated the question. But the policy of the old men was, that they should be allowed to stay in their village until harvest, and until they had time to dry their corn and shake out the grain. In consideration of this privilege, they each proposed to pay the commandant, in so many moons, a basket of corn and a fowl. * * * * The cupidity of the commandant made him accept the proposition with joy, and blinded him with regard to the consequences of his tyranny. He, however, pretended that he agreed to the offer out of favor, to do a pleasure to a nation so beloved, and who had ever been good friends of the French. The Sun appeared highly satisfied to have obtained a delay sufficient for taking the precautions necessary to the security of the nation, for he was by no means the dupe of the feigned benevolence of the commander.

Summer of 1729

"The Sun, upon his return, again caused the council to be assembled. * * * * He stated to them that it was necessary to avail themselves of this time, in order to withdraw themselves from this proposed payment and tyrannic domination of the French, who grew dangerous in proportion as they multiplied. That the Natchez ought to remember the war made upon them, in violation of the peace concluded between them. That this war, having been made upon their

CHAPTER VII.

village alone, they ought to consider of the surest means to take a just and bloody vengeance. That this enterprise being of the utmost importance, it called for much secrecy, for solid measures, and for much policy. That it was proper to cajole the French chief more than ever, and that the affair required reflection before it was proposed to the GRAND SUN.

"In the meantime, the old men had come to the determination, not only to revenge themselves, but to engage in the entire destruction of all the French in the province. When, therefore, the council again met, the most venerable man rose and delivered the following speech:

"'We have a long time been sensible that the neighborhood of the French is a greater prejudice than a benefit to us. We,

Summer of 1729

who are old, see this—the young see it not. The wares of the French yield pleasure to the youth, but to what purpose is it, except to debauch the young women, and taint the blood of the nation, and make them vain and idle? The young men are in the same condition—they must work themselves to death to maintain their families and please their children. Before the French came among us, WE WERE MEN, content with what we had, and walked with boldness every path. Now we go groping about, afraid of meeting briars. We walk like slaves, which we shall soon be, since the French already treat us as if we were such. When they are sufficiently strong, they will no longer dissemble. For the least fault of our young people, they will then tie them to a post and whip them. Have they not already done so to one of our young men, and is not death preferable to slavery? What wait we for? Shall we suffer the French to multiply till we are no longer in a condition to oppose them? What will the other nations say of the Natchez, who are admitted to be the greatest of all the Red men? Let us set ourselves at liberty. * * * * From this very day let our women get provisions ready, without telling them the reason. Go and carry the pipe of peace to all the nations of this country. Tell them that the French, being stronger here than elsewhere, enslave us the more; but when they spread out, they will treat all nations in like manner. That it is their interest to join us to prevent so great a misfortune. That they have only to join us, to cut off the French to a man, in one day and in one hour!'"

Here the speaker continued his address, and exhorted them to be prepared to fall upon the French at nine o'clock, on the morning of the day when they were to deliver to the commandant the corn and chickens, and that the warriors were to carry with them their arms, as if going to hunt. They unanimously approved of his views, and pledged themselves to carry them out. DuPratz continues:—"Notwithstanding the profound secrecy observed by the Natchez, the council held by the Suns and aged nobles gave the people great uneasiness, unable, as they were, to penetrate into the matter. The female Suns had alone, in this nation, the right to demand why they were kept in the dark in this affair. The young grand female Sun was a princess scarce eighteen. None but the Stung Arm, a woman of great wit, and no less sensible of it, could be offended that nothing was disclosed to her. In effect,

Fall of 1729

CHAPTER VII.

she made known to her son her displeasure at this reserve with respect to herself. He replied that the several deputations were made in order to renew their good intelligence with the other nations, to whom they had not, in a long time, sent an embassy, and who might imagine themselves slighted by such a neglect. This feigned excuse seemed to appease the princess, but not quite to rid her of all her uneasiness, which, on the contrary, was heightened, upon the return of the embassies, when she saw the Suns assemble in secret council together. She was filled with rage, which would have broken out, if her prudence had not set bounds to it. Happy it is for the French that she imagined herself neglected. I am persuaded that the colony owes its preservation to the vexation of this woman, rather than to any affection she entertained for the French, as she was now far advanced in years, and her French gallant long since dead. In order to get to the bottom of the secret, she prevailed on her son to accompany her on a visit to a relation that lay sick at the village of the Meal, and leading him the most distant and retired route, took occasion to reproach him with the secrecy he and the other Suns observed with regard to her. She insisted on her right, as a mother, and her privilege as a princess, adding, that although the world and herself, too, had told him he was the son of a Frenchman, yet her own blood was much dearer to her than that of strangers; that he need not apprehend she would ever betray him to the French, against whom, she said, you are plotting.

Fall of 1729

"The son, stung with these reproaches, told her it was

unusual to reveal what the old men of the council had once resolved upon, and as he was Grand Sun, he ought to set a good example in this respect; but seeing you have guessed the whole affair, I need not inform you further. You know as much as I do, myself, only hold your tongue."

"She replied that she was in no pain to know against whom he had taken his precautions, but as it was against the French, this was the very thing that made her apprehensive he had not taken his measures aright, in order to surprise them, as they were a people of great penetration, although their commandant had none. Her son told her that she had nothing to apprehend as to the measures taken; that all the nations had heard and approved their project, and promised to fall upon the French in their neighborhood, on the same day with the Natchez; that the Choctaws had resolved to destroy all the French lower down and along the Mississippi, up as far as the Tonicas, to which last people, he said, we did not send, as they and the Oumas are too much wedded to the French. He, at last, told her that the bundle of rods*

* By all ancient and modern Indians, rods or sticks were used to assemble the nation together. A Chief was accustomed to send forth a warrior, with a bundle of sticks, and as he journeyed towards the towns to which he was despatched, he would throw away one of these sticks, at the close of each day. When he gave them to the party to whom he was bearing them, the latter also continued, at the close of every day, to throw away a stick. The Chiefs, who sent these sticks, also kept a duplicate number, and each day threw away one, so that those at a distance, and those at the council house, would meet

CHAPTER VII.

lay in the temple, on the flat timber. The Stung Arm, being informed of the whole design, pretended to approve it, and leaving her son at ease, henceforward was only solicitous how she might defeat this barbarous design. The time was pressing, and the term fixed for the execution was almost expired. Unwilling to see the French cut off to a man in one day, she resolved to apprise them of the conspiracy through some young women who loved them, enjoining them never to tell from whom they had their information.* She desired a soldier, whom she met, to tell the commandant that the Natchez had lost their senses, and to desire him to be upon his guard. The soldier faithfully performed his commission, but the commandant treated him as a coward

Fall of 1729

together on the same day, when the last stick had been thrown away. In modern times, sending sticks was called "sending out the broken days."

* "The Sieur de Macé, ensign of the garrison of the fort at Natchez, received advice by a young Indian girl who loved him. She told him, crying, that her nation was to massacre all the French. M. De Macé, amazed at this discourse, questioned his mistress. Her simple answers and her tender tears, left him no room to doubt of the plot. He went immediately to give Chopart intelligence of it, who put him under arrest for giving false alarm."—Bossu's Travels through Louisiana, letter 3, addressed to the Marquis de L'Estrade, vol. 1, p. 62. London, 1771.

Bossu also states that Chopart, becoming enraged at Dumont, the second in command, for remonstrating with him against his tyranny towards the Natchez, in the commencement of the spring, placed that excellent officer and faithful historian in irons.—Vol. 1, p. 48.

and a visionary,—caused him to be placed in irons, and declared he would never take any steps towards repairing the fort, as the Natchez would then imagine he was a man of no resolution. The Stung Arm fearing a discovery, notwithstanding her precaution and the secrecy she enjoined, repaired to the temple and pulled some rods out of the fatal bundle. Her design was to hasten the time fixed, to the end that such Frenchmen as escaped the massacre might apprise their countrymen, many of whom had informed the commandant, who placed seven of them in irons. The female Sun, seeing the time approaching, and many of those punished whom she had charged to acquaint the governor, resolved to speak to the under-lieutenant,—but to no better purpose. Notwithstanding all these warnings, the commandant went out the night before on a party of pleasure, with some other Frenchmen, to the grand village of the Natchez, without returning to the fort till break of day, where he had no sooner arrived than he was admonished to be upon his guard. Still stimulated with his last night's debauch, he added imprudence to neglect, and despatched his interpreter to demand of the Grand Sun whether he intended to kill the French. The Grand Sun, though but a young man, knew how to dissemble, and spoke in such a manner to the interpreter as to allay his suspicions and fears.*

* DuPratz' Louisiana, pp. 79–90. In copying this author's statement, I have occasionally omitted some redundancies and uninteresting detail.

CHAPTER VII. We propose now to introduce the statement of Father Le Petit, who at the time of its occurrence was residing in New-Orleans, respecting the massacre itself. He was a learned and pious Jesuit priest. The following is his letter to Father D'Avaugour, procurator of the missions in North America.

"AT NEW-ORLEANS, 12th July, 1730.

My Reverend Father,—the Peace of our Lord be with you:

* * * * After having given you an imperfect idea of the character and customs of the Natchez Indians, I proceed, my reverend father, as I have promised you, to enter upon a detailed account of their perfidy and treason. It was on the second of December of the year 1729, that we learned they had surprised the French, and had massacred almost all of them. This sad news was first brought to us by one of the planters, who had escaped their fury. It was confirmed to us on the following day by other French fugitives, and finally, some French women, whom they had made slaves, and were forced afterwards to restore, brought us all the particulars.

"At the first rumor of an event so sad, the alarm and consternation was general in New-Orleans. Although the massacre had taken place more than a hundred leagues from here, you would have supposed that it had happened under our own eyes. Each one was mourning the loss of a relative—a friend—or some property; all were alarmed for their own lives, for there was reason to fear that the conspiracy of the Indians had been general. This unlooked for massacre began
1729 October 28 on Monday, the 28th of October, about nine o'clock in the morning. Some cause of dissatisfaction which the Natchez

thought they had with the commander, and the arrival of a number of richly laden boats for the garrison and the colonists, determined them to hasten their enterprise, and to strike their blow sooner than they had agreed with the other confederate tribes.* First they divided themselves, and sent into the fort, into the village, and into the two grants, as many Indians as there were French in each of these places. Then they feigned that they were going out for a grand hunt, and undertook to trade with the French for guns, powder and ball,—offering to pay them as much, and even more, than was customary; and, in truth, as there was no reason to suspect their fidelity, they made, at the time, an exchange of their poultry and corn for some arms and ammunition, which they used advantageously against us. It is true that some expressed their distrust, but this was thought to have so little foundation that they were treated as cowards, who were frightened at their own shadows. They had been on their guard against the Choctaws; but, as for the Natchez, they had never distrusted them, and they were so persuaded of their good faith, that it increased their hardihood. Having thus posted themselves in different houses, provided with the arms obtained from us, they attacked, at the same time, each his man; and in less than two hours they massacred more than two

* Father Le Petit is mistaken as to the causes which hastened the massacre. It will be recollected that DuPratz told us that Stung Arm pulled out several sticks from the bundle, and it was this which brought on the time sooner.

CHAPTER VII. hundred of the French. The best known are M. De Chopart, commander of the post; M. Du Codere, commander among the Yazoos; M. Des Ursins; Messieurs De Kolly, father and son; Messieurs De Longrays, Des Noyers, Bailly, &c.

"The Father Du Poisson had just performed the funeral rites of his associate, the brother Crucy, who had died very suddenly, of a sun stroke; he was on his way to consult Governor Perrier, and to adopt with him proper measures to enable the Arkansas to descend the banks of the Mississippi, for the accommodation of the voyagers. He arrived among the Natchez on the 26th of November, that is, two days before the massacre. The next day, which was the first Sunday of Advent, he said mass in the parish, and preached in the absence of the curé. He was to have returned in the afternoon, to his mission among the Arkansas, but he was detained by some sick persons, to whom it was necessary to

1729 October 28 administer the sacraments. On Monday, he was about to say mass, and to carry the holy sacrament to one of those sick persons whom he had confessed, the evening before, when the massacre begun. A gigantic Chief, six feet in height, seized him, and having thrown him to the ground, cut off his head with blows of a hatchet; the father, in falling, only uttered these words: "Ah my God! ah my God!" M. Du Codere drew his sword to defend him, when he was himself killed by a musket ball from another Indian, whom he did not perceive.

"These barbarians spared but two of the French, a tailor and a carpenter, who were able to serve their wants. They did not treat badly, either the negro slaves or the Indians who were willing to give themselves up; but they ripped up the abdomen of every pregnant woman, and killed almost all those who were nursing their children, because they were disturbed by their cries and tears. They did not kill the other women, but made them their slaves, and treated them with every indignity during the two or three months that they were their masters. The least miserable were those who knew how to sew, because they kept them busy in making shirts, dresses, &c. The others were employed in cutting and carrying wood for cooking, and in pounding the corn of which they made their *sagamité*. But two things, above all, aggravated the grief and hardness of their slavery; it was, in the first place, to have for masters, those same persons whom they had seen dipping their cruel hands in the blood of their husbands; and, in the second place, to hear them, continually, saying that the French had been treated in the same manner at all the other posts, and that the country was now entirely freed from them. 1729 October 28

"During the massacre, the Sun, or the Great Chief of the Natchez, was seated quietly under the tobacco shed of the company. His warriors brought to his feet the head of the commander, about which they ranged those of the principal French of the post, leaving their bodies a prey to the dogs, the buzzards, and other carniverous birds.* When they

* Dumont, in his "Memoires Historiques sur la Louisiane," tome 2, pp. 145–146, thus speaks of Chopart:

"In the midst of this general massacre of all the French, Chopart

CHAPTER VII.

were assured that no other Frenchmen remained at the post, they applied themselves to plunder the houses, the magazines of the Indian company, and all the boats which were still loaded by the banks of the river. They employed the negroes to transport the merchandize, which they divided among themselves, with the exception of the munitions of war, which they placed, for security, in a separate cabin. While the brandy lasted, of which they found a good supply, they passed their days and nights in drinking, singing, dancing, and insulting, in the most barbarous manner, the dead bodies and the memory of the French. The Choctaws and the other Indians being engaged in the plot with them, they felt at their ease, and did not at all fear that they would draw on themselves the vengeance which was merited by their cruelty and perfidy. One night, when they were

revived, as if Providence had wished to reserve him as a witness of the destruction of so many inhabitants who would not have perished but for his folly. He recognized it, at last, but too late, and raising himself from his seat, instead of taking his gun and placing himself on the defence, he fled to his garden, where he gave a whistle, in order to call the soldiers of the garrison. But they were no more. He could see all around him, by the sides of the palisades, which enclosed his garden, the earth strewn with their carcasses. At the same time he was surrounded by the savages, who breathed nothing more than his death, while none of them wished to lay hands upon him. They considered him as a "dog," unworthy of being killed by a brave man, and they made the chief stinking-man come, who killed him with the stroke of a club."

plunged in drunkenness and sleep, Madame Des Noyers wished to make use of the negroes to revenge the death of her husband and the French, but she was betrayed by the person to whom she confided her design, and came very near being burned alive.

"Some of the French escaped the fury of the Indians by taking refuge in the woods, where they suffered extremely from hunger and the effects of the weather.* One of them, on arriving here, relieved us of a little disquietude we felt in regard to the post we occupy among the Yazoos, which is not more than forty or fifty leagues above the Natchez by water and only from fifteen to twenty by land. Not being able to endure the extreme cold from which he suffered, he left the woods under cover of the night, to go and warm himself in the house of a Frenchman. When he was near it he heard the voices of Indians, and deliberated whether he should enter.

* In a despatch made by Governor Perrier to the Minister in France, dated the 18th March, 1730, he says:—" * * A general assassination of the French ensued, which occupied but little time; one single attack terminated it with the exception of the house of M. la Loire des Ursins, in which there were eight men, six of whom were killed, and the remaining two escaped during the night—the Indians having been unable to seize them during the day. M. la Loire des Ursins was mounted on a horse when the attack commenced, and being unable to regain his house, he defended himself until he fell, having killed four Indians. Thus it has cost the Natchez only twelve men to destroy two hundred and fifty of our people."—Gayarre's Histoire de la Louisiane, vol. 1, pp. 242–243.

CHAPTER VII. He determined, however, to do so, preferring rather to perish by the hands of these barbarians than to die of famine and cold. He was agreeably surprised when he found these savages ready to render him a service, to heap kindness upon him, to commisserate him, to console him, to furnish him with provisions, clothes and a boat to make his escape to New-Orleans. These were the Yazoos, who were returning from chanting the calumet, at Oumas. The Chief charged him to say to M. Perrier, that he had nothing to fear on the part of the Yazoos, that 'they would not lose their spirit,'—that is, that they would always remain attached to the French, and that he would be constantly on the watch with his tribe, to warn the French boats that were descending the river, to be on their guard against the Natchez.

"We believed, for a long time, that the promises of this Chief were very sincere, and feared no more Indian perfidy for our post among the Yazoos. But learn, my reverend father, the disposition of these Indians, and how little one is able to trust their words, even when accompanied by the greatest demonstrations of friendship. Scarcely had they returned to their own village, when loaded with presents they received from the Natchez, they followed their example and imitated their treachery. Uniting with the Corroys, they agreed together to exterminate the French. They began with Father Souel, the missionary of both tribes, who was then living in the midst of them, in their own village. On the

1730 December 11 11th of December, Father Souel was returning in the evening from visiting the Chief, and while in a ravine, received many musket balls, and fell dead on the spot. The Indians immediately rushed to his cabin to plunder it. His negro, who composed all his family and all his defence, armed himself with a wood-cutter's knife to prevent the pillage, and even wounded one of the savages. This zealous action cost him his life, but happily less than a month before he had received baptism, and was living in a most Christian manner.

"These Indians, who even to that time seemed sensible of the affection which their missionary bore them, reproached themselves for his death, as soon as they were capable of reflection; but returning again to their natural ferocity, they adopted the resolution of putting a finishing stroke to their crime, by the destruction of the whole French post. 'Since the Black Chief is dead,' said they, 'it is the same as if all the French were dead; let us not spare any.' The next day they executed their barbarous plan. They repaired, early in the morning, to the fort, which was not more than a league distant, and whose occupants supposed, on their arrival, that the Indians wished to chant the calumet to the Chevalier des Roches, who commanded that post, in the absence of M. de Codere. He had but seventeen men with him, who had no suspicion of any evil design on the part of the savages, and were, therefore, all massacred, not one escaping their fury. They, however, spared the lives of four women and five children, whom they found there, and whom they made slaves. One of the Yazoos having stripped the missionary, clothed himself in his garments, and shortly after announced to the Natchez that his nation had redeemed their pledge,

CHAPTER VII. and that the French, settled among them, were all massacred. In this city, there was no longer any doubt on that point, as soon as they learned what came near being the fate of Father Doutreleau. This missionary had availed himself of the time when the Indians were engaged in their winter occupations, to come and see us, for the purpose of regulating some matters relating to his mission. He set out on the first of this year, 1730, and not expecting to arrive at the residence of Father Souel, of whose fate he was ignorant, in time to say mass, he determined to say it at the mouth of the Little Yazoo river, where his party had cabined.

1730 January 1 "As he was preparing for the sacred office, he saw a boat full of Indians landing; they demanded from them of what nation they were. 'Yazoos, comrades of the French,' they replied, making a thousand friendly demonstrations to the voyagers, who accompanied the missionary, and presenting them with provisions. While the father was preparing his altar, a flock of bustards passed, and the voyagers fired at them the only two guns they had, without thinking of re-loading, as mass had already commenced. The Indians noted this, and placed themselves behind the voyagers, as if it was their intention to hear mass, although they were not Christians. At the time the father was saying the *Kyrie Eleison*, the Indians made their discharge; the missionary, seeing himself wounded in his right arm, and seeing one of the voyagers killed at his feet, and the four others fled, threw himself on his knees to receive the last fatal blow, which he regarded as inevitable. In this posture he received two or three discharges, but although the Indians fired while almost touching him, yet they did not inflict on him any new wounds. Finding himself then, as it were, miraculously escaped from so many mortal blows, he took to flight, having on, still, his priestly garments, and without any other defence than entire confidence in God, whose particular protection was given him, as the event proved. He threw himself into the water, and after advancing some steps, gained the boat, in which two of the voyagers were making their escape. They had supposed him to be killed by some of the many balls which they had heard fired on him. In climbing up into the boat, and turning his head to see whether any one of his pursuers was following him too closely, he received, in the mouth, a discharge of small shot, the greater part of which were flattened against his teeth, though some of them entered his gums and remained there for a long time. I have, myself, seen two of them. Father Doutreleau, all wounded as he was, undertook the duty of steering the boat, while his two companions placed themselves at the oars; unfortunately one of them, at setting out, had his thigh broken, by a musket ball, from the effects of which he has since remained a cripple. * * * As soon as they found themselves freed from their enemies, they dressed their wounds as well as they could, and for the purpose of aiding their flight from that fatal shore, they threw into the river every thing they had in their boat, preserving only some pieces of raw bacon, for their nourishment. It had been their intention to stop, in passing, at the Natchez, but having

1730 January

CHAPTER VII. seen that the houses of the French were either demolished or burned, they did not think it advisable to listen to the compliments of the Indians who, from the bank of the river, invited them to land. They placed a wide distance between them as soon as possible, and thus shunned the balls which were ineffectually fired at them. It was then that they began to distrust all the Indian nations, and, therefore, resolved not to go near the land until they reached New-Orleans, and supposing that the savages might have rendered themselves masters of it, to descend even to the Balize, where they hoped to find some French vessel provided to receive the wreck of the colony. * * * * * I cannot

1730 January 8 express to you, my reverend father, the great satisfaction I felt at seeing Father Doutreleau, his arm in a scarf, arrive (in New-Orleans) after a voyage of more than four hundred leagues, all the clothes he had on having been borrowed, except his cassock. My surprise was increased at the recital of his adventures. I placed him, immediately, in the hands of brother Parisel, who examined his wounds, and who dressed them with great care and speedy success. The missionary was not yet entirely cured of his wounds, when he departed to act as chaplain to the French army, as he had promised the officers, in accordance with their request.

* * * * * *

"Knowing as you do, my reverend father, the vigilance and the oversight of our governor, you can well imagine that he did not sleep in this sad crisis in which we now found ourselves. We may say, without flattery, that he surpassed himself by the rapid movements he made, and by the wise measures he adopted to revenge the French blood which had been shed, and to prevent the evils with which almost all the posts of the colony were threatened. As soon as he was apprised of this unexpected attack, by the Natchez Indians, he caused the news to be carried to all the posts, and even as far as the Illinois, not by the ordinary route of the river, which was closed, but on one side by the Natchitoches and the Arkansas, and the other by Mobile and the Chickasaw. He invited the neighbors, who were our allies, and particularly the Choctaws, to avenge this outrage. He furnished arms and ammunition to all the houses of the city and to the plantations. He caused two ships, that is, the Duc de Bourbon and the Alexandre, to ascend the river as far as the Tonicas. These ships were like two good fortresses against the insults of the Indians, and in case of attack, two certain asylums for the women and children. He caused a ditch to be dug entirely around the city, and placed guard houses at the four extremities. He organized for its defence many companies of city militia, who mounted guard during the whole night. As there was more to fear in the grants and in the plantations than in the city, he fortified them with the most care. He had good forts erected at Chapitoulas, Cannes, Brûles, Altemands, Bayagoulas, and Pointe Coupee.

"At first, our governor, listening only to the dictates of his own courage, adopted the design of placing himself at the head of the troops, but it was represented to him that he ought not to quit New-Orleans, where his presence was

CHAPTER VII. absolutely necessary; that there was danger of the Choctaws determining to fall upon the city, if it should be deprived of its troops; and the negroes, to free themselves from slavery, might join them, as some had done with the Natchez. Moreover, he could feel perfectly easy with regard to the

1730 January conduct of the troops, as the Chevalier De Loubois, with whose experience and bravery he was well acquainted, had been appointed to command them. Whilst our little army was repairing to the Tonicas, seven hundred Choctaws, mustered and conducted by M. De Sueur, marched towards the Natchez. We were informed, by a party of these people, that the Natchez were not at all on their guard, but passed all their nights in dancing. The Choctaws took them, therefore, by surprise, and made a descent on them, the 27th January, at the break of day. In less than three hours they had delivered fifty-nine persons, both women and children, with the tailor and carpenter, and one hundred and six negroes or negro women, with their children. They made eighteen of the Natchez prisoners, and took sixty scalps. They would have taken more, if they had not been intent on

1730 January 27 freeing the slaves, as they had been directed. They had but two men killed and seven or eight wounded. They encamped, with their prizes, at the grant of St. Catherine, in a mere park enclosed with stakes. The victory would have been complete, if they had waited the arrival of the French army, as had been agreed upon by their deputies.*

* Monette, Martin, and other modern authors, state that LeSeur advanced from the Tombigby, with six hundred warriors, and near

CHAPTER VII.

"The Natchez, seeing themselves attacked by the formidable Choctaws, regarded their defeat as certain, and shutting themselves up in two forts, passed the following nights in dancing their death dance. In their speeches, we heard them reproaching the Choctaws for their perfidy in declaring in favor of the French, contrary to the pledge they had given, to unite with them for our destruction. Three days before this action, the Sieur Mesplex landed at the Natchez with five other Frenchmen; they had volunteered to M. De Loubois, to carry to the Indians negociations for peace, that they might be able, under this pretext, to gain information with regard to their force and their present situation. But, in descending from their boat, they encountered a party who, without giving them time to speak, killed three of their men and made the other three prisoners. The next day they sent one of these prisoners with a letter, in which they demanded, as hostages, the Sieur Broutin, who had formerly been commander among them, and the Chief of the Tonicas. Besides, they demanded, as the ransom for the women, children and slaves, two hundred guns, two hundred barrels of powder, two thousand gun flints, two hundred knives, two hundred hatchets, two hundred pickaxes, five hogsheads of brandy, twenty casks of wine, twenty barrels of vermilion, two hundred shirts, twenty pieces of limbourg, twenty pieces

Pearl river increased his force to twelve hundred. Arriving near Natchez, and learning the unguarded condition of the Indians of that place, the Choctaws fell upon them, in spite the entreaties of LeSeur, who urged them to await the arrival of the French army.

CHAPTER VII. of cloth, twenty coats with lace on the seams, twenty hats bordered with plumes, and a hundred coats of a plainer kind. Their design was to massacre the French, who should bring these goods. On the very same day, with every refinement in cruelty, they burned the Sieur Mesplex and his companion.

"On the 8th February, the French, with the Tonicas and some other small tribes from the lower end of the Mississippi, arrived at the Natchez, and seized their temple, dedicated to the Sun. The impatience and impracticability of the Choctaws, who, like all these Indians, are capable of striking only one blow and then disperse—the small number of French soldiers, who found themselves worn down by fatigues—the want of provisions, which the Indians stole from the French—
1730 February the failure of ammunition, with which they were not able to satisfy the Choctaws, who wasted one part of it, and placed the other in reserve to be used in hunting—the resistance of the Natchez, who were well fortified, and who fought in desperation—all these things decided us to listen to the propositions which the besieged made, after the trenches had been opened for seven days. They threatened, if we persisted in the siege, to burn those of the French who remained; while, on the other hand, they offered to restore them, if we would withdraw our seven pieces of cannon. These, in reality, for want of a good gunner, and under present circumstances, were scarcely in a fit state to give them any fear.

"These propositions were accepted, and fulfilled on both sides. On the 25th of February, the besieged faithfully restored all that they had promised, while the besiegers retired with their cannon to a small fort which they had hastily built on the Escore, near the river, for the purpose of always keeping the Natchez in check, and ensuring a passage to the voyagers. Governor Perrier gave the command of it to M. D'Artaguette, as an acknowledgment of the intrepidity with which, during the siege, he had exposed himself to the greatest dangers, and everywhere braved death.

"Before the Choctaws had determined to fall upon the Natchez, they had been to them to convey the calumet, and were received in a very novel manner. They found them and their horses adorned with chasubles and drapery of the altars; many wore patterns about their necks, and drank, and gave to drink, of brandy in the chalices and the pyx. And the Choctaws themselves, when they had gained these articles by pillaging our enemies, renewed this profane sacrilege, by making the same use of our ornaments and sacred vessels in their dances and sports. We were never able to recover more than a small portion of them."* 1720 February

Here Father Le Petit discontinues his detail of the Natchez war, and ends his letter with some remarks upon the character of the Illinois and several other tribes of Indians. He appears to have deemed it a very great outrage that the Natchez thus

* "The Early Jesuit Missions in North America," compiled and translated from the letters of the French Jesuits, with notes by the Rev. Ingraham Kip, M.A., Corresponding Member of the New-York Historical Society. New-York: 1846. See Part 2, pp. 267–300.

CHAPTER VII.

prostituted their holy vessels and priestly robes, yet he announces that the French army "arrived at the Natchez and seized their temple, dedicated to the Sun," which they, no doubt, also destroyed. The religion of the Natchez was as sacred to the Natchez, as the religion of the Roman Catholics was to the good Father Le Petit.

The Natchez Chiefs proposed to surrender more than two hundred prisoners, if the French commander would remove his artillery and withdraw his forces, or else all the prisoners would be consumed by fire. Loubois, to save the lives of these miserable captives, consented, yet with the secret intention of wreaking his vengeance upon the Indians as soon as the prisoners were in his possession. But he was sadly disappointed, for the Indians, suspecting treachery on his part, took advantage of the suspension of hostilities, and one night evacuated the fort, and succeeded in gaining the opposite shore of the Mississippi with all their women and children. The prisoners were found in the fort, agreeably to the treaty. Loubois was astonished at the dexterous manœuvre, but he saw the folly of pursuing the foe, who had now secreted themselves in the vast swamps. He began the erection of a terraced fort upon the verge of the bluff, and leaving there a garrison of one hundred and twenty men, returned with his troops and the rescued prisoners to New-Orleans.

1730 February 25

The largest portion of the Natchez, conducted by the Great Sun, established themselves "upon the lower Washita, on the point between Little river and the Washita, just below the mouth of Little river, where the Washita assumes the name of

Black river."* Here the Natchez placed about four hundred acres of land in a state of defence, by the erection of large and small mounds and extensive embankments. Other portions of this tribe sought an asylum among the Chickasaws, while others wandered still further east, and took up their abode upon a portion of the territory now embraced in Talladega county, Alabama. The English traders of Carolina, it is said, rejoiced in the destruction of the French, and many of them, then residing among the Chickasaws, urged those people and the refugee Natchez, to engage in a vigorous warfare, and not only to defend their soil, but to exterminate the French. In the meantime, Governor Perrier made preparations to follow up the Natchez upon the Washita, but his exertions were, to some extent, defeated by a serious negro insurrection, which occurred upon the plantations in the vicinity of New-Orleans. CHAPTER VII.

However, upon the 10th of August, one of the company's ships arrived at the Balize with some troops and supplies. Although mortified that the reinforcement was so small, Perrier added them to the colonial troops, and, procuring a Choctaw force at Mobile, left New-Orleans with an army of six hundred and fifty, which was increased on the way to one thousand, by Indian allies. Reaching the mouth of Black river, they at length came in sight of the enemy's stronghold. The troops were disembarked, the fort invested, and for three days the besieged made a spirited resistance, when they made 1731 August 10 November 15 1732 January 20

* Monette's History of the Valley of the Mississippi, vol. 1, p. 267.

CHAPTER VII.

propositions which Perrier rejected. At length the Indians consented to surrender the Great Sun and one War Chief, which the governor refused. They then consented to surrender sixty-five men and about two hundred women and children, upon condition that their lives should be spared. Perrier once more opened his artillery upon them; but a heavy rain, which continued until night, silenced his batteries. When night set in, the Natchez began to escape from their defences, and make their way up the river, in the midst of a tempest of wind and rain. The Indian allies went in pursuit, and returned with one hundred prisoners. The next day Perrier demolished the outworks of the fort and began his voyage to

1732 February 5

New-Orleans, where he arrived, in due time, with four hundred and twenty-seven captives of the Natchez tribe. At the head of them were the Great Sun and several principal Chiefs. Soon afterwards, they were all shipped to St. Domingo and sold as slaves.* Those of the Natchez who escaped during the stormy night, rallied again and collected in one body, near the French settlements on Red river. They then marched

*"The French army re-embarked, and carried the Natchez as slaves to New-Orleans, where they were put in prison; but afterwards, to avoid the infection, the women and the children were disposed of on the King's plantation and elsewhere. Among these women was the Female Sun, called the Stung Arm, who then told me all she had done, in order to save the French. Sometime after, these slaves were embarked for St. Domingo, in order to root out that nation in the colony; * * * * and thus that nation, the most conspicuous in the colony and the most useful to the French, was destroyed."—Du Pratz, p. 95.

and attacked the post in a most furious manner, but St. Denys, the commandant, an intrepid officer, repelled them, with the loss of ninety-two braves, including all their Chiefs. The remnant escaped by flight. This was the closing scene in the Natchez drama, and ended the existence of these brave Indians as a distinct tribe.*

* In relation to the massacre at Natchez, and the final defeat of those Indians, I have carefully consulted the following authorities:—Du Pratz's Louisiana ; London, 1774.—Bossu's Travels in Louisiana, vol. 1 ; London, 1771.—Memoire Historique et Politique sur la Louisiane, par M. de Vergennes, Ministre de Louis XVI. ; A Paris, 1802.—Voyage a la Louisiane, par B*** D ; Paris, 1802.—Memoires Historique sur la Louisiane, par M. Dumont ; A Paris, 1753.—Kip's Early Jesuit Missions ; New-York, 1846.—Gayarre's Histoire de la Louisiane.—Martin's History of Louisiana ; New-Orleans, 1827.—Stoddart's Sketches, historical and descriptive, of Louisiana ; Philadelphia, 1812.—Monette's History of the Valley of the Mississippi ; New-York, 1846.

CHAPTER VIII.

THE ENGLISH IN GEORGIA.

CHAPTER VIII.

WE have shown that South-Carolina had been established as a colony for some years, that its seat of government was at Charleston, and that its inhabitants, in endeavoring to extend the English trade to all the Western Indian nations as far as the Mississippi river, had many conflicts and difficulties with the French, who occupied the territory of Alabama. They were also constantly opposed by the Spaniards of the Floridas. In order to interpose a barrier to these foes, as well as to protect the citizens from the attacks of the Creek Indians, the King of England and the British Parliament listened to a proposition of a great philanthropist, to plant a colony upon the western bank of the Savannah river. His motives, purely noble and disinterested, originated in a desire to ameliorate the condition of many unfortunate people in England. To carry out his plans of humanity, he was willing that the King should blend with them politic measures for the advancement of this, his most Southern province, and it was determined that "silk, wine, and oil should be cultivated most abundantly."

James Oglethorpe, a descendant of one of the oldest and most influential families of England, was born on the 22d December, 1688, and after graduating at Oxford University, was commissioned an ensign in the British army. In 1713, he accompanied the Earl of Petersbourg, then Ambassador to the Italian States, in the capacity of aid-de-camp. Returning to England, a year afterwards, he was promoted to a captaincy in the first troop of Queen Anne's Guard, and was soon an adjutant-general of the Queen's forces. He was next transferred to the post of aid-de-camp to Prince Eugene, the first general of the age, and was with him amid all the sanguinary battles fought between the Austrians and the Turks, upon the frontiers of Hungary. When these wars were over, Oglethorpe returned to England, and in 1722 was elected a member to the British Parliament, where he soon became useful and influential.

Oglethorpe caused an investigation to be made into the state of the English prisons, and it was ascertained that they groaned with thousands of poor wretches who had been imprisoned many years for debt. That the kingdom of England also contained thousands, "descended of good families," who were in destitute circumstances, and that hundreds of German exiles, driven from their native country by religious persecution, were starving among them. He brought this unhappy state of things before the King and Parliament, and, by his zeal and ability, succeeded in procuring a charter for the colonization of Georgia, the inhabitants of which were to consist of these distressed people. He

1732 June

CHAPTER VIII. resolved, himself, to embark with the first emigrants. They consisted of thirty families, numbering, collectively, one hundred and twenty-five souls. Entering the sea from the Thames, the vessel, after a long voyage across the Atlantic, 1733 January furled its sails in the harbor of Charleston. Oglethorpe landed, and was received with attention by the Governor and Council of South-Carolina. The King's pilot carried the ship into Port Royal, while small vessels were furnished to convey January 20 the emigrants to the Savannah river. Leaving his people at Beaufort, and accompanied by Colonel Bull, of South-Carolina, Oglethorpe ascended the Savannah, and launched his boat at the splendid bluff, which now forms the site of the commercial emporium of Georgia. At the northern end of this bluff, the great philanthropist came upon an Indian town, called Yamacraw, the chief of which was named Tomochichi, and where Musgrove, a Carolina trader, married to a half-breed named Mary, had established himself.*

This Indian, Mary, was born in the year 1700, at the town of Coweta, upon the Chattahoochie, in Alabama. Her Indian name was Consaponaheeso, and by maternal descent she was one of the Queens of the Muscogee nation, and the Indians conceded to her the title of princess. When ten years of age, her father took her to Ponpon, in South-Carolina, where she was baptised, educated and instructed in

* Stevens' History of Georgia, vol. 1, pp. 58–76–89. Georgia Historical Collections, vol. 1, pp. 9–11–12–167–174. McCall's History of Georgia, vol., 1, pp. 9–32.

Christianity. Afterwards, she fled back to her forest home, laid aside the civilization of the British, and assumed the ease and freedom of the happy Muscogee. In 1716, Colonel John Musgrove was despatched to the Chattahoochie, by the government of Carolina, to form a treaty of alliance with the Creeks, with whom that colony had been at war. It was there stipulated that the Creeks were to remain the free occupants of all the lands east, as far as the Savannah river. The son of the British negotiator, John Musgrove, had accompanied his father to Coweta, and falling in love with the princess Mary, made her his wife. After remaining in the nation several years, and after the birth of their only child, they removed to South-Carolina. There residing seven 1723
years in much happiness, they afterwards established themselves upon Yamacraw Bluff, at the head of an extensive 1732 June
trading house, and where Oglethorpe found them, as we have just observed. By his alliance with this remarkable woman, who was well versed in the Indian and English languages, Musgrove obtained considerable influence over the natives, and became exceedingly wealthy. Mary was, afterwards, the warm friend of Oglethorpe, and several times saved the early colonists of Georgia from savage butchery.

Oglethorpe returned to Beaufort, and, collecting his colonists, sailed up the Savannah, and landing at the bluff, where now stands the beautiful city, immediately disembarked and pitched four large tents. Here the emigrants spent their 1733 February 12
first night in Georgia. The Indians received them with hospitality, and gave pledges of future friendship. Ogle-

CHAPTER VIII. 1733 February 9 thorpe marked out the streets and squares; all was bustle and activity, and it was not long before Savannah assumed something of the appearance of a town. A small fort was established at the edge of the bluff, as a place of refuge, and some artillery was mounted upon it. Fort Argyle was built at the narrow passage of the Ogechee, above the mouth of Canouchee, to defend the inhabitants against inland invasion from the Spaniards of St. Augustine.

Soon after his arrival, Oglethorpe despatched runners to the Lower Creek nation, and having assembled eighteen
May 21 Chiefs and their attendants, at Savannah, he formed a treaty with them, in which they relinquished to the British government the lands between the Savannah and the Altamaha. It was also stipulated, among other things, that English traders should be allowed to establish themselves in any part of the Creek nation. Their goods were to be sold at fixed rates: thus, a white blanket was set down at five buckskins, a gun at ten, a hatchet at three doeskins, a knife at one, and so on. Returning to Charleston, after this important treaty, a dinner was given to the philanthropist by the legislative bodies, which he returned by a ball and supper to the ladies.

A company of forty Jews, acting under the broad principles of the charter, which gave freedom to all religions, save that of the Romish Church, landed at Savannah. Much dissatisfaction, both in England and America, arose in consequence of the appearance of these Israelites, and Oglethorpe was solicited to send them immediately from the colony.

He, however, generously permitted them to remain, which was one of the wisest acts of his life, for they and their descendants were highly instrumental in developing the commercial resources of this wild land. There also came, in the months of September and October, three hundred and forty-one Salzburgers, driven from Germany for their religious opinions, and Oglethorpe settled them above Savannah, on the river of that name, where they formed a town, and named it Ebenezer. These people were succeeded by many Highlanders, from Scotland, who, being brave and hardy, were located upon the banks of the Altamaha, the most exposed part of the colony, where they founded the town of Darien.

CHAPTER VIII.

1734

1736 January

In the meantime, Oglethorpe had made a voyage to England, taking with him Tomochichi, the Chief of Yamacraw, Senanky, his wife, Tooanhouie, their nephew, Hillipili, the War Captain, and five Chiefs of the Cherokees. He was most graciously received by the ruling powers of England, and by her citizens; and his noble and disinterested exertions were universally approved. In due time he returned to Georgia, with his Indian friends.

The lands, between Ebenezer and Briar Creek, belonged to the Uchees, who refused to dispose of them. But to secure this part of the country, two forts were built on the South-Carolina side of the river, which answered the purpose. Establishments were also made at Silver Bluff, and at the falls of the Savannah, where the town of Augusta was laid out, warehouses erected, and a garrison thrown into a small

1736

fort. Augusta immediately became a general resort for Indian traders, where they purchased annually about two thousand pack-horse loads of peltry. Six hundred white persons were engaged in this trade, including townsmen, pack-horse men, and servants. Boats, each capable of carrying down the river a large quantity of peltry, were built, and four or five voyages were annually made with them to Charleston. A trading highway was opened to Savannah on which few of the creeks were bridged, or marshes and swamps causewayed.

He who became the wealthiest and most conspicuous of all these Indian traders, was George Galphin, a native of Ireland. When quite a young man, he established himself upon the site of De Soto's ancient Cutifachiqui, where that remarkable adventurer first discovered the Savannah river, in 1540. Upon the site of this old Indian town, on the east bluff of the Savannah, in Barnwell District, South-Carolina, now called Silver Bluff, and at present the property of Gov.
1737 Hammond, young Galphin first begun to trade with the Creek Indians. Although he made Silver Bluff his headquarters, he had trading houses in Savannah and Augusta. He was a man of fine address, great sense, commanding person, untiring energy, and unsurpassed bravery. His power was felt and his influence extended even to the banks of the Mississippi. Among the Upper and Lower Creeks, Cherokees, Chickasaws and Choctaws, he sent forth numerous pack-horse men, with various merchandize, who brought back to Georgia almost countless skins and furs, kegs of bears' oil,

kickory-nut oil, snake root and medicinal barks, which he shipped to England. He often went himself into these nations, fearlessly trading in the immediate vicinity of the French Fort Toulouse, upon the Coosa. Commercial policy and an amorous disposition led him to form connections with several females, who were called his wives, and from whom descended many intelligent and influential persons, now inhabiting Georgia, Alabama, and the Arkansas Territory.

Among the passengers who came out with Oglethorpe, upon his return to America, were the celebrated Methodists, John and Charles Wesley, who eat at the table of the philanthropist, and who received from him much kindness and courtesy, during a stormy and dangerous voyage. Their object was to make religious impressions upon the minds of the Indians. Among the colonists, with whom they resided many years, they became not only unpopular, but very obnoxious. They finally returned to England much mortified and much disappointed. Stevens thus speaks of these talented and pious men :—"The proceedings of the Wesley's in Georgia have, indeed, been violently assailed; and even writers, who can offer no excuse for their ignorance, accuse them of immorality and blame. But it was not so. They were men delicately brought up, of fine sensibilities, of cultivated minds, of deep learning and of ardent devotion. * * Accomplished, though reserved in their manners,—associating from childhood with refined and learned society,—they could not conform at once to the tastes and habits of communities like those of Savannah and Frederica, but were rather repel-

CHAPTER VIII. led by the gross immoralities and offensive manners of the early colonists. Their error was, especially in John, of holding too high ideas of ecclesiastical authority, and the being too rigid and repulsive in their pastoral duties. They stood firmly on little things, as well as on great, and held the reins of church discipline with a tightness unsuitable to an infant colony. But no other blame can attach to them."*

The colony of Georgia had prospered under the wise guidance of Oglethorpe. Five principal towns had been 1738 surveyed and settled: Augusta, Ebenezer, Savannah, New Inverness, and Frederica, besides forts and villages. More than one thousand persons had been sent to Georgia, on the account of the trustees alone, while hundreds of other emigrants came at their own expense. The colonists being from different nations, were various in their characters and religous creeds. Vaudois, Swiss, Piedmontese, Germans, Moravians, Jews from Portugal, Highlanders, English, and Italians were thrown together in this fine climate, new world and new home. With all these people, in their various costumes, were often intermingled different tribes of Indians. What a field for a painter the colony presented! What materials for a scribbling tourist!

1737 January Having thus colonized the northern, southern, and eastern borders, Oglethorpe returned to England, and presented to his majesty and the Parliament an account of the affairs of Georgia. He asked, at their hands, a sufficient supply of

* Stevens' History of Georgia, vol. 1, pp. 339–349.

military stores and men to defend the province from an invasion contemplated by the Spaniards of the Floridas. The colonization of Georgia had given great offence to Spain. That power claimed the whole of Georgia, but made no serious opposition, so long as the English settlements were confined to Savannah river, but when Oglethorpe planted his Highlanders upon the Altamaha, the Spaniards resolved upon their expulsion. A long succession of border wars and difficulties ensued, which having but little connection with the history of Alabama, are omitted. It should be observed, however, that Oglethorpe succeeded in his applications to the Court, and was appointed general of the forces in South-Carolina and Georgia. In September, he was made colonel of a regiment to be employed in defence of the colony, which he had so successfully established. He returned to Georgia with his army, and disembarked his artillery at St. Simond's Island. 1738 September 19

No sooner had Gen. Oglethorpe placed his feet upon Georgia soil, than he saw the necessity of renewing his treaty with the Creeks, and of cultivating their alliance, for fear that they might form a dangerous connection with the Spaniards. He went immediately to Savannah, where he had an interview with the Chiefs of four towns, and succeeded in strengthening their fidelity to the English. But in order to accomplish a complete alliance with the brave Creeks, he resolved to attend the great council of that nation, which was to assemble at Coweta, in July and August following. It was a long and perilous journey. Coweta lay upon the west bank of

CHAPTER VIII. the Chattahoochie river, three miles below the falls, at which the city of Columbus is now situated, and within the limits of the present Russell county, Alabama. The distance from Savannah to that point was not only considerable, but lay over extensive pine forests, dismal swamps, and rapid and dangerous rivers, while the solitary trail was not unfrequently beset by Indian banditti. However, when the time arrived, he, who had so courageously fought under Prince Eugene, upon the frontiers of Hungary, was not to be dismayed by obstacles like these. With only a few attendants, and some pack-horses, laden with goods, designed as presents for the Indians, Oglethorpe set off on his journey. He crossed the Ogechee, Oconee, Ockmulgee, and the Flint, carrying over his effects in canoes, and sometimes upon rafts. Finally, he halted upon the banks of the Chattahoochie. He had camped out every night in the woods, exposed by day to the heat of the sun, and often to pelting showers of rain. Crossing the Chattahoochie, and ascending its western bank, the great and
1739 August 1 good Oglethorpe soon arrived in the town of Coweta, upon Alabama soil. Forty miles in advance, the Indians had met him and at various points upon the route, had deposited provisions for his subsistence. They now received him in their capital with every demonstration of joy.

Making Coweta his head-quarters, Oglethorpe occasionally rode to some of the towns in the vicinity, the most prominent of which were Uchee, Cusseta and Ositche, conversing with these people through his interpreters, and engaging their affections by his liberality and irresistible address. He drank with them the black drink—smoked with them the pipe of peace—and lounged with them upon the cool cane sofas with which their ample public houses were furnished. In the meantime, the Chiefs and warriors from the towns of Coweta, Cusseta, Ufaula, Hitchitee, Ositche, Chehaw, Oconee and Swagles, assembled in the great square. After many ceremonious preliminaries, they made a treaty of alliance with Oglethorpe. It was declared that all the lands between the Savannah and the St. John's, and from the latter to the Apalache bay, and thence to the mountains, by ancient right, did belong to the Creek nation. That neither the Spaniards nor any other people, excepting the trustees of the colony of Georgia, should settle them. That the grant on the Savannah river, as far as the river Ogechee, and those along the sea-coast as far as the St. John's river, and as high as the tide flowed, with the islands previously granted to the English at Savannah, should now be confirmed. The Chiefs again reserved all the lands from Pipe Maker's Bluff to the Savannah, with the Islands of St. Catharine, Osabow and Sapelo.

1739 August 21

After signing the treaty, Oglethorpe left with the Chiefs, for their protection against English encroachments, the following singular paper:—

By James Oglethorpe, Esquire, General and Commander-in-Chief of all His Majesty's forces in South-Carolina and Georgia, &c.: To all His Majesty's subjects to whom these presents shall come, greeting:—

KNOW YE, that you are not to take up or settle any land beyond the above limit, settled by me with the Creek nation,

CHAPTER VIII. at their estates held on Saturday, the eleventh day of August, Anno Domini, 1739, as you shall, through me, at your peril answer.

Given under my hand and seal, at the Coweta town, this, the 21st day of August, Anno Domini, 1739.

JAMES OGLETHORPE.

We desire it to be borne in mind, by the reader, that none of the Upper Creek Indians, who lived upon the Alabama, Coosa, and Tallapoosa rivers, were present at this treaty. They never recognized any of the treaties made in the Lower Creek nation with the Georgians. At this time, they were under the influence of the French; afterwards, they placed themselves under the wing of the Spaniards. Although the
1735 English built a fort and occupied it for many years, with a garrison, in the town of Ocfuske, on the east side of the Tallapoosa river, within forty miles of the French fortress, Toulouse, and partially succeeded in alienating some of the Upper Creeks from the French, yet the great body of these people forever remained the implacable enemies of the Georgians.

1739 September 22 Oglethorpe departed from Coweta, and after a disagreeable journey, reached Savannah. He there assisted in the funeral ceremonies of his friend, Tomochichi, who died at Yamacraw
October 5 Bluff. The body, brought down the river in a canoe, was received by Oglethorpe, and was interred in Percival Square, amid the sound of minute guns from the battery.*

* Stevens' History of Georgia, vol. 1, pp. 89–158. McCall's History of Georgia, vol. 1, pp. 32–142. Georgia Historical Collections, vol. 1, pp. 18–22–262–182.

CHAPTER IX.

JESUIT PRIESTS OR MISSIONARIES.

CHAPTER IX.

SINCE the revolt of the French garrison at Fort Toulouse, upon the Coosa, things at that place had remained in rather an undisturbed condition. It is true that the English had given them much uneasiness, and had occasionally cut off some of the *couriers de bois*. In order to cultivate a better understanding with the Lower Creeks, a Jesuit priest,—Father de Guyenne,—went to Coweta, upon the Chattahoochie, and succeeded in building two cabins, one at that place, and the other at Cusseta. His object was to learn the language of the Indians, and to instruct them in the Christian 1735
religion; but the English of the province of Georgia prevailed upon the Indians to burn up these houses. The zealous father was therefore forced to retreat to Fort Toulouse. Father Moran had been stationed, some years, at Fort Toulouse, and used to live occasionally at Coosawda.

"The impossibility, however, of exercising his ministry there, for the benefit of either the Indians or the French, has induced the superior to recall him, that he might be entrusted with the direction of the nuns, and of the royal hospital, which is

CHAPTER IX.

now under our charge. The English trade, as well as the French, among the Alabama Indians. You can easily imagine what an obstacle this presents to the progress of religion, for the English are always ready to excite controversy."* Among the Choctaws there were several missionaries, besides those stationed at Mobile. "The reverend Father Baudouin, the actual superior-general of the mission, resided eighteen years among the Choctaws. When he was on the point of reaping some fruits from his labors, the troubles which the English excited in that nation, and the peril to which he was evidently exposed, obliged Father Vitri, then superior-general, in concert with the governor, to recall him to New-Orleans."*

While the English of Carolina and Georgia engaged in various schemes to rid the territory of the present States of Alabama and Mississippi, of its French population, by unscrupulous intrigues with the natives, the French were but little behind them in similar enterprises. The Jesuits were adventurous and brave, and men of captivating address, and obtained much influence over the leading Chiefs, wherever they appeared. An account of the artful intrigues of a German Jesuit, named Christian Priber, as related, in his singular style, by James Adair, an old British trader, who lived forty years among the Cherokees and Chickasaws, will now be introduced.

* Letter of Father Vivier, of the company of Jesus, to a father of the same company.

"In the year 1736, the French sent into South-Carolina one Priber, a gentleman of a curious and speculative temper. He was to transmit them a full account of that country, and proceed to the Cherokee nation, in order to seduce them from the British to the French interest. He went, and though he was adorned with every qualification that constitutes the gentleman, soon after he arrived at the upper towns of this mountainous country, he exchanged his clothes and every thing he brought with him, and by that means made friends with the head warriors of the Big Tellico river. More effectually to answer the design of his commission, he ate, drank, slept, danced, dressed, and painted himself with the Indians, so that it was not easy to distinguish him from the natives; he married, also, with them. Being endowed with a strong understanding and retentive memory, he soon learned their dialect, and by gradual advances, impressed them with a very ill opinion of the English, representing them as a fraudulent, avaricious and encroaching people. He, at the same time, inflated the artless savages with a prodigious high opinion of their own importance in the American scale of power, on account of the situation of their country, their martial disposition and the great number of their warriors, which would baffle all the efforts of the ambitious and ill-designing British colonists.

CHAPTER IX.

1736

"Having thus infected them by his smooth, deluding art, he easily formed them into a nominal republican government. He crowned their old Archi-Magus, emperor, after a pleasing new savage form, and invented a variety of high sounding

CHAPTER IX. titles for all the members of his imperial majesty's *red* court and the great officers of state. He himself received the honorable title of his imperial majesty's principal secretary of state,
1739 and as such he subscribed himself, in all the letters he wrote to our government, and lived in open defiance of them. This seemed to be of so dangerous a tendency, as to induce South-Carolina to send up a commissioner, Colonel Fox, to demand him as an enemy to public repose. He took him into custody in the great square of their state house. When he had almost concluded his oration on the occasion, one of the warriors rose up and bade him forbear, as the man he intended to enslave was made a great beloved man, and had become one of their own people. Though it was reckoned our Agent's strength was far greater in his arms than in his head, he readily desisted, for, as it is too hard to struggle with the Pope in Rome, a stranger could not miss to find it equally difficult to enter abruptly into a new emperor's court, and there seize his prime minister by a foreign authority, especially when he could not support any charge of guilt against him. The warrior told him that the red people well knew the honesty of the secretary's heart would never allow him to tell a lie, and the secretary urged that he was a foreigner, without owing any allegiance to Great Britain. That he only travelled through some places of their country, in a peaceable manner, paying for every thing he had of them. That in compliance with the request of the kind French, as well as from his own tender feelings for the poverty and insecure state of the Cherokees, he came a great way, and lived with them as a

brother, only to preserve their liberties, by opening a water communication between them and New-Orleans. That the distance of the two places from each other proved his motive to be the love of doing good, especially as he was to go there and bring up a sufficient number of Frenchmen, of proper skill, to instruct them in the art of making gun-powder, the materials of which, he affirmed, their lands abounded with. He concluded his artful speech, by urging that the tyrannical design of the English commissioner towards him, appeared plainly to be levelled against them, because, as he was not accused of having done any ill to the English, before he came to the Cherokees, his crime must consist in loving the Cherokees. * * * An old war-leader repeated to the commissioner the essential part of the speech, and added more of his own similar thereto. * * * The English beloved man had the honor of receiving his leave of absence and a sufficient passport of safe conduct, from the imperial red court, by a verbal order of the secretary of state, who was so polite as to wish him well home, and ordered a convoy of his own life-guards, who conducted him a considerable way, and he got home in safety.

1741

"From the above, it is evident that the monopolizing spirit of the French had planned their dangerous line of circumvallation, respecting our envied colonies, as early as the before mentioned period. The choice of the man, also, bespoke their judgment. Though the philosophic secretary was an utter stranger to the wild and mountainous Cherokee nation, yet his sagacity readily directed him to choose a proper place,

CHAPTER IX. an old favourite religious man, for the new red empire, which he formed by slow and sure degrees, to the great danger of our Southern colonies. But the empire received a very great shock, in an accident that befel the secretary, when it was on the point of rising into a far greater state of puissance by the ac-
1731 quisition of the Muscogee, Choctaw, and the Western Mississippi Indians.

"In the fifth year of that red imperial era, Priber set off for Mobile, accompanied by a few Cherokees. He proceeded by land as far as the navigable part of the Tallapoosa river, and arriving at Tookabatcha, lodged there all night. The traders of the neighboring towns soon went there, convinced the inhabitants of the dangerous tendency of his unwearied labors among the Cherokees, and of his present journey. They then took him into custody, with a large bundle of manuscripts, and sent him down to Frederica, in Georgia. The governor committed him to a place of confinement, though not with common felons, as he was a foreigner, and was said to have held a place of considerable rank in the army. Soon
1744 March 22 after, the magazine took fire, which was not far from where he was confined, and though the sentinels bade him make off to a place of safety, as all the people were running to avoid danger from explosion of the powder and shells, yet he squatted on his belly upon the floor, and continued in that position without the least hurt. Several blamed his rashness, but he told them that experience had convinced him it was the most probable means of avoiding danger. This incident displayed the philosopher and soldier. After bearing his misfortunes a

considerable time with great constancy, happily for us, he died in confinement, though he deserved a much better fate. In the fifth year of his secretaryship, I maintained a correspondence with him. But the Indians becoming very inquisitive to know the contents of our papers, * * * he told them that in the very same manner, as he was their great secretary, I was the devil's clerk, or, an accursed one, who marked on paper the bad speech of the evil ones of darkness. Accordingly, they forbade him to write any more to such an accursed one. As he was learned, and possessed of a very sagacious, penetrating judgment, and had every qualification that was 1745 requisite for his bold and difficult enterprise, it is not to be doubted, that as he wrote a Cherokee dictionary, designed to be published at Paris, he likewise set down a great deal that would have been very accessible to the curious, and serviceable to the representatives of South-Carolina and Georgia, which may be readily found in Frederica, if the manuscripts have had the good fortune to escape the despoiling hands of military power."*

William Bacon Stevens, formerly professor of belles lettres and history, in the University of Georgia, and now an Episcopalian minister, in Philadelphia, has published one volume of the History of Georgia, in which we find the following interesting account of Priber, which we copy, at length, in his own style. In alluding to the arrival of Oglethorpe, at Frederica, Dr. Stevens says: "On the return of the general from Florida,

* Adair's American Indians: London, 1775; pp. 240–243.

CHAPTER IX. he ordered his strange prisoner to be examined, and was not a little surprised to find, under his coarse dress of deer-skins and Indian moccasins, a man of polished address, great abilities, and extensive learning. He was versed not only in the Indian language, of which he had composed a dictionary, but also spoke the Latin, French and Spanish fluently, and English perfectly. Upon being interrogated as to his design, he acknowledged that it was 'to bring about a confederation of all the Southern Indians, to inspire them with industry, to instruct them in the arts necessary to the commodities of life, and, in short, to engage them to throw off the yoke of their European allies of all nations.' He proposed to make a settlement in that part of Georgia which is within the limits of the Cherokee lands, at Cusseta,* and to settle a town there of fugitive English, French and Germans, and they were to take under their particular care the runaway negroes of
1745 the English. All criminals were to be sheltered, as he proposed to make his place an asylum for all fugitives, and the cattle and effects they might bring with them. He expected a great resort of debtors, transported felons, ser-

* If Doctor Stevens means the "Cusseta," on the east side of the Chattahoochie, and opposite old Fort Mitchell, it was within the limits of the Creek lands, and never belonged to the Cherokees. I am not aware of any town named "Cusseta," in any part of what formerly was the Cherokee nation, although there may have been, for, by reference to page 162 of the History of Alabama, it will be found that the Cherokees had towns named "Tallase" and "Tuskegee," and such towns were also in the Creek nation.

vants, and negro slaves from the two Carolinas, Georgia and CHAPTER Virginia, offering, as his scheme did, toleration to all crimes IX. and licentiousness, except murder and idleness. Upon his person was found his private journal, revealing, in part, his designs, with various memoranda relating to his project. In it he speaks not only of individual Indians and negroes, whose assistance had been promised, and of a private treasurer, in Charleston, for keeping the funds collected; but also, that he expected many things from the French, and from another nation, whose name he left blank. There were also found upon him letters for the Florida and Spanish governors, demanding their protection of him and countenance of his scheme. Among his papers was one containing articles of government for his new town, regularly and elaborately drawn out and digested. In this volume he enumerates many rights and privileges, as he calls them, to which the citizens of this colony are to be entitled, particularly dissolving marriages, allowing a community of women, and all kinds of licentiousness. It was drawn up with much art, method and learning, and was designed to be privately printed and circulated. When it was hinted to him that such a plan was attended with many dangers and difficulties, and must require many years to establish his government, he replied, 'proceeding properly, many of these evils may be avoided; and as to length of time, we have a succession of agents to take up the work as fast as others leave it. We never lose sight of a favorite point, nor are we bound by the strict rules of morality in the means, 1745 when the end we pursue is laudable. If we err, our general

CHAPTER IX. is to blame; and we have a merciful God to pardon us. But believe me,' he continued, 'before the century is passed, the Europeans will have a very small footing on this continent.'

"Indeed, he often hinted that there were others of his brethren laboring among the Indians for the same purpose. Being confined in the barracks at Frederica, he exhibited a stoical indifference to his fate; conversed with freedom, conducted with politeness, and attracted the notice and favorable attention of many of the gentlemen there. His death in prison, put an end to all further proceedings, and his plans died with him. Such was the strange being whose Jesuitical intrigues well nigh eventuated in the destruction of Georgia. A thorough Jesuit, an accomplished linguist, a deep tactician, far-sighted in his plans, and far-reaching in his expedients, he possessed every qualification for his design, and only failed of bringing down great evil upon the English, because he was apprehended before his scheme had been matured."*

1745 There were many curious characters roving over the territory of Alabama and Mississippi at this period. Traders from South-Carolina and Georgia, were found in almost every Indian village; while the French from Mobile and New-Orleans and the Spaniards from the Floridas continued to swell the number of these singular merchants. They encountered all kinds of dangers and suffered all kinds of privations to become successful in their exciting traffic. Adair, one of these British

* Steven's History of Georgia, vol. 1, pp. 165–167.

traders, thus describes the mode by which difficult streams were passed : CHAPTER IX.

"When we expect high rivers, each company of traders carry a canoe, made of the tanned leather, the sides overlapped about three fingers' breadth, and well sewed with three seams. Around the gunnels, which are made of saplings, are strong loop-holes, for large deer-skin strings to hang down both the sides. With two of these is securely tied to the stem and stern, a well shaped sapling for a keel, and in like manner the ribs. Thus they usually rig out a canoe, fit to carry over ten horse-loads at once, in the space of half an hour. The apparatus is afterwards hidden with great care on the opposite shore. Few take the trouble to paddle the canoe, for, as they are commonly hardy, and also of an amphibious nature, they usually jump into the river with their leathern barge ahead of them, and thrust it through the deep part of the water to the opposite shore. When we ride with only a few luggage horses, we make a frame of dry pines, which we tie together with strong vines well twisted. When we have raised it to be sufficiently buoyant, we load and paddle it across, and afterwards swim our horses, keeping at a little distance below them."*

* Adair's American Indians, p. 272.

CHAPTER X.

THE FRENCH BATTLES UPON THE TOMBIGBY.

CHAPTER X.

WHEN we suspended our review of the operations of the French upon the territory of Alabama and Mississippi, for the purpose of bringing to the notice of the reader the early colonization of Georgia by Oglethorpe, it will be borne in mind that the horrible massacre at Natchez had occurred. The tribe of that name had crossed the Mississippi, and fortified on Black river, near the Washita. Governor Perrier, attacking them at 1732 January that point, had captured many of the men, women and children, whom he conveyed to New-Orleans, and from thence March shipped to the Island of St. Domingo, where they were sold to work upon the plantations. Some of those who escaped the hands of the French at Black river, retreated to the vicinity of the fort at Natchitoches, upon which they presently made a furious assault. The brave St. Denys, the commandant, successfully repulsed them. A remnant of this warlike but unfortunate tribe had fled to the Chickasaw nation, while another small band sought a home among the Creeks, upon the Coosa.

Governor Perrier was guilty of excessive cruelty to many

of these poor fugitives who fell into his hands. In the streets of New-Orleans he publicly, and without any hesitation, caused four of the men and two of the women to be burned to death. 1732 He also cheerfully permitted the Tonicas, who brought down a Natchez woman whom they had discovered in the woods, to put an end to her existence in the same manner. A platform was erected near the Levee. The unfortunate woman was led forth, placed upon it, and, surrounded by the whole population of New-Orleans, was slowly consumed by the flames! What a stigma upon the character of the early inhabitants of the Crescent City! Gayarre says:—"The victim supported, with the most stoical fortitude, all the tortures which were inflicted upon her, and did not shed a tear. On the contrary, she upbraided her torturers with their want of skill, flinging at them every opprobrious epithet she could think of."*

As a nation, the Natchez were thus entirely destroyed. 1732
Great sympathy was felt for them by all the tribes in Mississippi and Alabama; even the Choctaws, who were so wedded to the French, being sad on account of their fate, and annoyed at the unparalleled cruelties which they experienced at the hands of their vindictive conquerors. The noble Creeks, upon the Coosa, received some of the refugees with open arms, while the still nobler Chickasaws not only welcomed others to their doors, but swore to shed the blood of their pursuers, in

* Louisiana, its Colonial History and Romance, by Charles Gayarre. New-York: 1851. pp. 444–445.

CHAPTER X.

a protracted war. These things made the condition of the French colony a very critical one. The English of Carolina did not fail to fan the fire which, they imagined, would soon 1734 consume their ancient colonial enemies. An expedition was fitted out in Charleston, composed of many traders and adventurers, with seventy pack-horses laden chiefly with munitions of war. Whether it was at the instance of the British government, or not, is unknown. They took the well-beaten path for the Chickasaw nation, and passing by the town of Coosa, then situated in the territory of the present county of Talladega, they prevailed upon some of the refugee Natchez to accompany them, and to assist in repelling the French invasion, which, it was known, was then contemplated. Arriving in the Chickasaw nation, they dispersed over the country, and not a few of them found their way to the towns of the Choctaws. Soon the whole Indian sky was crimsoned with flashing meteors, and then made dark with angry clouds.

France, apprised of the precarious situation of her distant children, once mcre resolved to send the veteran Bienville to take care of them. The King began to see that his services could not be dispensed with, and after he had passed eight 1733 March years in Paris, he sailed for the colony. His arrival at Mobile was hailed with joy and acclamations by the inhabitants. Diron D'Artaguette, a man of nerve and much ability, who had been longer absent from the colony than Bienville, accompanied him. He was presently stationed at Mobile as the King's commissary. Bienville, at first, occupied much of his time in visiting Mobile and New

Orleans, for the purpose of giving quiet to the inhabitants CHAPTER X.
and preparing them for a war of invasion. On one occasion, while he was in New-Orleans, Diron D'Artaguette aroused all the French settlers, towards the east, by despatches which he sent among them, in relation to the arrival of the English expedition, to which allusion has just been made, and of the determination of the Choctaws to act, in future, against the French. He warned everybody to be upon their guard, for it was probable they might be butchered at any hour. The people of Mobile were in a state of extreme terror; they 1735
never went to mass without carrying their guns in their hands. Indeed they, at one time, resolved to retire to New-Orleans; but Bienville arriving, commanded them to remain and fear nothing. He highly disapproved of the excitement which Diron D'Artaguette had produced, and thought there was no occasion for such officious watchfulness on the part of the commissary. This produced unpleasant feelings between them, and they indulged in recriminations of each other, in official reports to the government. Bienville was mortified at the conduct of D'Artaguette, in rebuking the Choctaw Chiefs, who had recently paid him a visit, for permitting the English to come among them. Further, he dismissed them without presents, upon which they returned home, highly offended. These things were represented to the government by Bienville, while D'Artaguette, on the other hand, stated, 1735 April 29
in one of his despatches, that Bienville's opposition to him arose from the fact that he had reported the "misconduct of his protéges or favorites, Lesueur and the Jesuit, Father

CHAPTER X. Beaudoin who, to the great scandal of the Choctaws, seduce their women."*

It is pleasant, to us, to be able to state that only a few of the missionaries, of the order of Jesuits, thus abused the holy offices with which they were entrusted. The great body of them led the most pious lives and suffered the greatest privations, in their efforts to redeem the savages from heathenism.

In the meantime, small parties of Natchez, with their generous allies, the Chickasaws, sought all occasions to annoy
1735 their enemy. From ambuscades on the hill tops and banks of the rivers, along the Indian paths in the interior, and from dark vallies in the mountains, they sprang upon the French trappers, hunters and traders, with the impetuosity of lions and the agility of tigers, and drank their hot blood with the voraciousness of wolves.

But Bienville was straining every nerve to complete his preparations for the invasion of the Chickasaw nation. He
1735 visited Mobile once more, and having assembled at that point a large delegation of Choctaw Chiefs, he, in a great measure, accomplished his object in gaining them over to his side. It was important that he should do so, for Red Shoes, a potent Chief of that tribe, had already declared in favor of the English. Bienville freely distributed merchandize, and promised a much larger amount, if they would assist him in the war,—to which they finally consented. Indeed, ever since his

* Louisiana, its Colonial History and Romance, by Gayarre, p. 469.

arrival from France, he saw the necessity of inspiring the Indian nations with awe and respect, by a bold and successful strike at the Chickasaws. Nor had he failed to demand the necessary men and military supplies from the mother country.

In the midst of these precarious times, a most unfortunate affair occurred in the bay of Mobile. A smuggling vessel, from Jamaica, cast her anchor twelve miles from the town. Diron D'Artaguette ordered her commander to leave the French coast; he refused. The commissary, then, placed Lieutenant DeVelles in a boat, armed with thirty men, and ordered him to capture the smuggler. When he approached near her, the latter opened an effective fire; seventeen Frenchmen were immediately killed. Before D'Artaguette could reinforce DeVelles, the smuggler had made her escape to sea. This affair again enraged Bienville, and the war of recrimination was fiercer than ever between him and the commissary. What a pity it was, that men of such worth and character did not better appreciate each other. In olden times they had been great friends.

1735 July 16

The commissary had a younger brother, who had behaved with distinguished gallantry in expeditions against the Natchez. He had recently been promoted to the command of the French fort in the district of Illinois. With him Bienville corresponded, respecting the invasion; he was ordered to collect the disposable French forces, and all the Indians in that country who would join him, and with them to march in a southern direction to the Chickasaw towns, while Bien-

CHAPTER X. ville would march from the south, and meet him in the country of the enemy, on the 31st March, 1736. Afterwards
1735 the governor informed young D'Artaguette that he had been unable to make his arrangements to join him at that time, but he would meet him at another time, which was also appointed.

Bienville, nine months before this period, had despatched M. De Lusser, with a company of soldiers and artizans, to a place upon the Little Tombigby, which is now called Jones' Bluff, with orders to erect there a fort and cabins to be used as a depot for the army, and, afterwards, to serve as a permanent trading post. That fearless officer had reached these wilds in safety, and it was not long before the forest resounded with the noise of axes and the heavy falling of timber. He was assisted in his labors by many of the Choctaws.

1736 March 22 At length the army left New-Orleans, and passing through the lakes reached Mobile. The vessels containing the supplies having entered the Gulf by way of the Balize, were retarded
March 28 by winds, and did not arrive until six days afterwards; and then it was discovered that a cargo of rice was destroyed by the salt water. To replace this loss, Bienville set his bakers to work, who made a large supply of biscuits for the army. He sent a despatch to De Lusser at Fort "Tombecbe," ordering him to build ovens, and to have made an abundant supply of biscuits by the time of his arrival at that place. When all
1736 April 1 things were ready, Bienville embarked his troops at Mobile, and turned his boats up the river of that name. Never before had

such a large and imposing fleet of the kind disturbed the deep and smooth waters which now flow by our beautiful commercial emporium. Every kind of up-country craft was employed, and they bore men nearly of all kinds and colors. The crews were composed of genteel merchants, gentlemen of leisure and fortune, loafers and convicts, rough but bold mariners, veteran soldiers, sturdy and invincible Canadians, monks and priests, Choctaws and Mobilians, and a company of negroes commanded by Simon, a free mulatto. The fleet comprised more than sixty of the largest pirogues and bateaux. Entering the main Tombigby, Bienville made his way up that stream to the confluence of the Warrior, and there, passing into the Little Tombigby, he at length arrived at the fort.* Heavy rains and much high water had retarded his passage.

The governor found that the fort was unfinished, and only some cabins, surrounded by stockades and covered with leaves, could be occupied. The bakers had prepared but few biscuits, for the fire cracked the prairie soil of which the ovens were made. After various unsuccessful efforts to make suitable ovens, they succeeded by mixing sand with the earth. Bienville was surprised to see, at the fort, four persons in irons—one Frenchman, two Swiss, and Montfort, a sergeant. They had formed the design of assassinating the commandant of the fort, M. De Lusser, and also the keeper of the store-house, and of carrying off Tisnet and Rosilié, who had recently been rescued from the Chickasaws, among whom they had

* Now Jones' Bluff.

CHAPTER X. been held in slavery. They intended to convey these unfortunate men back to their masters, in order to gain favor with the tribe, who would therefore be induced, after a time, to facilitate their escape to the British provinces. But these assassins were defeated in their plans; for Lieutenant Grondel, with the rapidity of action and the bravery which had ever distinguished him, arrested Montfort with his own hands. The prisoners were tried by a court martial, and being sentenced to be shot, were "presently passed by the arms at the head of the troops."*

When all the allied Choctaws had arrived, Bienville reviewed his troops upon the plain in the rear of the fort. He found that his army was composed of five hundred and fifty men, exclusive of officers, together with six hundred Indians. 1736 May 4 He now assumed the line of march for the country of the enemy. The larger number of the French troops embarked in the boats. Some of the Indians proceeded in their own canoes, while many hardy Canadians, called *couriers de bois*, marched with other Indians, sometimes along the banks, where the swamps did not intervene; and then again a mile or two from the river. It was truly an imposing scene to be exhibited in these interminable wilds. After encountering many difficulties, the redoubtable Bienville at length reached the spot where now stands the city of Columbus, in Mississippi; May 22 and pursuing his tedious voyage, finally moored his boats at or near the place now known as Cotton Gin Port. Here dis-

* Dumont's Memoires Historiques sur la Louisiane, p. 216.

embarking, he immediately began to fell the trees in the forest, and soon stockaded a place ample enough to secure his baggage and provisions, together with the sick; while the side fronting the river was arranged with loop-holes for muskets, to protect his boats, which were all unladen and drawn up close together. He was twenty-seven miles from the towns of the enemy, which lay in a western direction. He left twenty men here under Vanderek, besides the keeper of the magazine, the patroons of the boats, and some of the soldiers who were sick. With some difficulty he hired a sufficient number of the Choctaws to transport the sacks of powder and balls, for the negroes were already laden with other things. Taking provisions with him to last twelve days, the governor began the march in the evening, and that night encamped six miles from the depot. The rains which incommoded him in his voyage up the river, did not forsake him on his march upon the present occasion; for, scarcely had he formed his camp when a violent storm arose. The next day he passed three deep ravines,—the soldiers wading up to their waists,—and after gaining the opposite banks, slipping and falling constantly upon the slimy soil. Great difficulties were surmounted in transporting the effects of the army over these angry torrents. The banks on either side were covered with large canes, but Bienville took the precaution always to send spies in advance, to prevent surprise from ambuscades. Soon, however, the French were relieved by the appearance of the most beautiful country in the world. The prairies were stretched out wide before them, covered with green grass,

1736 May 23

May 24

CHAPTER X.

flowers and strawberries, while forests of magnificent trees were to be seen in the distance. A breeze gently played over the surface of the lovely plains, and a May day's sun warmed all nature into life. The sleek cattle were everywhere grazing upon these sweet meadows of nature. The nimble deer bounded along, and droves of wild horses, of every variety of color, with lofty tails and spreading manes, made the earth resound with their rapid tread. Alas! alas! to think that the inhabitants, whom the Great Spirit had placed in a country so lovely and so enchanting, were soon to be assailed by an army of foreigners, assisted by their own neighbors.

Drawing nearer and nearer to the enemy, Bienville finally encamped within six miles of their towns. His camp was formed upon the border of a delightful prairie, the view across which was not interrupted by trees, until it had reached far beyond the Indian houses. He had previously sent spies in all directions, to look for D'Artaguette and his troops, who were to have joined him there. The bands, chiefly composed of Indians, returned without having heard any thing of that unfortunate officer. The governor was sorely disappointed, and could no longer hope for aid from that source, and he resolved to rely upon his own forces. His intention, at first, was to march in a circuitous direction,
1736 May 24 around the Chickasaw villages, in order to attack the Natchez town which lay behind them, and which had recently been erected. But the Choctaws had become very impatient to assail an advanced village of the Chickasaws, which, they

insisted, could be easily taken, and which, they stated, contained a large amount of provisions. Their importunities were disregarded until strengthened by the entreaties of the Chevalier Noyan, the nephew of the governor, and many other French officers, whose impetuous disposition made them eager for an immediate attack. The houses of the enemy stood upon a hill, in the prairie, and spread out in the shape of a triangle. After some consideration, Bienville resolved to give the French an opportunity of gratifying a long sought revenge, especially when it was made known to him that his camp was then pitched near the last water which his men could procure for miles in a western direction. At two o'clock, in the afternoon, the Chevalier Noyan was placed at the head of a column consisting of a detachment of fifteen men drawn from each of the eight French companies, a company of grenadiers, forty-five volunteers and sixty-five Swiss.

1736 May 26

The Chickasaws had fortified themselves with much skill, and were assisted by Englishmen, who had caused them to hoist a flag of their country over one of their defences. The French troops, as they advanced, were not a little surprised to see the British Lion, against which many of them had often fought in Europe, now floating over the rude huts of American Indians, and bidding them defiance. The Chickasaws had fortified their houses in a most defensive manner, by driving large stakes into the ground around them. Many loop-holes were cut through the latter, very near the ground. Within the palisades, entrenchments were cut, deep enough to protect the

CHAPTER X.

persons of the Indians as high as their breasts. In these ditches they stood, and when the battle began, shot through the loop-holes at the French. The tops of these fortified houses were covered with timbers, upon which was placed a thick coat of mud plaster, so that neither ignited arrows nor bomb shells could set the houses on fire. What added still more to the security of the Chickasaws, was the position of some of their houses, which stood in nearly opposite directions, so as to admit of destructive cross-firing. Bienville having previously learned that there were several of the British in the village, had, with much humanity, as it may at that time have seemed, directed the Chevalier Noyan to give them time to retire before he brought on the attack. The division then marched briskly on. It was protected by moveable breastworks, called mantalets, which were now carried by the company of negroes. As their lives appear not to have been esteemed of as much value as those of the French,
1736 May 26 these negroes were used in the same manner as *shields* are in battle. When the troops advanced within carbine shot of the village of Ackia, where waved the British flag, one of the negroes was killed, and another wounded. They all now threw down their mantalets and precipitately fled. The French, with their usual impetuosity, rapidly advanced. They entered the village. The grenadiers led. And now, no longer protected by the mantalets, they received a severe fire from the Chickasaws, which killed and wounded many. Among the former was the gallant and accomplished Chevalier de Contre Cœur; and when he fell dead it produced an unplea-

sant feeling among those around him, by whom he was greatly esteemed. Upon his right and left soldiers lay dead, discoloring the green grass with their hot blood. But the troops carried three fortified cabins, and reached several smaller ones, which they presently wrapped in flames. The chief fort, and other fortified houses, lay some distance in the rear of those they had in possession. The Chevalier Noyan was eager to advance upon them, but turning round to take a rapid survey of his forces, he was mortified to perceive that only the officers, a dozen of the volunteers, and some grenadiers remained with him. Dismayed by the fall of Captain de Lusser,* who was now killed, and seeing a popular sergeant of grenadiers, and several soldiers, also fall, the troops retreated to the cabins which were first taken. In vain did the officers, who belonged to the rear, endeavor to drive them on to the scene of action. A panic had seized them, and no exhortation, threats, promises of promotion, or hopes of military glory, could induce them to make the slightest advance from their cowardly position. But the officers resolved more than ever, to do their duty, and placing themselves at the head of a few brave soldiers, essayed to storm the fort: But just at the moment of their contemplated charge, the brave Chevalier De Noyan, Grondel, an invincible lieutenant of the Swiss, D'Hauterive, a captain of the grenadiers, Montbrun, De Velles, and many

1736 May 26

1736 May 26

* It will be recollected that De Lusser, who was now killed, was the officer whom Bienville sent to construct Fort "Tombecbe," upon the site of the present Jones' Bluff.

CHAPTER X. other officers and soldiers received severe wounds. The balls of the Chickasaws came thick, and whizzed over the prairies. The bleeding De Noyan stood his ground, and despatched his aid to assist in bringing up the soldiers, who still screened 1736 May 26 themselves behind the cabins; but as he left to perform the order, a Chickasaw ball put an end to his existence. The death of this officer, whose name was De Juzan, increased the panic which had so unfortunately seized upon the larger number of the troops. A party of Indians, at this moment, rushed up to scalp Grondel, the Swiss officer, who had fallen near the walls of the fort. A brave sergeant, with four fearless soldiers, rushed to the rescue. Driving off the savages, they were about to bear him off in their arms, when a fire from the fort killed every one of these noble fellows! But the bleeding Grondel still survived, although those who come to protect his head from the blows of the hatchet, lay dead by his side. Another act of heroism is worthy of record. Régnisse now rushed out alone, and making his way to the unfortunate Grondel, who still lay bleeding from five wounds, dragged him out from among the bodies of those who had just fallen in his defence, placed him on his back, and return-
1736 May 26 ed to the French lines, without receiving a solitary wound from the showers of Chickasaw balls. The almost lifeless Grondel received, however, another severe wound as he was borne off by the noble Régnisse.*

* This Grondel was an officer of indomitable courage. His life was full of romantic events. He had fought several duels at Mobile. He

But where were the six hundred Choctaws, while the French were thus expiring in agony upon the prairie? Painted, plumed, and dressed in a manner the most fantastic and horrible, they kept the plain, on either side of the French lines, at a distance where the balls of the enemy could not reach them, sending forth yells and shouts, and occasionally dancing and shooting their guns in the air. The brave Chickasaws maintained their positions in the fortified houses, and, from loop holes, riddled the French with their unerring rifles. They, too, yelled most awfully. The scene was one calculated to excite deep interest, for, added to all this, the looker-on might have viewed the flames rising up from the burning cabins, and sending above them volumes of black smoke, which a May breeze wafted to the far off forests. 1736 May 26

The Chevalier De Noyan now ordered a retreat to the advanced cabins, and when he had arrived there, he despatched an officer to Bienville, bearing an account of their critical condition. Noyan sent him word that, although severely wounded himself, he was determined to keep the position which he had just taken. He requested that a detachment should be sent to his assistance, to bear off the dead and wounded, and assist those who were alive to make a retreat, as, now, no further hope remained of storming the fortifications of the Chickasaws. Bienville was hastened in 1736 May 26

recovered from the wounds which he received in this battle, and was promoted to high military stations.

CHAPTER X. his determination to send aid, by observing that a Chickasaw force on the flank, which had not yet participated in the battle, were about to sally from their houses, and immolate the French officers and the few soldiers who had remained with them. He then immediately despatched Beauchamp, with eighty men, to the scene of action. Arriving there he found the French officers huddled together, keeping their ground at the imminent peril of their lives. Beauchamp, in advancing, had already lost several men. The Chickasaws now redoubled their exertions, and made the plains resound with their exulting shouts. Beauchamp began the retreat, 1736 May 26 carrying off many of the wounded and the dead, but unfortunately was forced to leave some behind, who fell into the tiger clutches of the Chickasaws. When the French had retreated some distance, towards Bienville's head quarters, the Choctaws, by way of bravado, rushed up to the Chickasaw fortifications, as if they intended to carry them by storm, but receiving a general volley from the enemy, they fled in great terror over the prairie.

The battle of Ackia had lasted three hours, and resulted in glory to the Chickasaws, and disgrace to the French. When the French troops arrived at the camp, proper attention was paid to the wounded and the dying. It was not long before this brilliant and exciting scene was made to give place to one which presented an aspect at once quiet, calm and beautiful. The sun, in his retirement for the night, had 1736 May 26 just sunk to the tops of the trees in the far off distance. A cool and delicious breeze was made sweet with the odour of wild flowers. The Chickasaws were as quiet as the boa-constrictor after he has gorged upon his prey. The cattle and horses, much disturbed during the fight, now began to move up and feed upon their accustomed meadows. What a contrast had been produced by the lapse of only two hours!

During this quiet scene, a collection of French officers were on one side of the camp, summing up the misfortunes of the day. Among them stood Simon, the commander of the negroes who fled from the field. Simon was a favorite with the officers, and had resolutely maintained his ground during the engagement. Some of them rallied him upon the flight 1736 May 26
of his company, which annoyed him excessively. At that moment, a drove of horses came down to the stream to slake their thirst, not far from the fortified houses of the Chickasaws. The desperate Simon, in reply to those who made sport of his company, seized a rope and ran off towards the horses, saying: "I will show you that a negro is as brave as any one." He passed around the horses in full range of the Chickasaw rifles, from which balls were showered upon him, and making his way up to a beautiful white mare, threw a rope over her head, and thus securing her, passed it around her nose, mounted upon her back with the agility of a Camanche Indian, and pressed her with rapid speed into the French lines. He did not receive a wound,—and he was welcomed with shouts by the soldiers, and was no more jeered on account of the cowardice of his company.* 1736 May 26

* Dumont's Memoires Historique sur la Louisiane.

CHAPTER X.

Bienville, pleased with the gallantry which Régnisse had displayed in bearing off the wounded Grondel, immediately from under the guns of the Chickasaws, had him brought to the marquee, complimented him upon the generous and heroic act which he had performed, and proposed to promote him to the rank of an officer. The brave Régnisse modestly replied that he had done nothing more than what could have been accomplished by any of his brother grenadiers, and stated that as he could not write, he was unfitted for an officer; therefore he declined the intended honor.

Night now shrouded the scene with its sable mantle, and the French troops reposed behind some trees which had been felled for their protection. The Chickasaws remained quiet within their intrenchments. At length day dawned, and exhibited to Bienville a painful sight. On the ramparts of the Chickasaws were suspended the French soldiers and officers, whom Beauchamp was forced to leave upon the field. Their limbs had been separated from their bodies, and thus were they made to dangle in the air, for the purpose of insulting the defeated invaders. Many of the officers wished to rush again upon the villages, but Bienville determined to retreat, as the Choctaws were of no assistance to him, and he was without cannon to batter down the fortifications. In the
1736 May 27 afternoon, at two o'clock, he began the retrograde march. The soldiers, worn down with the fatigue produced by the battle and the mortifications arising from its disgraceful termination, were unable, in addition to their heavy loads of baggage, to carry the wounded, who were placed in litters. Conse-

quently night set in by the time Bienville had marched only four miles; here the camp was again made. The Choctaws were highly exasperated on account of this slow movement, and Red Shoes, who had long endeavored to wean his people from the French interest, now vociferously threatened to take with him the greater portion of the Choctaws, and thus leave the French to the mercy of the Chickasaws in this wild and distant region. Bienville was startled when he was informed of this determination. He sent for the main Chief of the Choctaws, and by his eloquence and the force of that mysterious influence which he possessed, he succeeded not only in getting the Choctaws to remain with the army, but made them consent to assist in the transportation of the wounded. Red Shoes rebuked the head Chief, for consenting to such terms, in a manner so insulting, that the latter drew his pistol from his belt, and was in the act of shooting him, when Bienville seized his arm, saved the life of Red Shoes, and, for a while, put an end to an affair which threatened the most serious consequences. The next morning Bienville put his troops upon the march, and he arrived at the depot, upon the Tombigby, on the 29th May, after he had buried two of his men, on the way, who had died of their wounds. 1736 May 28

Bienville was astonished to observe how much the river had fallen, and he hurried his effects into the boats, for fear that the delay of a day longer would leave him without a stream sufficient to convey him to Mobile. When the troops had embarked, the ropes which bound the boats to the banks were untied, and then the discomfited French party passed down

19*

CHAPTER X. the stream. The channel of the Little Tombigby was here so crooked and narrow, that the boats had frequently to stop until logs and projecting limbs were cut out of the way. If the Chickasaws had followed up the French, they could easily have destroyed Bienville's army at this time. At length the
1736 June 2 army reached Fort "Tombecbe," now Jones' Bluff. Bienville, sending on a portion of the troops, and the sick and wounded to Mobile, disembarked at the fort. He remained there, however, but one day, which he consumed in planning upon paper, and tracing upon the ground additions which he directed to be made to the defences. Then, leaving Captain De Berthel in command of Fort "Tombecbe," with a garrison of thirty Frenchmen and twenty Swiss, provisions to last for the remainder of the year, and an abundance of merchandize intended to be used in a commerce with the Indians, the
June 3 governor entered his boats, and continued the voyage until they were moored at the town of Mobile.

But where was the brave and unfortunate D'Artaguette? Why did not his army join Bienville at the Chickasaw towns? The reader will presently see. That officer had assembled the tribes of the Illinois at Fort Chatres, and had made them acquainted with the plans of Governor Bienville. With these Indians, and others which De Vincennes had collected upon the Wabash, together with thirty soldiers and one hundred volunteers, D'Artaguette floated down the Mississippi river until he reached the last of the Chickasaw Bluffs. He had expected to have been joined by De Grandpré, who commanded at the Arkansas, and that officer had sent twenty-eight warriors of that tribe to ascertain whether D'Artaguette was at Ecores à Prudhomme. These scouts were instructed to return with the necessary information; but upon arriving at that place, and finding that D'Artaguette had set out upon his expedition, they hastened to follow him into the enemy's country. Disembarking at the Chickasaw Bluffs, D'Artaguette marched across the country, at a slow pace, hoping to be overtaken by De Grandpré, and also by Montcherval, who had been ordered to bring on his Cahokias and Mitchigamias. Pursuing the march in an eastward direction, D'Artaguette advanced among the sources of the Yalobusha, and there encamped on the 9th May. He was but a few miles east of the site of the present town of Pontotoc, in Mississippi, near the place where he and Bienville were to have met each other, and not more than thirty miles from the spot where the latter, afterwards, moored his boats,—near the present Cotton Gin Port. D'Artaguette sought, in vain, for intelligence of the commander-in-chief. He was assisted by Lieutenant Vincennes, the young Voisin, and Sénac, a holy father of the order of Jesuits, in arranging and conducting the spy companies, who roamed the forests in search of Bienville. But nothing could be heard of him until a courier brought to D'Artaguette a letter, in which he was informed that unexpected delays would prevent Bienville from reaching the Chickasaw towns before the last of April. The red allies had become impatient, for, by this time, D'Artaguette had occupied his camp for eleven days. He now resolved to advance upon the Chickasaws, as his allies had threatened to

1736 May

May 20

CHAPTER X.

abandon him if he did not soon bring on the attack. They represented to him that the advance town was inhabited by the refugee Natchez, and by taking it they could return to their encampment with an abundance of provisions, where they might remain entrenched until Bienville's arrival. This plausible proposition found advocates in the French officers. The allied forces consisted of one hundred and thirty Frenchmen, and three hundred and sixty Indians. The French advanced within a mile of the village, on Palm Sunday. Frontigny was here left at the camp, with thirty men, in charge of all the baggage. D'Artaguette advanced rapidly to the attack, which he presently brought on with his accustomed gallantry. At that moment, thirty Englishmen and five hundred Indians, who were concealed behind an adjacent hill, rose up and fell upon the invaders with such impetuosity that the Miamis and the Illinois fled from the battle field. Indeed, all the Indians took to their heels, except a few Iroquois and Arkansas, who behaved in the bravest manner. The guns of the enemy brought to the ground Lieutenant St. Ange, Ensigns De Coulanges, De La
1736 May 20 Graviere and De Courtigny, with six of the militia officers. By this time the French were almost surrounded, but they still continued to keep their position. Presently, Captain Des Essarts was seen to fall, and also Lieutenant Langlois and Ensign Levieux. So great was the loss of the French, in this short, but desperate conflict, that D'Artaguette determined to retreat to the camp, for the double purpose of saving his baggage, and of being reinforced by the men he had left

there. But the retreat could not be conducted with the least order, for the Chickasaws were close upon their heels, and at length again surrounded them. D'Artaguette now fell, covered with wounds, and was taken prisoner, together with Father Sénac, Vincennes, Du Tisné, an officer of the regulars, a captain of the militia, named Lalande, and some soldiers, making nineteen in all. Not one man would have escaped the clutches of the brave Chickasaws, if a violent storm, which now arose, had not prevented further pursuit. It was a great victory; all the provisions and baggage of D'Artaguette fell into the hands of the Chickasaws, besides eleven horses, four hundred and fifty pounds of powder and twelve hundred bullets. With this powder and these bullets they, afterwards, shot down the troops of Bienville, as we have already seen.

1736 May 20

Voisin, a youth of only sixteen years of age, conducted the retreat for many miles, without food or water, while his men carried such of the wounded as they were able to bear. This noble youth,—one of the bravest that ever lived,—stood by the side of D'Artaguette in all this bloody engagement. At length, on the second day of his painful retreat, he halted his men at a place, where Montcherval, who was following D'Artaguette with one hundred and sixty Indians, had encamped. The latter, collecting the fragments of the army, fell back to the Mississippi river.

May

At first, the unfortunate D'Artaguette and his equally unfortunate companions in captivity, were treated with kindness and attention by the Chickasaws, who dressed their wounds.

CHAPTER X. 1736 May

Hopes of a high ransom prompted this conduct, so unusual with Indians. They expected not only to receive money from Bienville, who was known to be approaching, but imagined that, by holding these men as prisoners, the governor would consent to leave their towns unattacked. But at length they received intelligence that Bienville had been defeated, and they now resolved to sacrifice the prisoners. They led them out to a neighboring field, and D'Artaguette, Father Senac, Vincennes, and fifteen others were pinioned to stakes and burned to death! One of the soldiers was spared to carry the news of the triumph of the Chickasaws, and the death of these unhappy men, to the mortified Bienville.*

The Chickasaws have never been conquered. They could not be defeated by De Soto, with his Spanish army, in 1541; by Bienville, with his French army and Southern Indians, in 1736; by D'Artaguette, with his French army and Northern Indians; by the Marquis De Vandreuil, with his French troops and Choctaws, in 1752; nor by the Creeks, Cherokees, Kickapoos, Shawnees and Choctaws, who continually waged war

* MS. letters obtained from Paris. I have also consulted Gayarre's Histoire de la Louisiane, vol. 1, pp. 311–331, which contains the despatches of Bienville to the French Court, in relation to these battles. Also, Dumont's Memoires Historiques sur la Louisiane—Bancroft's History of the United States, vol. 3—The South West by Alexander B. Meek, of Mobile—Martin's Louisiana—Stodart's Louisiana—Monette's History of the Mississippi Valley, vol. 1, pp. 283–288—Louisiana, its Colonial History and Romance, by Charles Gayarre: New-York, 1851; pp. 476–495.

against them. No! they were "the bravest of the brave;" and even when they had emigrated to the territory of Arkansas, not many years ago, they soon subdued some tribes who attacked them in that quarter.

Young men of North Western Alabama and North Eastern Mississippi! Remember that the bravest race that ever lived, once occupied the country which you now inhabit—once fished in your streams, and chased the elk over your vast plains. Remember, that whenever that soil, which *you* now tread, was pressed by the feet of foes, it was not only bravely defended, but drenched with the blood of the invaders. Will you ever disgrace that soil, and the memory of its first occupants, by submitting to injustice and oppression, and finally to invasion? We unhesitatingly give the answer for you—"No—no—never!"

CHAPTER XI.

BIENVILLE LEAVES THE COLONY—HIS CHARACTER.

CHAPTER XI. In our investigations of the French Colonial History of Alabama and Mississippi, for a period of sixteen years from the conclusion of the campaigns of Bienville and D'Artaguette, in the Chickasaw nation, we find but little to interest the reader. The same difficulties as heretofore, continued to exist with the Indian tribes, with the colonial authorities and with the English of Carolina. Bienville began, soon after his defeat near Pontotoc, to lose favor with the King and the West India Company. To recover the ground which he had lost in their confidence, he exerted himself to organize another expedition against the Chickasaws; and having perfected it, he sailed up the Mississippi to Fort St. Francis, and disembarking, brought his army to a place near the mouth of the Margot or Wolf river. Here his troops remained a long time, until, reduced by death from various diseases, and by famine, he was left with but few soldiers. Finally, with these
1740 March M. Celeron was ordered to march against the Chickasaw

towns. As he advanced, the Chickasaws, supposing that a large French army had invaded their country, sued for peace. Celeron took advantage of their mistake, and immediately come to terms with them. The Chickasaws promised to expel the English traders from their country, and, from that time, to remain true to the French interest. When the result of this expedition, which terminated forever the military operations of Bienville, became known in France, the governor began to receive despatches dictated in a spirit of much harshness and censure. The pride of Bienville was wounded—his spirit was humbled; and, being too sensible a man to retain a position the duties of which it was believed he had failed creditably to perform, he now requested to be recalled. He wrote to the Minister as follows:— 1742 March 26

"If success had always corresponded with my application to the affairs of the government and administration of the colony, and with my zeal for the service of the King, I would have rejoiced in devoting the rest of my days to such objects; but, through a sort of fatality, which, for some time past, has obstinately thwarted my best concerted plans, I have frequently lost the fruit of my labors, and, perhaps, some ground in your excellency's confidence:—therefore have I come to the conclusion, that it is no longer necessary for me to struggle against my adverse fortune. I hope that better luck may attend my successor. During the remainder of my stay here, I will give all my attention to smooth the difficulties attached to the office which I shall deliver up to him; and it is to me

CHAPTER XI.

a subject of self-gratulation that I shall transmit to him the government of the colony, when its affairs are in a better condition than they have ever been."*

Bienville was, unquestionably, not only a great and good man, but a modest one. We find in this letter none of that disgusting cant indulged in by American politicians and American office holders, when they lose their places. In these days it is common for such men to say that they have been treated with ingratitude by the government, if they are removed from an office,—or by the people, if an opposing candidate is elected to Congress, and to whine and complain about having "grown gray in the service of their country," when, in truth, they have lived at their ease and feasted upon the contents of the public treasury, time out of mind. Some of these men have received over a hundred thousand dollars for occupying seats in the Senate and the House of Representatives, and much larger sums for filling the office of President, and for foreign missions, and yet, after all these favors, from the government and the people, they complain of being treated with ingratitude, if they lose their position. The people who permitted them so long to hold these trusts, often to their own injury, should never be charged with the crime of ingratitude; but the recipient of all these political favors

* Louisiana, its Colonial History and Romance, by Charles Gayarre, pp. 526–527. See also Bienville's letter in French, contained in Histoire de la Louisiane, par Charles Gayarre.

should ever feel grateful, and retire with dignity and grace, like the good and wise Bienville.*

The successor of Bienville, the Marquis De Vaudreuil, arrived at New-Orleans, and shortly afterwards the former sailed for France. Although sixty-five years of age when he left the colony, Bienville lived to the advanced age of ninety. What a constitution for a man who had passed through such trials and hardships! In the whole of the twenty-five years that he passed in France, he never, for one moment forgot, the colony in Alabama, Mississippi and Louisiana. He nursed it in his remembrance, as does the aged grandfather who is far off from his beloved descendants. He sympathized with its misfortunes, and exulted in its triumphs and prosperity. Whenever a vessel, from the colony, reached the shores of France, Bienville was the first to go on board, and learn tidings of his beloved bantling. And when the French King, towards the last of Bienville's days, ceded the colony of Louisiana to Spain, the good old man implored him with tears in

1743 May 10

* If Alabama should, hereafter, change the names of any of her present counties, or form new ones, we very respectfully suggest that one be named "De Soto," and another "Bienville." The former was the first to discover our territory, and the latter was the French governor of it for forty years! We have a sufficient number of counties, rivers, creeks and towns bearing Indian names, to preserve a remembrance of the former residence of the Red Men here. We have counties also named for politicians and warriors, but unlike Mississippi, Louisiana and Georgia, we have not one named for a person whose name would lead us to think of the history of our country.

CHAPTER XI. his eyes, not to place the French subjects of the colony under the control of the tyrannical Spaniards.

Another distinguished person departed from our country about the time that Bienville sailed for France—Diron D'Artaguette, the royal commissary, who had lived so long at Mobile. As we have seen, he came to our country in 1708,
1742 where he filled several high offices until 1742. It was his younger brother whom the Chickasaws burned to death, near Pontotoc, in the present State of Mississippi. It is not known whether the royal commissary and Bienville ever again became friends. They ought, really, never to have disagreed, as they were both men of ability, honor and fidelity.

The colony, at length, became prosperous. Capitalists embarked in agriculture and commerce, after the restrictions upon the latter had been set aside by the King. Cargoes of flour, hides, pork, bacon, leather, tallow, bear's oil and lumber found their way to Europe. These articles came chiefly from the Illinois and Wabash countries, and the inhabitants of that region, in return, received from New-Orleans and Mobile, rice, indigo, tobacco, sugar and European fabrics. But a war broke out between France and Great Britain, and the Chickasaws again becoming the allies of the English, the Marquis De Vaudreuil determined to invade their country. He organized
1752 his army, and embarking in boats, at Mobile, made his way up the Tombigby river. After resting a few days at Fort "Tombecbe," he renewed his voyage until he reached the place where Bienville, sixteen years before, had disembarked his army. Marching from this point with his troops, com-

posed of French and Choctaws, he reached the Chickasaw towns, and endeavoring to storm them, lost many of his men; and was finally beaten, and compelled to retreat to his boats near Cotton Gin Port. All he accomplished was to destroy the fields and burn some cabins of the enemy. Arriving at Fort "Tombecbe," he caused it to be enlarged and strengthened—leaving there a strong detachment to prevent the incursions of the Chickasaws. Like Bienville, the Marquis re- 1752
turned to Mobile not at all satisfied with the laurels which he had won in his expedition against the Chickasaws.*

* It has been stated to me, by several persons, that cannon have been found in the Tombigby, at or near Cotton Gin Port, and it has been supposed that they were left there by De Soto. De Soto brought from Cuba but one piece of artillery, and that he left behind him in Florida. If any such cannon have been found in the Tombigby, they belonged to the Marquis De Vaudreuil. He carried with him a few pieces to operate against the Chickasaws upon the occasion just referred to. After he had fought the Chickasaws, and returned to his boats, he found that the Tombigby had fallen considerably, and it is probable he threw these cannon into the river to lighten his boats.

CHAPTER XII.

HORRIBLE DEATH OF BEAUDROT AND THE SWISS SOLDIERS.

CHAPTER XII.

In 1757, Kerlerec was governor of the colony. He had succeeded the Marquis De Vaudreuil, who had been transferred to the government of New France. Some of the officers, stationed at the different posts, were great tyrants. One of them, named Duroux, was sent to command a detachment of troops of the Swiss regiment of Halwyl, who were station-
1757 ed at Cat Island, which, we believe, is now within the jurisdiction of the State of Alabama. He forced his soldiers to work his gardens, and to burn coal and lime, which he disposed of in trade for his own emolument. Some of them, who refused to work for him, he caused to be arrested, stripped and tied naked to trees, where, for hours, the mosquitoes tortured them with their poisonous stings. These soldiers, repairing to New-Orleans, received no satisfaction from Governor Kerlerec, who presently sent them back to Duroux. That officer was now still more tyrannical, and in addition to his other severe usage, gave them no meat to eat, and fed

them upon stale bread. One day he entered a boat, and was CHAPTER
rowed to an adjacent island, for the purpose of hunting deer. XII.
Returning in the evening, a party of the soldiers prepared themselves to kill him, and, as soon as he put his foot upon shore, he was instantly despatched, by the discharge of several guns. His body, stripped of its apparel, was contemptuously thrown into the sea. They then rifled the King's stores, and, for once in a long while, fared sumptuously. Becoming masters of the
island, the soldiers set at liberty an inhabitant, named Beau- 1757
drot, who had been unjustly imprisoned by Duroux. He had been long in the colony, and was often employed upon dangerous missions in the Creek nation. Indeed, he well understood the language of these Indians, besides that of neighboring tribes. Often had he made journeys to Fort Toulouse, upon the Coosa, both in boats and upon foot. He was a great favorite of Bienville. Beaudrot was a powerful man, as to strength, and almost a giant in size, and these qualities, together with his bravery and prowess, endeared him to the Indians. The soldiers, who now released him from prison, compelled him to conduct them towards Georgia. Advancing rapidly through the woods, after they had touched the main land in their boats, the veteran Beaudrot led them around Mobile, up to the Tombigby, and, crossing that stream, and afterwards the Alabama, in canoes which belonged to the Indians, Beaudrot conducted them from thence to Coweta, upon the Chattahoochie. Here he was dismissed by the fugitives, whom he compelled to give him a certificate, stating

CHAPTER XII. that he had been *forced* to act as their guide, and was not in any way concerned in the killing of Duroux.

Some of these soldiers, who pursued their journey, made safe their retreat to the English in Georgia; but others loitered in Coweta and Cusseta, enjoying the hospitality of the Indians. 1757 In the meantime, Montberaut, who then commanded at Fort Toulouse, had been made acquainted with the murder of Duroux and the flight of the soldiers. Hearing that some of them were upon the Chattahoochie, a small detachment of soldiers, and some Indians, under Beaudin, were sent across the country, to arrest them. Beaudin returned with three of the men, who, after being chained in the prison for a week, were put in canoes, and conveyed down the Alabama river, to Mobile, and there thrown into the dungeon, to await trial.

Beaudrot arrived in Mobile, and was quietly living in his hut, when two of his sons, who had just arrived from New-Orleans, were the innocent cause of his arrest. Governor Kerlerec sent by them a sealed package to De Ville, the commandant at Mobile, authorizing his imprisonment. The poor fellow knew nothing of the arrest of the soldiers, until his eyes fell upon them in prison. Notwithstanding that he exhibited, upon the trial, his certificate, which declared his innocence of the murder, and which stated that he was compelled to facilitate the escape of the authors of it, a court martial condemned him to die. The soldiers, of course, were also condemned to share the same fate. As soon as Governor Kerlerec confirmed the judgment, the innocent and unfortunate

Beaudrot was led forth, and broken upon a wheel! The people of Mobile were shocked at the spectacle, for some of their lives had been saved by the sufferer. Not many years before that, Beaudrot, while trading in the town of Autauga, among the Alabamas, ransomed a French boy, who had been captured near Mobile, by the Lower Creeks of the Chattahoochie, and who had sold him to those Indians. Beaudrot paid away all his profits for the boy, and immediately carried him to Mobile, and restored him to his uncle. On another occasion, a party of the Lower Creeks had taken a Frenchman, who had gone up to his little plantation on the Tensaw river. They stripped the man, and, having pinioned him well, took the trail for the Chattahoochie. It so happened that Beaudrot was returning, upon that trail, from Fort Toulouse, whither Bienville had some weeks before despatched him, with a letter to the French commandant. Night drew apace, and the wearied Beaudrot sought repose upon the pine straw, behind a log, without a spark of fire. It was his custom, when alone, to sleep in the dark, for fear of being discovered by Indian enemies. He lay quietly, with his head resting upon his knapsack. Presently three stout warriors made their appearance, with the Frenchman to whom we have just alluded. They presently collected lightwood, which lay in profusion around, and kindled a large fire. Ten of the party, after the capture of the Frenchman, went in another direction, to see if they could not do more mischief in the French settlements, and, entrusting the prisoner to the three warriors who now guarded him, had not yet overtaken them.

1757

CHAPTER XII.

The fire threw a glare over the woods, and Beaudrot would have been discovered, had he not, fortunately, been behind a log. The warriors eat their supper, and, tying the Frenchman to a tree, where he would have been compelled to stand all night upon his feet, they dropped off to sleep. The heart of the generous Beaudrot beat quick; he longed to rescue the man, whom he well knew, but endeavored to compose himself. After a while, when the wearied warriors snored in profound sleep, he cautiously approached. His first intention was to unloose the prisoner, and place a pistol in his hand, when they would both instantly fall upon the Indians; but a moment's reflection warned him that, if he approached the prisoner first, the latter would be startled, and cry aloud, which would arouse the savages. This reflection altered his plans, and he now crept up to the camp, keeping a large pine tree between him and the warriors. Two of them lay together. Beaudrot's carbine was heavily charged, and, raising himself suddenly, he fired, and the warriors were both killed. The third one rose up, and rushed at Beaudrot with his hatchet, having, in his haste, forgotten his gun. Beaudrot had already a pistol in his hand, and now discharged its contents into the stomach of the Creek, who whooped and fell dead. Rushing to the tree, he untied his friend, who immediately sank in the arms of his generous deliverer. But they had no time to tarry here. The rescued prisoner informed Beaudrot that the other party were probably upon their trail. They immediately left the spot, and, reaching the Alabama river, Beaudrot constructed a raft, on which he now placed the prisoner, and they both floated down the river some distance, and landed on the western side. He tore the raft to pieces, and set the fragments adrift. Beaudrot took all this precaution to keep the Indians from tracking him. About this time it was daylight, and he and the Frenchman were in a swamp, and quite secure. Beaudrot now drew forth his bottle of brandy, and gave his companion a drink, which did much to revive him. They also shared some bread and dried venison. After they had rested here some hours, Beaudrot and his companion arose, and, after a tedious march through the woods, subsisting upon what game Beaudrot could kill, he arrived safe in Mobile, with the Frenchman. CHAPTER XII.

Such a man was Beaudrot, whom the French authorities in Mobile broke upon a wheel! His life was worth a thousand such lives as that of the tyrannical wretch whom he was accused of having killed. On the same day that he was thus made to suffer death, in the most barbarous and excruciating manner, one of the fugitives, a French soldier, was also broken upon a wheel, while two poor Swiss soldiers were subjected to a still more horrible fate. The authorities placed each one of them in a long narrow box, like a coffin, nailed it up, and then cut the box in two with a cross-cut saw.* 1757

* French MS. letters in my possession, obtained from Paris. See also Bossu's Travels, vol. 1, pp. 320–325. But Bossu *incorrectly* states that these men suffered death in New-Orleans. Some years previously, Fort Conde, a large brick fortress, had been built at Mobile, and it was in front of the gate of that fort that these men met such a terrible death.

CHAPTER XIII.

BOSSU'S VISIT TO THE FRENCH FORTS UPON THE ALABAMA AND TOMBIGBY RIVERS.

CHAPTER XIII. GOVERNOR KERLEREC having ordered Bossu, a Captain of the French Marines, to depart from New-Orleans with a detachment, destined for Fort Toulouse, among the Creek Indians, 1758 December 20 that officer reached Mobile, and was there received by D'Aubant, adjutant of that place. The latter, the same officer who married the Russian Princess, and lived with her in Mobile, as we have seen, had recently been appointed to the command of Fort Toulouse, and was instructed to accompany Bossu to that point; but sickness, for a while, detained him in Mobile. In the meantime, Bossu embarked his soldiers and Choctaws in several boats. 1759 March After a tedious voyage, of fifty days, up the Alabama river, he moored his boats at the French fort, upon the Coosa. Here he had the pleasure of meeting D'Aubant, who, having recovered from his indisposition, had come from Mobile on horseback, across the vast wilderness. Montberaut, who was still in command of the fort, received D'Aubant with politeness, and, for three months previous to his departure to Mobile, instructed him in regard to the condition of the fort, and of the policy which it was necessary for him to pursue with the tribes around. Montberaut was an officer of high reputation among the Creeks and Alabamas, and "was remarkable for the spirited speeches which he delivered, in a manner analogous to the way of thinking of these nations."* He despised the Jesuits, and, as they were formally stationed at Fort Toulouse, he always lived upon bad terms with them. Father Le Roi, one of these missionaries, wrote a letter to the Governor, in which he abused Montbéraut in unmeasured terms, and advised his removal. The soldier to whom the letter was delivered, and who was to convey it to Mobile, handed it to Montberaut, who noted its contents. When the Jesuit met him the next morning, he showed him many civilities, as Bossu says, "according to the political principles of these good fathers." The commandant asked him if he had written any thing against him. The Jesuit, not suspecting that his letter was in the officer's hands, assured him, by all that was sacred, that he had not. Montberaut then called Father Le Roi an impostor and cheat, and fixed his letter at the gate of the fort. Since that time no Jesuits have been among the Creeks and Alabamas.†

1759 April

When Bossu visited Fort Toulouse, upon the Coosa, he found that the Creeks and Alabamas were happy people. They lived with ease, had an abundance around them, and

* Bossu's Travels, vol. 1, p. 228. † Ibid., p. 229.

CHAPTER XIII. were at peace with the surrounding savages. While at the fort, Bossu heard a Chief deliver the following beautiful speech:

"Young men and warriors! Do not disregard the MASTER OF LIFE. The sky is blue—the sun is without spots—the weather is fair—the ground is white—every thing is quiet on the face of the earth, and the blood of men ought not to be spilt on it. We must beg the MASTER OF LIFE to preserve it pure and spotless among the nations that surround us."

Not only were the Creeks and Alabamas at peace with other nations, at this time, but gave evidences of warm and
1759 April generous hospitality. They thronged the banks of the river, which now meanders along the borders of the counties of Autauga, Montgomery, Dallas and Lowndes—as Bossu slowly made his way up the beautiful stream, greeted him with friendly salutations, and offered him provisions, such as bread, roasted turkies, broiled venison, pancakes baked with nut oil, and deers' tongues, together with baskets full of eggs of the fowl and the turtle. The GREAT SPIRIT had blessed them with a magnificent river, abounding in fish; with delicious and cool fountains, gushing out from the foot of the hills; with rich lands, that produced without cultivation, and with vast forests, abounding in game of every description. But now the whole scene is changed. The country is no longer half so beautiful; the waters of Alabama begin to be discolored; the forests have been cut down; steamers have destroyed the finny race; deer bound not over the plain; the sluggish bear has ceased to wind through the swamps; the

bloody panther does not spring upon his prey; wolves have ceased to howl upon the hills; birds cannot be seen in the branches of the trees; graceful warriors guide no longer their well-shaped canoes, and beautiful squaws loiter not upon the plain, nor pick the delicious berries. Now, vast fields of cotton, noisy steamers, huge rafts of lumber, towns reared for business, disagreeable corporation laws, harrassing courts of justice, mills, factories, and everything else that is calculated to destroy the beauty of a country and to rob man of his quiet and native independence, present themselves to our view.

The heart yearns to behold, once more, such a country as Alabama was the first time we saw it, when a boy. But where can we now go, that we shall not find the busy American, with keen desire to destroy everything which nature has made lovely?

Fort Toulouse, at various times, had many commandants, who filled each others' places according to the will or whim of the colonial Governor and the different companies. At one time, the Chevalier D'Ernville commanded here, when a young warrior killed a French soldier, and fled to the forests. According to an agreement formed between the French and the Indians, when the fort was first established, the killing of a person was to be atoned for by the immediate execution of him who committed the deed, whether he was a Frenchman or an Indian. D'Ernville demanded the Indian of the Chiefs, who stated that they were unable to find him. He next required that the mother of the guilty warrior should be made

CHAPTER XIII. to expiate the crime. They replied that the mother had not killed the Frenchman; but the officer only reminded them of the agreement, and further, of the previous customs of their country. Deeply embarrassed, in consequence of the escape of the criminal, and unwilling that the old woman should be put to death, the Chiefs, to compromise the case, offered the French officer furs and horse-loads of booty. But D'Ernville was unyielding, and had the mother brought out before Fort Toulouse, to suffer death. Her relatives followed her with sad countenances, one of them exclaiming, in a loud voice, "My mother-in-law dies courageously, as she has not struck the blow." In a few minutes the son rushed through the cane-brake, boldly walked up to D'Ernville, gave himself up, saved the life of his mother, and was then—killed!

1759 May One day it was announced at Fort Toulouse that the Emperor of Coweta, a town on the Chattahoochie, was advancing to pay the French a visit. Bossu walked some distance upon the pathway, towards the present Grey's Ferry, which was, at that early day, a great crossing-place for the Indians. He was accompanied by some soldiers, and, to surprise the Emperor, they fired their muskets as soon as Bossu took him by the hand, which was also the signal for a general discharge of the artillery from the fort. The woods presently resounded with the noise of the cannon, and the Emperor felt that he was greatly honored. He was mounted on a Spanish horse, with an English saddle, which was bordered with a beautiful spotted skin. He alighted from his horse, and advanced to the fort with an air of great dignity and importance. His costume was so singular as to excite the subdued risibilities of the Frenchmen, who marched behind him. He wore on his head a crest of black plumes; his coat was scarlet, with English cuffs, and beset with tinsel lace; he had neither waistcoat nor breeches; under his coat he wore a white linen shirt. His attendants were naked, and painted in a variety of colors. Being only eighteen years of age, the Emperor was accompanied by his Regent, a noble and wise old man, who ruled the Lower Creeks during his minority. When they reached the fort, the old man delivered a speech to D'Aubant, which was reported by Laubene, the King's interpreter, who had been long stationed at that place.

CHAPTER XIII.

Being anxious to alienate the Lower Creeks, upon the Chattahoochie, from the relations which they had formed with the Georgians, D'Aubant paid the visitors unusual attention. The next day, at ten o'clock, he received the Emperor, his War-Chief, Regent, Doctor, and followers, in considerable state. They were marched before the officers and soldiers, who were all drawn up in full uniform. At noon they were conducted to the dining table, where they and the officers took seats together. The Emperor was much puzzled in what manner to employ the knife and fork, and was extremely awkward and embarrassed. But the old Regent seized the back-bone and breast of a turkey, and broke them in two with his fingers, saying, "The MASTER OF LIFE made fingers before knives and forks were made."

1759 May

Towards the end of the repast, a servant of the Emperor,

CHAPTER XIII. who stood behind his chair, perceived that the French ate mustard with their boiled meat. He asked Beaudin what it

1759 May was that they relished so much? This officer, the same who went to the Chattahoochie, and arrested the soldiers who fled from Cat Island, and who had lived forty years in the Creek nation, replied, that the French were by no means covetous of what they possessed. He handed the Indian a spoonful of the mustard, who swallowed it. He thereupon made many ridiculous contortions, giving several whoops, and affording the whole company much merriment. The Indian imagined himself to be poisoned, and D'Aubant, the commandant, could only appease him by a glass of delightful brandy.*

About this time, the celebrated Russian Princess, whom, as we have seen, D'Aubant had long since married, at Mobile, becoming tired of his protracted absence, determined to join him, which, indeed, had been planned when the chevalier left her at Mobile. Going on board a boat which was starting

1759 June for Fort Toulouse, this remarkable and romantic woman, after a long voyage, arrived at this place with her little daughter and a female servant. She was affectionately received by D'Aubant, and had many lively adventures to relate of her passage up the Alabama. Not having pleasant quarters in

* Travels through that part of North America formerly called Louisiana, by M. Bossu, Captain in the French Marines. Vol. 1, pp. 226–278.

the fort, a cabin was built for her in the field, not far from the fort, to which was attached a brick chimney, the fragments of which still remain there. Here this gay woman was accustomed to converse with the Indians and prattle with their pickaninnies. So, then, citizens of Wetumpka, there was once living, within three miles of your city, a Russian Princess—so represented to be—who had married the son of Peter the Great!*

CHAPTER XIII.

1759 June

While at Fort Toulouse, Bossu received an order to repair to Mobile, for the purpose of serving under the orders of De Ville, the King's lieutenant, stationed at that place. He entered a boat, and, after a prosperous voyage, reached Mobile. Some time afterwards he was ordered to command a convoy to Fort "Tombecbe." He left Mobile with three boats, in which were soldiers and Mobile Indians. He entered the Tombigby river, after a voyage of seven days, which now can be performed in four hours. Mooring his boats near some land, a little elevated above the water, he pitched his camp, and prepared to pass the night on shore, as was the custom of all voyagers of that day. While wrapped in a corner of his tent-cloth, and reposing upon his bear's skin, with a string of fine fish, which he designed for his breakfast, lying at his feet, he was awakened from a profound sleep, by finding himself suddenly carried away, by an extroardinary force. Terribly alarmed, he cried out for help. An enormous alligator,

1759 August

* French MS. letters in my possession, obtained from Paris.

CHAPTER XIII. intent upon seizing the string of fish, had caught in his teeth a portion of the tent-cloth, and was hurrying Bossu, tent cloth, bear-skin, fish and all, rapidly to his accustomed element. Fortunately, just before the alligator plunged into the river, Bossu saved himself and the bear-skin; but the fish and the tent-cloth disappeared with the monster.

The voyage up the river was remarkably tedious, for, it being at a low stage, Bossu was often compelled to drag his boats over the bars. He camped upon the banks every night, and, to protect himself as much as possible from the mosquitoes, he placed canes in the ground, and, making their tops meet by bending them over, formed an arch. Over this rude frame
1759 August he threw a linen sheet, and slept under it most comfortably, reposing on his bear-skin. On one occasion, provisions became so scarce that Bossu sent out some of his men to procure game in the forests. Discovering the nest of a large eagle, built in the branches of a lofty tree, the Indians soon prostrated the latter with their axes. They obtained from this immense nest, several fawns, rabbits, wild turkies, partridges and wild pigeons, together with four eaglets.* The old eagles fought desperately for their young; but the famished party bore off the nest and the abundance of game which it contained, all of which had recently been taken for

* Bossu must be mistaken as to the number of eaglets. According to my reading of natural history, I am under the impression that not more than *two* eaglets are ever found in the same nest.

the eaglets to devour. Bossu and his party lived sumptuously during the remainder of their voyage, which was at length terminated at Fort "Tombecbe," the site of which is now familiarly known as Jones' Bluff. De Grandpré, a Canadian of much bravery, and possessed of much experience in relation to the habits and customs of the Indians, commanded the garrison at this post. Bossu's journal, kept at this place, is wholly occupied with the manners and customs of the Choctaws. As we have already referred to him, upon this subject, in our description of that tribe, we will omit here what would be a mere repetition, only submitting to the reader the following extract: 1759 August

"I saw an Indian of the Choctaws who had lately been baptized. As he had no luck in hunting, he imagined himself bewitched. He went immediately to Father Lefevre, the Jesuit missionary, who was stationed at Fort 'Tombecbe,' and who had lately converted him. He told him that his *medicine* was good for nothing, for, since he had practised it upon him, he could kill no deer. He therefore desired the priest to take off his enchantment. The Jesuit, in order to avoid the resentment of this Indian, acted as if he had annihilated the baptismal ceremony. Some time after this, the Indian killed a deer, and, thus thinking himself forever free from the enchantment, was a most happy fellow."*

But the colony of Louisiana, so vast in extent, and embra-

* Bossu's Travels, pp. 226–318.

CHAPTER XIII. cing within its limits the territory of our own State, and that of Mississippi, was soon to be taken from the French. It has been seen that the English and the French had long been competitors for the commercial patronage of the Indians, in Lower Louisiana, and also for the right to the soil. Far more bitter were their jealousies, and far more bloody their feuds upon the borders of Ohio, Virginia and Pennsylvania. For some time, a serious colonial war had been raging between the North American provinces of France and those of England. The French lost post after post. The victorious Britons garrisoned them with troops, and then captured others. In this manner, the King of France lost all his Louisiana possessions, and, with them, the soil of Mississippi and Alabama. Spain, too, had allied herself with France, in the war. At
1763 February 18 length the three belligerant powers concluded a peace, the conditions of which are stated in the commencement of our second volume.

Agreeably to the provisions of that treaty, Pierre Annibal
October de Ville, lieutenant of the King, commandant at Mobile, and Jean Gabriel Fazende, d'ordonnatuer, delivered that town and its dependances to Major Robert Farmar, commissary of His Britannic Majesty.

Pierre Chabert, captain of infantry and commandant of Fort "Tombecbe," and Valentine Duboca, keeper of the
November 23 magazine, delivered that post to Captain Thomas Ford, who garrisoned it with English troops.

The Chevalier Lavnoue, commanding Fort Toulouse, upon

the Coosa, not being relieved by the appearance of any British officer, spiked his cannon, broke off the trunnions or ears, and left them in the fort. The river being shallow, during a dry fall, and having his soldiers and all the provisions and military effects to convey to Mobile, in boats, he caused to be cast into the Coosa all which the magazine contained, among which was a large quantity of powder.*

CHAPTER XIII.

1763 November

* Histoire de la Louisiane, par Charles Gayarre, vol. 2, pp. 108–9.

END OF VOLUME I.

www.ingramcontent.com/pod-product-compliance
Lightning Source LLC
LaVergne TN
LVHW020059110826
845151LV00001B/24

* 9 7 8 1 4 2 5 5 4 4 9 3 5 *